Jim Peyton's

New
Cooking
Old FROM
Mexico

Jim Peyton's
New Cooking
from
Old Mexico

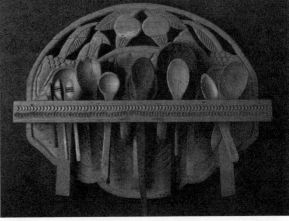

R · E · D
CRANE
B∞KS

FIRST EDITION

Manufactured in the United States of America.
Book and cover design by Jos. Trautwein and Beverly Miller Atwater.
Food photographs by Murrae Haynes and Michael O'Shaughnessy. Author photograph by Murrae Haynes.
Cover photograph by Michael O'Shaughnessy. Table setting by The Clay Angel, Santa Fe, NM.
Endsheet detail from "Map of Mexico, Central America, and the West Indies" by S. Augustus Mitchell,
    from his *New General Atlas*, Philadelphia, 1860.

Library of Congress Cataloging-in-Publication Data

Peyton, James W.
    Jim Peyton's new cooking from old Mexico / James W. Peyton. — 1st   ed.
        p.   cm.
    Includes bibliographical references (p.   ).
    ISBN 1-878610-70-8
    1. Cookery, Mexican.   I. Title.

TX716.M4P488   1999
641.5972—dc21

99-38892
CIP

Red Crane Books
2008-B Rosina Street
Santa Fe, NM 87505
www.redcrane.com
email: publish@redcrane.com

ACKNOWLEDGMENTS

I wish to give my sincere thanks to the following who were especially helpful in this project:

Graciela and Luis Jaime, owners of Saltillo's incomparable La Canasta restaurant for their encouragement and hospitality. José Ortega, Louise Martinez, Alicia Quiles and Madeline Coleman for helping with the translations. Amanda Villarreal for the fine travel arrangements. Michael Nye for the loan of a lens at a critical time during the photography. Murrae Haynes and Mabel Chen for the photography. The Barraca Orraca restaurant chain for both recipes and inspiration. Truman and Karen Smith and Bonnie Ivancic for the use of their folk art collections. Lucinda Hutson for the loan of some difficult-to-find cookbooks. Roger Chenburg and Frances Chenburg for helping to check the text, and the School of American Research for quotes from *The Florentine Codex*. Judith Espinar who graciously shared her home and pottery collection for the cover photo. All the great people at Red Crane Books who are simply the best at what they do: Michael and Marianne O'Shaughnessy, Ann Mason, Kathi Long, Beverly Miller Atwater, and Daniel Kosharek.

A very special thanks to Blanca de Loera for sharing the recipe for the best flan I have ever tasted, and to Emilio and Amparo Alcazar for terrific meals, recipes and ideas, and for their friendship. And an extra special thanks to Elena Hannan who found and sent me everything from information and recipes to cooking equipment, ingredients and books, and who lent her considerable expertise to the editing process.

And most importantly to my wife Andrea for her unstinting support and to my mother for everything.

CONTENTS

"La historia de México es, en gran medida, la historia de su cultura, y la historia de su cultura es, en gran medida la historia de su cocina."

"The history of Mexico is, in great measure, the history of its culture, and the history of its culture is, in great measure, the history of its cooking."

From the foreword by Enrique Krauze to
La cocina mexicana a través de los siglos, by Yoko Sugiura and Fernán González de la Vara.

PREFACE

Mexican-American restaurants, supermarket shelves stacked with salsas, and an avalanche of cookbooks have made tacos, enchiladas, tamales, and burritos as familiar as hamburgers and pizza throughout the United States. However, few people know the fascinating history behind such popular dishes or, more importantly, that a much more sophisticated side of Mexican cuisine from Mexico's interior awaits discovery. Even fewer people realize that there is a recent development in Mexican cuisine called *nueva cocina mexicana*—Mexico's answer to "new Southwest" and other styles of "fusion" cooking. Richly varied, with remarkable substance and flavor, Mexican cuisine is more accessible to North American cooks than is currently imagined.

Jim Peyton's New Cooking from Old Mexico traces the roots of traditional Mexican cooking and of *nueva cocina mexicana* with the hope of providing an understanding and a passion for one of the world's most important but least understood cuisines. The book follows the development of the cuisine from the cooking of pre-Hispanic Mexico through the centuries of Spanish rule to the innovative cooking style currently practiced by Mexico's most creative chefs.

With the goal of making the book as rewarding as possible, I selected recipes using four criteria: First, in the section on traditional cuisine, recipes were chosen to illustrate historical events and important cooking techniques. Second, in both sections recipes were selected for excellence. They had to be not just good but belong to an elite category that some cooks call the "A list." Third, with the exception of a few historically important dishes, recipes were included which contained only ingredients readily available either in stores or through mail-order sources. Finally, recipes were chosen for their ease of preparation.

INTRODUCTION

High on a mountain overlooking Mexico City, the metropolis the Aztecs once called Tenochtitlán, a slight breeze drew wisps of smoke up through the thick pine forest. Below, Doña Juana stooped over the rocks circling her small fire and adjusted one of her *ollas* (pots). The movement was deft for she had been preparing the same dishes in this place for over thirty years. Although it was midmorning, the forest was nearly deserted—except for her customers: two women, a man, and two children, who were seated around the fire on rough-cut timbers. The people had traveled far to sample Doña Juana's renowned *tlacoyos* (a snack).

From a basket the famed cook pulled a chunk of bluish green *masa* (corn dough), which had been recently ground by hand from corn of the same color, and rolled it into a flat oblong shape. Carefully she encased a freshly picked, perfectly formed squash blossom in the dough, patted it delicately, and placed the completed package on a *comal* (griddle). After flicking a little melted fat into the fire to rekindle it, she pulled another chunk of *masa* from the basket and repeated the process, filling the dough alternatively with tender *nopalitos* (cactus paddles), inky *huitlacoche* (corn smut), and avocado. While her guests waited for the *tlacoyos*, Doña Juana served them a soup made from wild mushrooms, *epazote* (herb), and *chile de árbol* (hot chile). Into small clay cups she poured sweet, fresh, home-made *pulque* (fermented maguey juice), and handed them to the adults. When the *tlacoyas* were cooked, she dabbed them with drops of fat and placed them on clay plates with small dishes of red and green chile sauce. After the guests were finished, she served each a small clay cup of *café de olla* (Mexican-style coffee) that she had somehow managed to prepare without anyone noticing.

I was one of the people at this alfresco meal served in the mountain park above Mexico City called El Desierto de los Leones. With the exception of the *café de olla*, the exact same meal could have been served in precisely the same place a thousand or more years earlier.

Later that day our party dined at a glitzy new restaurant on Avenida Presidente Masarik in the chic Polanco District of Mexico City. Outside the restaurant, chauffeurs and bodyguards waited for their employers from the capital's political, business, and media elite. The restaurant featured the city's newest culinary rage, *nueva cocina mexicana*. This cooking style resembles our fusion cooking except that unlike other styles of nouvelle and fusion cooking, many of the techniques and ingredients are derived from the various aspects of Mexican cooking rather than from a variety of cuisines. This is feasible because the range of possibilities within the Mexican tradition is so extensive and because Mexican cooking itself is the result of fusion.

The menu consisted of dishes named for their creators, some of

Mexico's most famous cooks. I chose one by my friend Lula Bertrán consisting of a *sábana* (a filet mignon pounded into a paper-thin circle), which was then folded in half around some freshly fried *chicharrones* (pork rinds). This package was placed on a plate, half of which had been covered with a mild, strained tomatillo sauce, and the other half with a very thin layer of refried beans. It was delicious, as were the creations served to the rest of our party.

In the days that followed, I ate many other meals in various restaurants, alternating between traditional Mexican cooking and *nueva cocina mexicana* until the distinctions began to blur. During this experience, I was constantly reminded that this cuisine was far different from what most people in the United States think of as Mexican food and kept wondering why such cooking of Mexico's interior had not yet achieved great popularity north of the border. After all, the dishes are not only delicious and aesthetically pleasing but have the powerful appeal of foods that have developed organically through centuries of trial and error. Adding to the mystery of why such cooking is not better known is the fact that Diana Kennedy first published *The Cuisines of Mexico*, featuring interior Mexican cooking, in 1972, and it has been selling well ever since, as have other books on the subject by experts such as Rick Bayless. Nevertheless, while the salsas, tacos, enchiladas, tamales, and quesadillas—the snacks of interior Mexico and the mainstay of Mexican-American restaurant cooking—are wildly popular, the moles, *barbacoa* (pit cooking), and soups from Mexico's interior remain nearly unknown in most parts of the United States.

In searching for an explanation of why the cooking of Mexico's interior is not more widely known, I found several reasons. First and probably most important, is the fact that, with the exception of the Southwest, the United

States has tended to focus first on cultures across the Atlantic and then across the Pacific for culinary inspiration—rather than south of the border. In the past, Mexican food has not been of great interest to the culinary establishment. This may have been partly because some people thought of Mexican cooking as peasant food rather than sophisticated cooking. Another factor that may have hindered the popularity of Mexican cuisine is that some of the classic Mexican recipes like the moles are time-consuming to prepare and require ingredients that may be difficult to obtain.

However, I believe that all these views of Mexican cuisine are rapidly changing. Exotic ingredients are becoming more readily available in the United States, and Americans are gaining increased awareness of the great variety and sophistication of cooking from various areas of Mexico.

I have written *Jim Peyton's New Cooking from Old Mexico* with the hope of increasing knowledge about Mexican cooking. I want the book to do four things: First, by revealing the roots of Mexican cuisine as well as its development, I hope to create a passion for Mexican food, and thus a desire to explore the cuisine. Second, I want to present excellent recipes that would reward readers for their efforts in preparing them. Third, I want to introduce *nueva cocina mexicana*, an aspect of the cuisine that is as sophisticated and aesthetically pleasing as any in the world and largely unknown outside of Mexico. Finally, I wish to encourage restauranteurs to consider offering both traditional interior and new wave Mexican cooking.

I reflected on what it was that so attracted me to Mexican cooking, concluding that along with its pleasing flavors, a major factor was its history. I discovered that in English language books, the real story of Mexican cooking has only been told on a superficial level; therefore, Part I of *Jim Peyton's New Cooking from Old Mexico* focuses on the history of Mexican cuisine in order to contribute additional dimensions to an understanding of Mexican cooking. It includes chapters on the roots of Mexican cuisine in both Spain and pre-Hispanic Mexico; on the importance and characteristics of various New World ingredients; and on the development of traditional Mexican cooking from the time of the Spanish conquest to the present day, highlighting recent developments of *nueva cocina mexicana*.

In Part II, in addition to presenting an excellent collection of recipes, I have provided a basis upon which readers can build to create their own dishes.

I hope you will join me on this culinary journey through the centuries, which begins—and ends—with a style of cooking that stands with the world's greatest.

Buen provecho,

Part I

THE HISTORY OF MEXICAN CUISINE

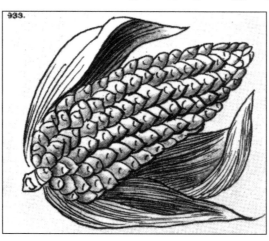

CHAPTER 1

THE ROOTS OF MEXICAN COOKING

Unlike our current so-called fusion cooking, Mexican food was not fashioned in a few years by a sprinkling of creative chefs. It was forged over many centuries, through peaceful times of plenty and violent times of need, by rich and by poor, organically evolving into a cuisine that remains as extraordinarily true to its roots as the people of Mexico themselves.

Mexican cuisine emerged over the centuries as a result of an integration between Old World and New World ingredients and cooking techniques. So, to comprehend and appreciate this remarkable cuisine it is necessary to know something about both the Old World and the New World food baskets, including their characteristics and their contributions to Mexican cooking. Perhaps most important is the ability to understand the origin of various dishes as we prepare and consume them, for it is only with this knowledge that the enjoyment of food transcends sensual pleasure to become something much more profound—a cultural experience.

The principal actors of this cuisine, which has all the drama of a theater production, are the Mexican Indians and the Spanish, with lesser parts being played by the French and Orientals. Indian customs and foods of pre-conquest Mexico contributed vital aspects to Mexican cuisine. Moreover, natural forces such as climate, topography, and soil conditions created regional variations in food and its preparation, as did the food preferences of the Indians themselves.

The Spanish also made critical contributions during five centuries of settlement. Of nearly equal importance was the influence of the Catholic Church, which introduced saints' days and other occasions for which special meals were prepared, and which regulated what and when foods could be eaten, as well as the workday of the Indians. In addition, the prodigious cooking skills of nuns in Catholic convents were crucial to the development of certain dishes.

Just as the Old World and New World players were different, so were their ingredients. While the New World provided a truly revolutionary array of foods—largely plants—including corn, tomatoes, chiles, potatoes, chocolate, and vanilla, the Old World placed wheat, rice, meat, chicken, milk, cheese, fats, and citrus fruits on the communal table.

When people first migrated to the Americas, meat from enormous pre-historic animals constituted the major portion of the diet, supplemented by vegetables and fruits gathered when available. After the large animals disappeared, the diet of early hunter-gatherers consisted of smaller species such as rabbits, turkeys, deer, and fish, as well as fruits, wild grasses, and plants. Not only did these people survive, they gradually discovered how to take control of growing food, selecting seeds from the best fruits and vegetables, directing water into primitive irrigation systems, and removing weeds with both tools and fire.

The discovery of how to plant seeds to produce life-sustaining grains resulted in the greatest revolution in the history of agriculture. Wheat in

Europe, rice in Asia and the Middle East, and corn and potatoes in the Americas created the basis for subsequent civilizations. Freed from the unrelenting search for game and edible plants, people were able to create communities and other aspects of culture.

However, there was still another threat to food supplies: weather, with its floods, droughts, freezes, heat waves, and windstorms. But people adapted to these circumstances as well, developing calendars to determine when to plant and harvest crops, and creating ways to dry, smoke, preserve in salt, and store food for times of inevitable crop failure. And when these measures proved inadequate the people turned to the gods, who they believed controlled the hostile elements. Having learned that nothing good came without cost, they assumed that in return for providing conditions that would permit plentiful harvests, the gods expected sacrifice. Over time attempts to placate the gods through human sacrifice became customary throughout the region. Given the life and death nature of their circumstances, it is not surprising that these early people came up with radical measures to assure an adequate food supply. Though tragic, such rituals do not invalidate the many positive contributions of these early people to the world.

As agriculture spread throughout Mesoamerica and people began to form communities, farmers produced more food than their families could use, enabling the emerging military, political, and religious elite to exact tributes in return for protection from both worldly and otherworldly dangers. Much of what was ordained by the leadership was interpreted from calendars kept by the priests.

The first Indian calendar used was the 260-day sacred almanac, which, according to Vincent H. Malmström in *Cycles of the Sun, Mysteries of the Moon*, was developed around the middle of the fourteenth century B.C. The count of the days began with the zenith of the sun as it began its passage to the south, and ended with the next zenith on the northward passage, 260 days later. These 260 days were divided into 13 groups of 20 days, and were identified by 13 numbers combined with the names of 20 different animals, plants, and other natural objects, for example 1 Snake or 2 Wind. Malmström states:

> Here was a tool for alerting the farmer to the beginning of the rainy season that was easily understood by everyone: The rains would start on or about the time of the sun's northward passage (April 30), and the corn would be ready to harvest by the time of its southward passage (August 13). In short, it seemed that the stargazer had unlocked one of the most important secrets of the heavens. (Malmström 1997, 55)

However, the 260-day calendar had a fatal flaw. While there were always 260 days between the southward and northward passages of the sun, the zeniths did not always appear on the same day. This discrepancy was addressed by observing that when the sun reached its northward extreme it rose precisely over some readily identifiable landmark and that a more accurate measurement could be made by counting the days between the times that the sun rose at this marker, the result being 365. These 365 days were then divided into 18 groups of 20 days, with an additional 5 "lost" days.

Because only priests and soothsayers knew the secrets of the calendar and were able to decree precisely what should be done and when, the priests became extremely powerful and were obeyed without question. It is known that the Aztecs preferred to let a crop rot rather than harvest it before the elders gave the word. And calendars, first developed for determining when to plant and harvest crops, later were used to control almost every phase of life.

Early agriculture in Mexico was further influenced by the climatic conditions of various areas. The region is divided into three basic climatic zones: northern Mexico is arid to semiarid desert land with sandy soil and very little precipitation. Most of central Mexico sits on a high plateau where the climate fluctuates. Much of southeastern Mexico is tropical.

The varying climates of these three regions determined the type and extent of agriculture. Because the desert lands of northern Mexico were not conducive to cultivation, the population there, nomadic warriors called the *Chichimeca*, existed more nearly as their hunter/gatherer ancestors had. In the central plateau, where the soil was good, there were permanent agricultural units, many with creative irrigation systems. It was here that the advanced civilizations of the Toltecs, Zapotecs, and Aztecs developed. The most ingenious agricultural system of the region were the *chinampas* of the Aztecs, which consisted of soil-covered rafts anchored by the roots of living trees to the bottom of lake Texcoco.

In the tropical south, although the rains were heavier and more frequent, the soil was often poor because the nutrients were leached out. The soil was especially poor and rocky in the Yucatán Peninsula. In these areas the slash and burn type of agriculture was often used—with land being cleared by burning and used only for a season or two before the cycle was repeated in a new area. Nevertheless, it was in the tropical regions that Mesoamerican civilization really began with the Olmecs and later flourished with the Mayas.

Around 1500 B.C., the Olmec civilization emerged in the lowlands near the Gulf coast, a civilization that would determine the development of future pre-Hispanic Mesoamerican culture. The Olmecs developed extensive agriculture, a dating system, long-distance trade networks, and pyramids and ceremonial centers. Although ruins of this culture remain, including huge stone sculptures of broad-faced human heads, the Olmecs left few clues to their identity. However, T.R. Fehrenbach stresses the importance of this culture:

> It is difficult to make direct links with the prehistoric Magician-Olmec age and the Meso-American culture that came afterward. But it seems certain that the Magicians developed much, if not all, of the cultural patina that overlaid the basic maize-culture. This era was a great turning point for Meso-American man. (Fehrenbach 1985, 17)

Although the origin and decline of the Olmec civilization are shrouded in mystery, we do know that this was the first society in the Americas to conduct widespread trade throughout the region, and to have a sophisticated calendar, knowledge of the solar system, a leadership cadre, and an elaborate religious doctrine. The spread of Olmec culture can be traced through their method of orienting their cities to the solar system, and their style of pottery and sculpture that has been found from El Salvador to Mexico City.

Between 600 B.C. and A.D. 1, the Olmecs were gradually replaced by other Mesoamerican cultures. The most influential of these was Teotihuacán, which, at its apex in about A.D. 500, along with Rome and Beijing was one of the world's three greatest cities. (Malmström 1997, 184) Located just north of present-day Mexico City, Teotihuacán had a population estimated at 200,000. The Teotihuacán culture is nearly as much a mystery as the Olmec culture; even the name, which means "place of the gods," came from the Aztecs centuries later. However, historians are fairly certain that the achievements of Teotihuacán culture resulted from expertise at trade rather than bounties of war. (Viola and Margolis 1991, 28)

During this period, referred to as the Classic Period (A.D. 300–900), the Mayas refined the science of astronomy and mathematics and built spectacular cities that would eventually be buried in the jungles of the Yucatán, Chiapas, and Guatemala. Their remarkable structures, the tallest of which rose to the height of a twenty-story building, were constructed of massive pieces of stone without the use of beasts of burden or the wheel, and they were often oriented so that the sight lines between them pointed precisely to the rising or setting sun at the summer and winter solstices.

Simultaneously, other Mesoamerican peoples were developing sophisticated societies, including the Zapotecs of Oaxaca, who oriented their magnificent ceremonial city of Monte Albán astronomically in a way similar to other great classic civilizations.

While these people were racially the same, they were of different tribes with different languages, and developed well-defined regional characteristics. Still, it was the striking similarity of their way of life in terms of religion, architecture, art, political organization, and foodways, that set them apart from the cultures of Europe. The similarities of Mesoamerican cultures are usually explained by the fact that while Europe was open to influence from the Orient and Middle East the New World peoples had no contact with the outside world. However, this view poses an interesting question concerning foodways. While there are distinct regional differences in the cuisine of present-day Mexico, why is it still dominated by the same common elements after nearly 500 years of exposure to other world cultures?

One of the greatest mysteries of Mesoamerica is how cultures that developed sophisticated calendars based on scientific observation of the heavens, expert mathematical calculations, and widespread trade abruptly disappeared. One theory stresses that while Mesoamerica's magnificent cities were thriving, there remained in the arid desert lands to the north and west the fierce group of hunter-gatherer tribes collectively known as the *Chichimeca*, who were prevented from developing agricultural economies because of the climate and who during a serious drought attacked the more prosperous people to the south.

Another theory about why these advanced cultures rapidly disappeared surmises that when, in spite of precisely following the dictates of the elite, droughts and other natural disasters caused widespread starvation, the people rose in defiance. In *Everyday Life of the Maya*, Ralph Whitlock states:

> It may well be that a contributory reason for the abandonment of some of the religious sites was the failure of the priests concerned to make correct prognostications. A peasant people which spends all its leisure time building splendid temples to the gods in anticipation of future favours is entitled to expect results. (Whitlock 1987, 35)

If such circumstances occurred, and the small group of educated leaders were killed in a rebellion, an entire civilization could have been left without the cultural and scientific benefits related to higher learning.

Two slightly different scenarios have been proposed to specifically explain the decline of the Mayan culture, which began in the A.D. 800s—one attributing the decline to soil depletion and other environmental problems, and the other to constant wars between different cities and clans.

Whatever the reasons for the decline of these civilizations, the first city to fall was Teotihuacán, initially overrun by the Otomís and then finally destroyed by the Toltecs around A.D. 750. Subsequently, the Toltecs established their own capital at Tula, fifty-five miles north of present-day Mexico City, from which their influence spread far and wide—into Guerrero to the south, to Tlaxcala in the northeast, and even to the Yucatán Peninsula.

However, waves of invaders kept coming, and the Toltecs themselves soon lost power. According to legend, even their principal deity, Quetzalcoatl the "Plumed Serpent," was forced to flee to the Yucatán, where he also reached divine status among the Mayas. From there he disappeared into the eastern sea, promising to return again in the year 1 Reed, the very year Hernán Cortés landed at present-day Veracruz.

The last Mesoamericans to build a great empire were the Mexicas, later known as the Aztecs. This tribe migrated to the Valley of Mexico during the twelfth century from their homeland, Aztlán, a region alternately thought to have been along the coast of present-day Nayarit or Florida, or in the present-day state of Zacatecas from which the name Aztec derived.

After approximately 187 years, the Aztec odyssey culminated at Lake Texcoco, one of three large adjoining lakes in the Valley of Mexico. According to legend, throughout the Aztecs' arduous journey, their gods had instructed them that they would find their new home at the place where they would see an eagle perched on a cactus eating a snake. This occurred at Tenochtitlán, a name derived from the word for prickly pear in the Nahuatl language. The settlement of the Aztecs at Tenochtitlán is described in the *Crónica Mexicayotl* as follows:

> Here it is told, it is recounted
> how the ancients who were called, who were named,
> Teochichimeca, Azteca, Mexitin, Chicomoztoca came,
> arrived,
> when they came to seek,
> when they came to gain possession of their land here,
> in the great city of Mexico Tenochtitlán....
>
> In the middle of the water where the cactus stands,
> where the eagle rises up,
> where the eagle screeches,
> where the eagle spreads his wings,
> where the eagle feeds,
> where the serpent is torn apart,
> where the fish fly,
> where the blue waters and the yellow waters join,
> where the water blazes up,
> where the feathers come to be known,
> among the rushes, among the reeds where the battle is joined,
> where the people from four directions are awaited,
> there they arrived, there they settled.... (Knab and Sullivan 1994, 85–86)

The divine selection of this location was auspicious since upon their arrival, the Aztecs were given no other choice by their more powerful, established neighbors at Culhuacán and Azcapotzalco, cities inhabited by remnants of the Toltecs and other tribes. This area, which had no land to cultivate and no stone or wood for building, was deemed appropriate for the uncultured newcomers. Consequently, for practical reasons the Aztecs built their settlements on two nearby islands in the lake, Tlatelolco and Tenochtitlán.

Although their condition might have been primitive at first, living on newts, salamanders, algae, worms, grasshoppers, and native grasses, the Aztecs were also ingenious and accustomed to back-breaking work. Beginning in about A.D. 1325 with a few huts and a shrine to their most important deity, Huitzilopochtli, the god of the sun and war, they soon developed their famous *chinampas,* or floating gardens, and by extensive infilling built Tenochtitlán into a fabulous metropolis described as follows by Bernal Díaz del Castillo, who accompanied Cortés on his expedition of conquest:

> This accursed temple was so high that from the top of it everything could be seen perfectly. And from up there we saw the three causeways that lead into Mexico—the causeway of Iztapalapan, by which we had come four days earlier; the causeway of Tlacopan, by which we were later to flee, on the night of our great defeat…and that of Tepeyacac. We saw the aqueduct that comes from Chalpultepec to supply the town with sweet water, and at intervals along the three causeways the bridges which let the water flow from one part of the lake to another. We saw a multitude of boats upon the great lake, some coming with provisions, some going off loaded with merchandise…and in these town we saw temples and oratories shaped like towers and bastions, all shining white, a wonderful thing to behold. And we saw the terraced houses, and along the causeways other towers and chapels that looked like fortresses. So, having gazed at all this and reflected upon it, we turned our eyes to the great market-place and the host of people down there who were buying and selling: the hum and the murmur of their voices could have been heard for more than a league. And among us were soldiers who had been in many parts of the world, at Constantinople, all over Italy and at Rome; and they said they had never seen a market so well ordered, so large and so crowded with people. (Hernández Díaz 1992, 355–56)

As the power of the Aztecs grew and they turned their Venice-like city to military advantage, they conquered their neighbors creating a vast empire that stretched from the Pacific to the Atlantic and as far south as Guatemala. Mandatory tributes of food and other valuable commodities, including chocolate, tobacco, gold, jade, jaguar skins, and colorful feathers, flowed into Tenochtitlán in immense quantities.

As the Aztecs conquered their more cultured neighbors, they also grew to admire them. Their sense of history was limited, and they ascribed the culture they found to the Toltecs and their god Quetzalcoatl. They even selected a nobleman of Toltec lineage to be their ruler. His descendants formed the core of the ruling class, from which future kings, priests, and noblemen were selected.

At the time the Spanish landed, the Aztecs were the major Mesoamerican power, and it was with this culture that the Spanish first mixed. And it is from Spanish historians like Father Sahagún and Bernal Díaz del Castillo that we have obtained most of our knowledge of pre-Hispanic life, including cooking.

Between 1375 and the arrival of Cortés in 1519, nine kings ruled the Aztecs, culminating with the rise to power in 1502 of Montezuma. Montezuma was much enamored of the rituals and spiritualism of the priesthood, probably realizing the importance of religion for the Aztec civilization. As Fehrenbach states:

> While the *Mexica* hegemony was held together by armies, disciplined training, and pervasive justice, the whole civilization still rested on the forces that had created it—the ancient religions, which permeated all life styles, custom and law. (Fehrenbach 1985, 92)

Aztec society consisted of various classes. As part of the ruling class, the priests conducted religious ceremonies and human sacrifice, kept and interpreted the calendars, and taught the tribe's traditions. It is believed that their use of hallucinogens, including mushrooms and peyote, contributed to their surrealistic worldview. Below the ruling class were the common people who were given parcels of land on which they lived communally. Below them was yet another class consisting of both temporary and permanent slaves. (León-Portilla 1990, xxiii) In spite of not sharing privileges accorded the rulers, common people had the use of slaves and were given enough of the tribute booty to make them content.

For the most part the Aztecs dressed simply, with the men wearing loincloths made of agave fiber or white cotton called *maxtlatl,* and for warmth and more formal occasions a cloak over one shoulder called a *tilmatli.* Women wore ankle-length skirts called *cueitl* secured with embroidered belts. As Jacques Soustelle relates:

> Among the lower classes and in the country the women often left their bosoms uncovered, but in the town and among the women of the middle class or the better sort a kind of blouse called *huipilli* was worn outside the skirt: it was embroidered at the neck. Everyday clothes were plain and white, but ceremonial or holiday clothes displayed a great variety of colours and patterns. (Soustelle 1993, 135)

The *huipilli* (in Mexican Spanish *huipil*) is still widely used all over the south and east of Mexico.

Aztec life was almost puritanical. While women in other tribes often wore garish makeup and even colored their teeth black and red, only Aztec courtesans did so. Drunkenness was often punished with death, and there was no sexual freedom except among the most important nobles, who were allowed harems. In other ways, though, the rulers were kept to a high standard, often receiving much harsher punishment than a commoner for the same crime. Moreover, the ruling class felt a sense of responsibility toward the common people, as stated by Bernardino de Sahagún:

> The ruler took care of the directing of the market place and all things sold, for the good of the common folk, the vassals, and all

dwellers in the city, the poor, the unfortunate, so that [these] might not be abused, nor suffer harm, nor be deceived nor disdained. (Sahagún 1981, 8:67)

Another example of the rulers' benevolence was the distribution of food to the common people between harvests when supplies were short. During the eighth twenty-day month of their eighteen-month calendar, food, especially tamales, was distributed. As Sahagún remarks:

This [feasting] the lords brought about in order to give comfort to the poor; for at this time, ordinarily, there is a want of the necessities of life. (Sahagún 1981, 2:14)

In managing their extensive empire, the Aztecs were far more interested in economic gain than political domination. Often they let the people they conquered administer their own affairs, leaving only an Aztec tax collector among them to assure that tributes were paid in a timely manner. But although Aztec commoners were reasonably content, this was not true of the people from whom increasing tributes were demanded. These tribes lacked the means to rebel against the Aztecs until the Spanish arrived. Other groups such as the Tarascans of present-day Michoacán and Tlaxcalans to the northeast remained free of Aztec domination but developed a hatred of them that Cortés was later able to exploit.

Despite puritanical tendencies, like most successful imperialists the Aztec nobility quickly developed a taste for luxuries, including sandals decorated with gold and immense feathered headdresses. Much of this finery came from their subjects to the south and east. Referring to the *Crónica Mexicayotle* (a chronical attributed to Tezozomac, originally in Aztec), Jacques Soustelle states:

The Mexicans had adopted the feather ornaments of the tropical races, the amberlip-ornaments of the Mayas of Tzinacantlan, the particoloured and embroidered clothes of the Totonacs, the golden jewels of the Mixtecs, as well as the Huextecs' goddess of carnal love and the feast that the Mazatecs held every eighth year in honour of the planet Venus. (Soustelle 1993, xxiii, xxiv)

Moreover, the Aztecs, who had originally subsisted on what others did not eat, developed extravagant tastes in food, as reflected in the following description by Bernal Díaz del Castillo of a typical meal in Montezuma's palace:

His cooks had upwards of thirty different ways of dressing meats, and they had earthen vessels so contrived as to keep them always hot. For the table of Montezuma himself, above three hundred dishes were dressed, and for his guards, above a thousand. Before dinner, Montezuma would sometimes go out and inspect the preparations, and his officers would point out to him which were the best, and explained of what birds and flesh they were composed; and of those he would eat. But this was more for amusement than anything else. It is said that at times the flesh of young children was dressed for him; but the ordinary meats were domestic fowls, pheasants, geese, partridges, quails, venison, Indian hogs, pigeons, hares, and rabbits, with many other animals and birds peculiar to the country. This is certain; that after Cortés had spoken to him relative to the dressing of human flesh, it was not practiced in his palace. At his meals, in the cold weather, a number of torches of the bark of a wood which makes no smoke and has an aromatic smell, were lighted, and that they should not throw too much heat, screens ornamented with gold, and painted with figures of idols, were placed before them. Montezuma was seated on a low throne, or chair, at a table proportioned to the height of his seat. The table was covered with white cloths and napkins, and four beautiful women presented him with water for his hands, in vessels which they call Xicales, with other vessels under them like plates, to catch the water; they also presented him with towels. Then, two other women brought small cakes of bread, and when the king began to eat, a large screen of wood, gilt, was placed before him, so that the people should not during that time see him. The women having retired to a little distance, four ancient lords stood by the throne, to whom Montezuma from time to time spoke or addressed questions, and as a mark of particular favor, gave to each of them a plate of that which he was eating. I was told that these old lords, who were his near relations, were also counsellors and judges. The plates which Montezuma presented to them, they received with high respect, eating what was in them without taking their eyes off the ground. He was served on earthenware of Cholula, red and black. While the king was at table, no one of his guards, or in the vicinity of his apartment, dared for their lives make any noise. Fruit of all the kinds that the country produced was laid before him; he eat [*sic*] very little, but from time to time, a liquor prepared from cocoa, and of a stimulative, or corroborative quality, as we were told, was presented to him in golden cups. We could not at that time see if he drank it or not, but I observed a number of jars, above fifty, brought in, filled with foaming chocolate, of which he took some, which the women presented to him. At different intervals during the time of the dinner, there entered certain Indians, humpbacked, very deformed, and ugly, who played tricks of buffoonery, and others who they said were jesters. There was also a company of singers and dancers, who afforded Montezuma much entertainment. To these he ordered the vases of chocolate to be distributed. The four female attendants then took away the cloths, and again with much respect presented him with water to wash his hands, during which time Montezuma conversed with the four old noblemen formerly mentioned, after which they took their leave with many ceremonies. One thing I forgot, and no wonder, to mention in its place, and that is, that during the time Montezuma was at dinner, two very beautiful women were busily employed making small cakes with eggs and other things mixed therein. These were delicately white, and when made they presented them to him on plates covered with napkins. Also another kind of bread was brought to him in long loaves, and plates of cakes resembling wafers. After he had dined, they presented to him three little canes highly ornamented, containing liquid amber, mixed with an herb they call tobacco; and when he had sufficiently viewed and heard the singers, dancers, and buffoons, he took a little of the smoke of one of these canes, and then laid himself down to sleep; and thus his principal meal concluded. (Díaz del Castillo 1927, 32)

Another testimonial to the importance the Aztecs placed on food was the practice of exempting potential sacrificial victims from their fate if they showed important skills, including culinary proficiency:

Likewise, if a woman could sew or if she prepared food well, or made good cacao—from whose hand good food and drink came; [or if she was] a good interpreter; her also they set aside. The nobles took [such women] as wives. (Sahagún 1981, 1:20)

That historian Friar Bernardino de Sahagún and his native informants saw fit to include a firsthand description of what, to the Aztecs, constituted both a good and bad cook emphasizes the importance of food in the Aztec empire as well as the Aztec view of women, who prepared virtually all the food:

The good cook is honest, discreet; [she is] one who likes good food—an epicure, a taster [of food]. She is clean, one who bathes herself; prudent; one who washes her hands, who washes herself; who has good drink, good food.

The bad cook [is] dishonest, detestable, nauseating, offensive to others—sweaty, crude, gluttonous, stuffed, distended with food—much distended, acquisitive. As one who puts dough into the oven, she puts it into the oven. She smokes food; she makes it very salty, briny; she sours it. She is a field hand—very much a field hand, very much a commoner. (Sahagún 1981, 10:52–53)

Although the warrior-oriented Aztec society was dominated by men, women, as the bearers of children and cooks of life-sustaining meals, had a separate but equal status:

> It is women's work that sustains life on the earth and in the holy earth. It is the Aztec woman who can still be seen "feeding" the ancestors, tossing a bit of tortilla, perhaps unconsciously, into the home fire under her griddle. (Knab and Sullivan 1994, 122)

As with clothing, meals of the common people were much simpler than those of the upper class. Typically, working people ate their first meal around midmorning consisting of a bowl of boiled ground corn, sometimes with honey and/or chiles, called *atole*. In the afternoon they had the main meal, of tortillas, tamales, squash, and beans with sauces of tomato or *tomatillo* and chiles. While the rich imbibed frothy chocolate beverages, the common people drank water.

Despite the extensiveness and power of the Aztec empire, its influence abruptly ended when Cortés arrived in 1519. Undoubtedly, Montezuma's predilection for the occult, particularly his knowledge of the legend of Quetzalcoatl and his belief in mystical omens, was a major reason why only a handful of Spaniards and their Indian allies were able to conquer the Aztecs, whose capital city had a population of up to 250,000 with tens of thousands of armed warriors.

CHAPTER 2
NEW WORLD INGREDIENTS

The basic diet of preconquest Mexico consisted of corn, beans, squash, and chiles, although it varied according to location. These plants were often planted together in the classic Indian growing scheme called a *milpa*. In this cleverly symbiotic arrangement, the vines of the beans and squash were (and are still in many parts of Mexico) supported by the cornstalks, and the bean plants supplied the soil with nitrogen. Friar Diego de Landa described the typical Mayan *milpa*, which was similar to those in other areas, as follows:

> For each married man and his wife it was their custom to plant a space of 400 feet, which was called *hun vinic* [one man], a plot measured with a 20-foot rod, 20 in breadth and 20 in length. (Landa 1978, 38)

In Mexico, as in most of Central America, the development of corn was the key to a new agricultural life. The fact that for corn to reproduce the husks must be removed and the seeds planted is evidence that corn was not found by early man in its present form but developed. While the exact origin of corn has been intensely debated, virtually all experts agree that it was cultivated by trial and error from either a primitive corn plant, from teosinte, a plant very similar to corn, or from a combination of both.

The profound impact of corn on early American civilization was actually the result of two discoveries: the discovery of corn itself and—perhaps more important to the inhabitants of Mesoamerica and of greater concern to people interested in Mexican cooking—the discovery of nixtamalization, the process of treating corn in a heated alkaline solution.

For many years anthropologists and historians believed that the Mexican Indians and those in other areas simmered corn in water made alkaline by the addition of either slaked lime, sifted wood ashes, or ground seashells for culinary reasons alone. And indeed, nixtamalization loosens the pericarp, or "skin," of corn enough so that it can be removed, and the corn easily ground into a dough smooth enough to make tortillas and tamales. However, it is now known that the process facilitates the body's use of needed nutrients while inhibiting the absorption of toxic substances.

After the discovery of the New World, corn was exported around the world, but wherever corn was taken—Romania, Italy, Spain, Egypt, Africa, and the southern United States—people who ate it became seriously ill with "corn sickness," the disease we now call pellagra. This disease causes skin problems, depression, and if not treated, internal hemorrhaging, damage to the central nervous system, and death. Theories advanced as early as 1786 blamed this disease on contamination; but it was not until this century that the exact cause was determined—and why people who processed their corn by nixtamalization remained healthy.

The solution to the mystery was fully explained in an article in the May 1974 issue of *Science* by S. H. Katz, M. L. Hediger, and L. A. Valleroy entitled "Traditional Maize Processing Techniques in the New World." At the heart of the matter is the fact that the human body requires amino acids to perform vital functions. While some of these amino acids are synthesized within the body itself, others, called the essential amino acids, must come from dietary sources. Corn contains insufficient quantities of the essential amino acids lysine and tryptophan. The deficiency of tryptophan is of particular consequence because it is instrumental in the body's manufacture and utilization of niacin, which is deficient in corn. The absence of niacin has been found to be a major cause of pellagra. Scientists believe that pellagra can also be caused by a ratio of too much leucine to isoleucine in the diet (which inhibits the conversion of tryptophan to niacin). Corn has three times the desired amount of leucine in relation to its content of isoleucine. It was ancient chemistry that resulted in the widespread use of corn in Mexico. Unfortunately, people were unaware of the value of this critical process when corn was first dispersed throughout the world. If they had been, perhaps John Gerard, a noted English herbalist of the sixteenth and seventeenth centuries, would have had something different to say about corn than the following:

> Wee have as yet not certaine proofe or experience concerning the vertues of this kinde of corne; although the barbarous Indians, which know no better, are constrained to make a vertue of necessitie, and think it a good food whereas we may easily judge, that it nourisheth but little, and is of hard and evill digestion, a more convenient food for swine than for man. (Heiser 1990, 92)

Because of its role as the primary sustenance of the human body, corn had a spiritual as well as material significance for the Indians. As Octavio Paz states in his introduction to *Mexico: Splendors of Thirty Centuries:*

> The great economic revolution came with the domestication of maize, which transformed nomads into sedentary peoples. It is not surprising that they deified the grain. (Paz 1990, 9)

In the *Popol Vuh*, the famous creation myth and counsel book of the Quiché Mayas, corn is the material from which the gods finally created man. The gods were determined to create men who would order their activities according to the sacred calendar, and who would revere and honor their makers. The first attempt produced creatures who could only screech and howl, could not speak to each other, and whose progeny became the animals of the world. The second attempt, using clay, only resulted in creatures who could not move properly and eventually melted. The third attempt, using wood, produced beings who were the closest yet to what the gods wanted, but they lacked self-discipline and did not revere their creators. It was only with the fourth attempt, when corn dough was used, that beings were finally created who had attributes the gods desired, made in the form of four individuals: Jaguar Quitze, Jaguar Night, Not Right Now, and Dark Jaguar:

> The making, the modeling of our first mother-father,
> with yellow corn, white corn alone for the flesh,
> food alone for the human legs and arms,
> for our first fathers, the four human works. (Tedlock 1996, 146)

The Nahuas, to which the Toltecs and Aztecs belonged, believed that corn came to the people through the god Quetzalcoatl. According to legend, after seeing red ants carrying corn and being unable to find the source, Quetzalcoatl transformed himself into a black ant and followed a red ant into Food Mountain, where he found the secret cache and brought it to human beings.

In describing Aztec beliefs, the historian Friar Bernardino de Sahagún not only notes the importance of maize and Chicome Coatl, the goddess of food and drink, but also hints at the immense variety of corn that was available:

> And it was said, it was indeed this Chicome Coatl who made all
> our food—white maize, yellow maize, green maize shoots, black

maize, black and brown mixed, variously hued; large and wide; round and ball-like; slender maize; thin, long maize; speckled red and white maize as if striped with blood, painted with blood—then the coarse brown maize (its appearance is as if tawny); popcorn; the after fruit; double ears; rough ears; and maturing green maize; the small ears of maize beside the main ear; the ripened green maize. (Sahagún 1981, 2:64)

Sahagún gives additional insight into the reverence with which maize was held when he writes of the ways in which he considered how people were deceived by their gods:

As to dried grains of maize, in many ways were the women none the less deluded. First, when they cooked it or set it in ashes—behold their folly: when they would place it in the olla with ashes, first of all they breathed upon it. It was held that in this way it would not take fright; thus it would not fear the heat. It was said that thus they mitigated the heat.

Second, they deceived themselves in this way: if they saw or came upon dried grains of maize lying scattered on the ground, then they quickly gathered them up. They said: "Our sustenance suffereth: it lieth weeping. If we should not gather it up, it would accuse us before our lord. It would say: "O our lord, this vassal picked me not up when I lay scattered upon the ground. Punish him! Or perhaps we should starve." (Sahagún 1981, 5:184)

Sahagún's meticulous research is evident in his description of growing maize as it was practiced both then and now:

The best seed is selected. The perfect, the glossy maize is carefully chosen. The spoiled, the rotten, the shrunken falls away; the very best is chosen. It is shelled, placed in water. Two days, three days it swells in the water. It is planted in worked soil or in similar places.

First a hole is made. The land is sought where there is

moisture. The grains of maize are tossed in. If there is no moisture, it is watered. At the same time it is covered over with soil, and the soil which is placed on it is pulverized. Then it is gathering moisture; then it swells; then the grain of maize bursts; then it takes root. Then it sprouts; then it pushes up; then it reaches the surface; then it gathers moisture; it really flies. Then it forks, it lies dividing; it spreads out, it is spreading out. And they say it is pleasing. At this time it is hilled, the hollow is filled in, the crown is covered, the earth is well heaped up.

Also at this time beans are sown or cast. They say that at this time this [maize] once again begins to grow, also begins to branch out. Then it reaches outward; then it spreads out; then it becomes succulent. Once again at this time it is hilled. Then the corn silk develops; then the corn tassels form. At this time, once again it is hilled; it is, they say, the hatching of the green maize ear. Then an embryonic ear forms. Then the green maize ear begins to form; the green maize ear shines, glistens, spreads glistening. Its maize silk spreads blanketing the green maize ear; its maize silk spreads blanketing it. [The maize silk] spreads becoming coveted—spreads becoming desired. Then, it is said, the maize silk dries up, withers away.

[The kernels] spread forming little droplets; it is said that they spread taking form. Then [the kernels] form milk. Then the surface [of the kernels] becomes evened. Then it becomes the *nixtamal* flower; now it is called *chichipelotl*. Then [the milk] thickens, at which time it is called *elotl*. Then, at this time, it begins to harden; it turns yellow, whereupon it is called *cintli*. (Sahagún 1981, 11:283)

Today, as it was in the past, corn is still grown in tens of thousands of *milpas* throughout Mexico. While people in the United States are primarily acquainted with sweet corn and popcorn, there are several other varieties:

For convenience, five main types of maize are recognized: (1) popcorn, probably the most primitive type, with extremely hard grains that allow pressure to be built up within them upon heating; "popping" results when the sudden expansion of the soft starch turns the grain inside out (other varieties of maize and other cereals can also be popped and are commonly prepared in this way as breakfast foods, but special methods are necessary to allow the pressure to build up); (2) flint corns, which have kernels of hard starch; (3) flour corns, which have soft starch, of particular value to the Native Americans because it is easily ground, but disadvantageous in being quite subject to insect damage; (4) dent corn, so called because there is a dent in the top of the kernel in which a soft starch overlies an area of hard starch; modern dent corns are responsible for the high productivity of the corn belt and were originated in the nineteenth century by crossing a southern dent corn with a northern flint variety; and (5) sweet corn, which has sugary instead of starch kernels and is today a favorite fresh vegetable. (Heiser 1990, 95)

Virtually all inhabitants of Mesoamerica and most of the tribes in other parts of North and Central America used maize in essentially the same ways. Although the sprout, spike, or baby corn could be eaten whole, the mature corn was so much larger and more valuable that this was often prohibited. When it was fully grown but still tender, the "green" corn was often either boiled, roasted, or made into *tamales verdes* but most frequently allowed to dry. Then the kernels were removed and used in three basic ways: they were put through the process of nixtamalization and ground into *masa* (dough), from which tortillas or tamales were made, or used whole for *pozole* (hominy); they were toasted and then ground into flour to make corn-based drinks such as *atole* or *pinole*; or they were dried and toasted to make popcorn, much as we do today.

In addition to kernels, the Indians used other elements of corn in a variety of ways. They used *huitlacoche*, corn smut, in foods. This black, mushroom-like fungus is often found growing on corn and was and is used in Mexico as a filling for tacos. Despite its unappealing description, *huitlacoche* has a delicious, subtle flavor and a dramatically inky-black color. Today, this delicacy is gaining popularity in the United States and is being used in new and interesting ways in *nueva cocina mexicana*. Moreover, Aztecs relished a corn worm called *gusano elotero*. The Indians also utilized corn-husks to wrap tamales for steaming and to make teas to serve as diuretics. Even the cobs were used after they were dried, either as abrasive scrapers or as kindling.

The use of wild beans in Mexico dates from as early as 8750 B.C., and their domestication from about 5000 B.C. (Coe 1994, 31)

In Mexico, domesticated beans belong to the genus *Phaseolus* and include the scarlet runner bean, the tepary bean, the lima and sieva bean, and the pinto and black bean. Pintos and black beans are most frequently used today. The earliest discoveries of domesticated beans in the Americas were of *Phaseolus vulgaris* in Peru, dating to 8,000 years ago, and in Mexico 6,000 to 7,000 years ago. Sieva and tepary beans have been found dating back 1,000 to 1,200 years, and scarlet runner beans up to 6,000 years old were discovered in the state of Tamaulipas. (Foster and Cordell 1992, 63–65)

Beans are an excellent nutritional companion for maize since not only is their protein content fairly high, but their amino acid content complements that of corn. (Heiser 1990, 117) A combination of these two foods normally provides all the protein required for adequate nutrition, except for people with the greatest protein needs, such as nursing mothers and newly weaned infants. (Coe 1994, 30)

The bottle gourd may be the earliest squash used in Mexico, but it was utilized as a container rather than for food. Thought to be native to the Old World, this plant has been found to date back to 7000 B.C. or earlier in Mexico, before trade was established between the

Old World and the New World. This mystery could be explained by the fact that, given their ability to float, gourds with seeds might have come across the ocean and washed up on Mesoamerican shores. (Heiser 1990, 180, 181)

When it comes to squash as a food source, other than the chayote, most of Mexico's (and the New World's) squash varieties, including zucchini, yellow summer squash, pumpkin, and acorn squash, come from the genus *Cucurbita*. (Coe 1994, 38)

A vine plant like beans, squash can also be grown in a *milpa*. However, squash was far more versatile than beans. While beans were boiled and eaten alone or mixed with corn to make bean tamales, squash was eaten in several different forms. The seeds were consumed raw, roasted, or ground, and added to stews to provide flavor, texture, or serve as a thickening agent. Pumpkin seeds are still a major ingredient in *moles* and *pipians*, and are often eaten as snacks. Squash blossoms were considered a delicacy in ancient Mexico, just as they are today. They are most commonly wrapped in tortillas or used as an ingredient in soups and stews. The meat of the squash was used both fresh and dried, and possibly cooked with honey to make a sweet.

I n *America's First Cuisines*, Sophie D. Coe points out that while archaeologists dismiss chile as being nothing more than a condiment, its omnipresence among the Indians and their abstinence from chiles during virtually every important religious fast indicates that it was of much greater significance to them than is usually thought. It is a fact that throughout pre-Hispanic Mesoamerica, the common way to fast was to forego both chiles and salt. (Coe 1994, 62)

It is not just the heat of chiles that make them significant in Mexican cooking. Many cuisines, including those of India, Thailand, and China, use chiles but with a far different effect. It is the various flavors, textures, and smells of the chiles used in Mexico, as well as the way they are utilized in

Mexican cooking, that make the cuisine unique.

Excavations at Tehuacán, where many of the oldest examples of foods were found, indicate that chiles were used by people as far back as 7500 B.C. While these early chiles were probably wild, further evidence indicates that man learned to domesticate them by 3300 B.C. (DeWitt and Gerlach 1990, 73)

When Christopher Columbus landed in the New World, he encountered chiles, naming them *pimiento* after the product he was really after, black pepper, or *pimienta*. The fact that there was no word for chile in any Old World language prior to 1492 is evidence that chile is a New World plant. (Andrews 1992, 81, 82) However, the pungent fruits were quickly circulated around the world and soon became part of local cuisines in Africa, Asia, and parts of Europe.

While chiles are the most important aspect of Mexican cooking after corn, they are often intimidating to individuals new to the cuisine. This is because many people have the impression that there are countless chiles that are both difficult to identify and to obtain, which is simply not true. Virtually all Mexican dishes can be prepared with about seven varieties. The confusion about chile varieties is exacerbated by the fact that chiles cross-pollinate and that, in Mexico, different chiles are often called by different names in various regions and villages. For example, in most of Mexico *cascabel* refers to a distinctive, medium-sized, round, dried chile; however, in the state of Coahuila, *cascabel* is the name given to the chile that is called *guajillo* almost everywhere else.

All the world's chiles belong to the genus *Capsicum*, and from an original pool of around twenty-five species botanists now recognize five domestic ones. Of these, it is believed that *Capsicum frutescens*, *Capsicum chinense*, *Capsicum baccatum*, and *Capsicum pubescens* were all originally cultivated in South America. *Capsicum annuum*, economically the most important, was domesticated in Mexico. Today, the major chiles used in Mexico belong to the latter species, except for the *habanero*, which belongs to *Capsicum chinense*.

Amaranth, which produces beautiful foliage and tiny seeds, was probably nearly as important as squash and beans to the first inhabitants of Mexico. It is estimated that this plant, which was called *huautli*, constituted about 14 percent of the Indian diet. And in an historical document, the *Mendocino Codex*, it is recorded that in the Aztec empire eighteen granaries were reserved for amaranth as compared to twenty-one for beans and maize. (Foster and Cordell 1992, 18, 19)

Amaranth's importance was due to the fact that it is high in protein and amino acids and was the first crop of the year, maturing before corn, thus becoming the first major sustenance after winter deprivation. The seeds were used much like corn kernels; they were ground and made into dough or diluted with water to make a drink. The tender new leaves were eaten as a vegetable.

One reason there is not much amaranth in Mexico today is that a dough made of amaranth seeds, combined with either honey or syrup made from the maguey plant and often blood as well, was used extensively by the Aztecs in religious ceremonies. Considered by them to be the essence of their gods, this mixture was used much the way Christians use Communion bread. Juan Ruiz Alarcón described the use of amaranth in the following way:

> Where there is manifestly a formal practice of idolatry is [*sic*] at the close of the rainy season, with the first fruits of a seed smaller than a mustard, which they call *huauhtli*, for also the devil wishes the first fruits to be offered to him. This seed is the earliest to ripen, hardening and maturing before any other....Of this seed they make a drink like gruel for drinking cold, and they also make certain dumplings (*bollos*) of it which in their language they call *tzoalli*, and these they eat cooked like their tortillas.
>
> The idolatry consists in giving thanks for its having ripened. Of the first seed which they gather, well ground and made into paste, they make certain idols with human shape, a quarter of a

AMARANTH

yard, more or less, in size. For the day on which they are made they have prepared a quantity of their wine [*pulque*, fermented from the sap of the agave] and the idols having been made and cooked, they put them in their oratories, as though placing some sacred image, and putting candles and incense before them, they offer up among bouquets of flowers some of the wine prepared for the dedication…; and for all this all those unite of that party, which is the fraternity of Beelzebub, and seated in a circle with much applause, the calabashes [of *pulque*] and bouquets placed before the said idols, there begins in their honor and praise, and in that of the devil, the music of the Teponazatli, which is a drum entirely of wood, and with it is accompanied the singing of the old people, and when they have finished their wonted drumming and singing, the patrons of the feast and the other principals of the ceremony arrive, and as a sign of sacrifice they pour out the wine contained in the calabashes, a part or the whole of it, before the little idols of Huautli, and this ceremony they call Tlatotoyahua; and then they all begin to drink what is left in the said calabashes and then they fall upon the jars of pulque until they are exhausted and their reason as well, winding up with what usually follows idolatrous ceremonies and debauches. However, the owners of the idols keep them with care for the following day, when all of those assisting at the feast in the said oratory, divide the idols into pieces, as for relics, and eat them all up. (Foster and Cordell 1992, 23, 24)

As a result of such ritual use of amaranth, the Catholic Church did not encourage its production. Nevertheless, it is still used in a limited way today but for a different purpose, in nearly the same form—in the form of the popular *alegría*, or "joy," candy that is made with popped amaranth seeds and syrup or molasses and compressed into squares.

In terms of its significance to the Indians of Mesoamerica and later to the rest of the world, chocolate may be second only to corn in importance. It is believed that chocolate was first planted by the Izapans, who inhabited the area along the Pacific Coast of southern Mexico and northern Guatemala, and who are believed to have been the inventors of the Mesoamerican calendrical system. (Coe and Coe 1996, 39–40)

Both the Mayans and Aztecs used chocolate extensively, almost exclusively as a drink, which the Mayans drank hot and the Aztecs cold. To these people, chocolate was not just the fairly simple concoction we enjoy today, but was mixed with ground corn, chile, honey, vanilla, achiote, and numerous other flavorings. Moreover, chocolate was not only valued for its culinary uses but was also utilized as money and had religious significance.

A testimonial to the importance of cacao is that it was widely cultivated in spite of the difficulties involved in growing it and producing chocolate. First, the cacao tree will not bear fruit outside of a zone extending from 20 degrees south of the equator to 20 degrees north of the equator, and will not even produce in this zone if the altitude is too high or the temperature is too cold. (Coe and Coe 1996, 19) Further, this tree is susceptible to many diseases and requires a great deal of water. (The Mayans of the dry Yucatán even planted it in *cenotes*, or sink holes.) In addition, cacao is pollinated by midges that prefer the sweltering compost of the jungle floor to the cleaner environment of organized agriculture. (Coe and Coe 1996, 21) And finally, the flowers of the cacao tree develop into pods with thirty to forty beans, which have to be opened and the seeds spread by either humans or monkeys if trees are to reproduce. (Coe and Coe 1996, 22) Moreover, even after the tree was grown, the flowers were pollinated, and the seeds were extracted, it was necessary to complete four additional processes before the chocolate was usable. First, the seeds were fermented for up to six days, during which time they would germinate, creating the chocolate flavor. Second, the seeds were dried in the sun, which stopped the

CHOCOLATE

germination process. Third, the seeds were roasted at 210 to 219 degrees Fahrenheit. And finally, the seeds were peeled. (Coe and Coe 1996, 23) Today, chocolate is still made in essentially the same way.

Cacao belongs to the genus *Theobroma*, and the two species that we know as chocolate, *Theobroma bicolor* and *Theobroma cacao*, are the sources of chocolate. In Mexico, *Bicolor*, while it does not actually produce cacao, is the source of *pataxte*, which is utilized to make a chocolate-like product used to imitate or dilute chocolate. The principal varieties of *Theobroma cacao* are *Forestero*, from South America, and *Criollo*, from the southern tropical region of Mesoamerica.

Chocolate is, by weight, about 50 percent fat, or "cocoa butter" (the part of the bean from which white chocolate is now made), and about 10 percent protein and starch. The remainder is made up of literally hundreds of compounds, two of which have a significant effect on people physiologically—caffeine and theobromine. The scientific opinion differs widely on the effects of these compounds, although many scientists will agree that cacao has a physiological effect on hormones.

145.

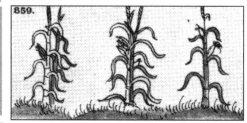

859.

CHAPTER 3
THE DEVELOPMENT OF MEXICAN CUISINE

There are many intriguing aspects of the history of food in the New World following European contact and the development of traditional Mexican cuisine. It is interesting to remember that even the Spanish discovery of America occurred as a result of interest in better-tasting food and profits that could be made from its enhancement. Christopher Columbus was not in search of gold and silver, but a new passage to the Orient to procure the spices so necessary for the preservation of food. After the fall of Constantinople, the old routes had been closed to Europeans.

IMPORTS FROM SPAIN

The Spanish who went into Mesoamerica brought their food customs and food stuffs along with them. It is the unique fortune of Mexican cooking that it is a blend of Mediterranean ingredients with the exciting new foods cultivated by the Native Americans. For the most part, the ingredients that the Spanish brought to Mexico became common elements in Mexican cuisine familiar to us, and do not require lengthy description. Perhaps the greatest Spanish contribution was meat and its byproducts, especially milk, cheese, and lard. The Native Americans had no herd animals. Their main sources of animal protein were wild and domestic turkeys, domestic dogs, and wild game. What little fat they used in cooking came from *chia*, pumpkin seeds, and game animals. Consequently, Spanish cattle, sheep, and goats, from which meat, milk, cheese, and cooking fat could be obtained, had a great impact on the Mexican cuisine.

The list of ingredients the Spanish contributed to Mexican cuisine includes the following: wheat, rice, beef, pork, goat, chicken, cinnamon, pepper, thyme, marjoram, bay laurel, saffron, olives and olive oil, milk and cheese, grapes and wine, sugar, parsley, onion, lettuce, and spinach. Two other culinary factors played prominent roles in the development of Mexican cuisine—the cooking expertise of nuns and the process of distillation.

We know that the Native Americans spiced their foods with salt, chiles, allspice, *achiote*, and a myriad of lesser herbs and spices. Thus the culinary possibilities created by the addition of Spanish ingredients such as cinnamon, black pepper, thyme, marjoram, bay laurel, saffron, garlic, onion, parsley, and sugar were boundless.

Unlike Mexico, Spain had a considerable diversity in terms of climate, soil, population, and commerce with other Mediterranean peoples. Moreover, Spanish cooking at that time had distinct regional variations—partly because Spain had been settled for over 1,500 years by Romans, Visigoths, and Moors and people had isolated themselves into various regions. With a few exceptions, Spanish cuisine was not particularly noteworthy until after the conquest of Mexico when dishes such as paella, gazpacho, the Spanish tortilla or potato omelet, and tapas were able to incorporate New World ingredients.

In Spain, the Romans cultivated olives and wheat, producing olive oil and bread, which may have been used as additions to soups and stews. Under the Visigoths, the raising of cattle, pigs, and sheep spread across the peninsula. However, meat always remained a luxury item. The Moors brought with them Middle Eastern agricultural products, poultry, and a knowledge of irrigation. Realizing their inability to forecast growing conditions, they sometimes planted several crops together, such as wheat and rye, to ensure that regardless of climatic variations there would be something to harvest.

As in most societies, the privileged lived with luxuries unavailable to average citizens. There are numerous accounts and paintings of banquet tables piled with huge plates of roast meat and fowl, presided over by servants especially trained to serve meat and poultry. Included were beef, veal, kid, lamb, deer, chicken, duck, pigeon, partridge, and pheasant. If the banquet was near the sea, platters might be filled with such seafoods as tuna, swordfish, whale, dolphin, pollock, sole, flounder, shad, sea bream, sardines, eels, shrimp, crab, and squid. On the table with these foods were others we regard as wild animals, such as herons, sparrows, swallows, bitterns, hedgehogs, and badgers.

In *Historia de la gastronomía española,* Manuel Martínez Llopis describes a fascinating dish of this period called *gallinas o capones armados,* in which poultry was roasted to produce something that must have been an early fowl version of beef Wellington. Another interesting dish was made of sliced liver with onion, bread, vinegar, sweet wine, and ground cinnamon. (Martínez Llopis TK, 172)

Most roasted foods were served with sauces based on wine, sour grapes, lemon juice, pomegranate juice, and vinegar; sweetened with sugar or rose water; and seasoned with salt, mustard, thyme, garlic, parsley, ginger, cinnamon, and black pepper. A passage by Martínez Llopis, loosely translated, states, "There is no doubt that the elegance of medieval cooking was in the stews and sauces, complicated mixtures—saturated with herbs and spices."

Martínez Llopis also relates that due to the lack of proper meat storage, sauces were often chosen to mask the flavor of spoiled food and were selected based on the season. In fact, both the tenderness and flavor of spoiled meat came to be so desirable that freshly killed animals were frequently held to age. Young animals were not slaughtered for food, except for lamb and kid. In summer, strongly acidic sauces made with vinegar, combined with parsley and ginger and toasted bread, were popular. In winter, the sour sauces were replaced by those containing wine, meat juices, very weak vinegar, and larger amounts of spices like mustard and garlic. Depending on the season, the entrées were accompanied by plums, peaches, cherries, oranges, figs, pears, grapes, melons, pomegranates, and apples; and by vegetables such as cucumbers, turnips, nettles, purslane, carrots, lettuce, onions, celery, mustard greens, parsley, cabbage, and fennel.

To drink, the well-to-do were served wine, sometimes diluted with water or fruit juices, or wine distilled into a crude brandy called *aguardiente*. Instead of wine from grapes, lower-class Spanish people drank *hidromiel*, which was a mead made with fermented honey and water. Nonalcoholic drinks included fruit juices and lemonade.

Grains, including wheat, rye, and oats, hardly provided basic subsistence for most Spaniards during the Middle Ages. Sometimes these grains were ground into flour, then made into bread in communal ovens, and sometimes they were made into porridge that might also contain fruits, nuts, vegetables, and meat, not unlike the Mesoamerican *atole*. Often these porridges were sweetened with sugar. Martínez Llopis describes one of these dishes, *potaje de sémola,* as being made of coarsely ground, washed wheat in chicken broth with almonds, and sweetened with sugar.

For the majority of Spaniards, lima beans, kidney beans, garbanzo beans, and lentils, cooked with stews, supplemented grains. Green vegetables were not particularly popular, and were thought to be difficult to digest. Those most frequently eaten included cabbage, eggplant, spinach, and onion.

When meat was available to the less affluent, it was most frequently pork, mutton, or beef. These meats were preserved by then salting and drying them. This product could then be fried, grilled, or cut up and added to stews. Because of the lack of refrigeration, fresh seafood was only available along the coasts of Spain, but dried, salted fish, especially cod, was popular everywhere.

Spanish desserts of the time included fruit compotes made with apples, quinces, peaches, figs, pears, nuts, sugar, rose water, ginger, and cinnamon. Further, numerous custards were made with sweetened milk and cream, eggs, cinnamon, cloves, and other spices. In addition, rice pudding, the famous Spanish dessert introduced by the Moors was popular. There were also pies and *empanadas,* such as those of Jewish origin, which were filled with dried fruits, poppy seeds, and mild cheeses; desserts made of bread with milk or cream, sugar and fruits, almonds and pine nuts; and marzipan, a favorite sweet made with sugar and almonds. In a particularly interesting old Moorish recipe, cream was beaten with very fine sugar, almonds, pistachios, raisins, either cardamom or anise seeds, a little rose water, small pieces of cheese, and cinnamon.

Following European discovery of the New World, numerous colonizers sailed from Spain to Mexico, an arduous journey that usually took about three months but could take much longer because of the danger of unexpected calms, especially in the Sargasso Sea. For such extended voyages it was difficult to accurately predict the need for food and drink. Passengers usually brought their own food, which frequently consisted of hard, unleavened bread, salted fish and meat, lemons, oranges, rice, garbanzo beans, and olives. Meals requiring preparation were cooked in the ships' galleys.

Although there was limited room on ships to carry livestock, there was usually some access to fresh meat. Water and wine were the beverages of choice. (Brokmann Haro 1996, 17) Most passengers arrived in Mexico in bad health due to illnesses caused by vitamin deficiencies and the generally unsanitary conditions prevailing on the ships. These weary, ill travelers must have been overwhelmed by the sight of the little port of Veracruz with its throngs of seamen, soldiers, clerics, merchants, and colorful Indians.

Food Production & Mixing of Cuisines in the Sixteenth Century

The first order of business for the conquerors was to assure an adequate, reliable, and affordable food supply. One of the first things to strike the newcomers was the size and organization of native markets, such as the one at Tlatelolco described by Bernal Díaz del Castillo as teeming daily with 60,000 buyers and sellers. (Brokmann Haro 1996, 20) Initially, food was so abundant that the average Spaniard was able to eat far better in Mexico than in Europe, with some soldiers receiving two to three times the rations of their European counterparts. But with the increasing number of people arriving from Spain more attention began to be focused on the production of European meats, vegetables, and fruits in Mexico itself.

The Spanish began to raise cattle in the New World. Because they had earlier developed a thriving beef industry in the Antilles and wanted to maintain a monopoly on the supply of this product in New Spain, the authorities hindered competitors. Due to this monopolization and the difficulty of transporting breeding stock from Spain, the growth of cattle herds was slow at first. In order to promote the industry, it was forbidden to slaughter breeding stock until 1531. After five years the number of cattle in the country was estimated to be about 15,000. (Brokmann Haro 1996, 33)

Soon the rapid proliferation of huge haciendas, with 75,000 head of cattle or more, promoted the growth of the cattle industry. Less than a century later the number of cattle was calculated to be between 1 and 3 million.

(Brokmann Haro 1996, 33) And the price of beef, which had been originally imported from the Antilles, dropped from two to three times the price in Spain to one-eighth of the price in Europe. (Brokmann Haro 1996, 37)

Differences of Spanish and Indian styles of farming and agriculture sometimes caused misunderstandings and hostility. In addition to the huge *ranchos*, Spanish farmers also kept smaller numbers of cattle close to the major population centers. Often these animals were used for production of milk, butter, and cheese. Since the Indians viewed pasturelands as communal property, they simply helped themselves to the cattle or sheep they wanted, causing problems with the Spanish. Sheep and goats were kept because they could graze pastures unfit for cattle and survive in arid conditions. (Brokmann Haro 1996, 33) The Indians never grazed large herds of cattle, sheep, or goats, partly because they were difficult to move. The Indians sometimes disappeared into the mountains to avoid taxes they considered unfair. Moreover, in response to the new source of food provided by cattle, goats, sheep, and pigs, the largely vegetarian Indians were warned by some of their sorcerers that eating these animals could literally cause them to become what they ate. (Brokmann Haro 1996, 30) Further, because they had never kept animals, the Indians had never protected their *milpas* with fences. They were angered when Spanish pigs began to multiply into packs and range into their cornfields, destroying crops. However, the Indians adapted by using the pigs in their own cooking and eventually learning to raise them themselves.

While the Indians did not raise herd animals, raising pigs, which ate garbage and provided a large amount of meat, suited them perfectly. Consequently, although the Spaniards raised pigs in areas where cattle did not thrive, such as the Yucatán, the Indians raised them everywhere.

Moreover, the Indians also quickly became accustomed to raising chickens, which in addition to producing meat provided an ample supply of nutritious eggs. In spite of disease, which nearly wiped out the entire supply of chickens from time to time, these birds proliferated to the extent that they were soon very inexpensive.

To make agriculture more efficient, the Spanish introduced new methods, including irrigation techniques from the Romans and Moors, and plows. However, these new methods created additional problems, such as erosion and soil depletion. (Brokmann Haro 1996, 26)

Just as the introduction of herd animals to Mexico proved difficult, growing European crops also presented problems. For example, Spain's most important crop, wheat, required a cooler, less damp environment than existed in southern Mexico. Moreover, the Spanish settlers had little inclination to manual labor, and so depended almost entirely on Indians to perform tasks like planting and harvesting. Because these Indians soon realized that unlike growing corn the planting and processing of wheat required equipment and labor, when not required to produce wheat for tribute, they often abandoned its cultivation and focused instead on corn. Although in this war of the grains, corn triumphed, remaining Mexico's principal staple, in northern Mexico, which had better growing conditions and a high population of Spaniards and mestizos, wheat became a successful crop. Thus, today in northern Mexico you can find wheat flour tortillas as often as corn tortillas, whereas in southern Mexico flour tortillas are seldom seen.

Other crops, especially vegetables, were grown by the Spanish with success, partially due to their prior experience of farming in the Antilles. However, radishes, lettuce, and carrots did not initially thrive in Mexico, and required considerable experimentation. Quince, a favorite fruit of the Spanish, also did poorly; instead of using it fresh the colonists utilized it to make jams, and later a mild alcoholic beverage. (Brokmann Haro 1996, 29) Interestingly, grapes and olives, two of Spain's most important crops, never really caught on in Mexico, because Spain restricted the growing of these items to protect domestic industries. Also the first efforts to grow them in Mexican soil produced poor results. (Brokmann Haro 1996, 30)

In general, the growing of fruits and vegetables caused fewer problems between the Spanish and Indians than raising livestock because this development required no fundamental change in Indian approaches. Nevertheless, the groups had different tastes, and the Indians were not impressed with beets and eggplant any more than the Spanish accepted amaranth and guava.

Once they had established food production, the Spanish built facilities to store food in times of plenty and legislated price controls designed to stabilize the cost of basic food commodities, most notably wheat flour. Nevertheless, both the supply and price of basic staples remained erratic for many years. In fact, the periodic famines that struck Mexico have been partly blamed on government regulations regarding the pricing and storing of food, as well as on bad weather, insect infestations, and crop failure. When a government sets prices lower than what the market is willing to pay, producers hold back or hide production, creating a black market, and this also happened in early Mexico.

In preconquest Mexico, separate kitchens were a rarity, except in the ruler's palaces. The *tecuil*, or Indian hearth, was simply located in the center of the living area. The *comal* and cooking pots were placed on three stones, which were considered sacred; to step on them was considered disrespectful to Xiuhtecutli, the god of fire. (Long 1997, 39)

The Spanish monks and nuns brought Mexico their tradition of medieval kitchens, which were set apart from the main living areas and had high-vaulted masonry ceilings with large fireplaces and side rooms for smoking meats. This model was based on the monasteries and convents, which in Spain were cultural centers and inns for travelers. Because the monks and nuns worked in the kitchens themselves with the servants, the rooms were open, well lighted, and ventilated—in contrast to the kitchens of the Spanish nobility, which were usually located in dank, smoky cellars with poor lighting.

In Puebla, home of the New World version of Talavera tile, artisans transformed kitchens through the use of tile to decorate nearly everything. Made in a profusion of geometric shapes, designs, and colors, tile was utilized to cover walls, floors, ceilings, counters, hearths and even cooking pots, so that kitchens were no longer simply functional but also decorative. In these kitchens, the mixing of cultures was reflected in the use of utensils and methods. For example, because nuns worked with Indian cooks, the *metate* and *molcajete* were placed alongside pots of Spanish design and knives of Toledo steel. In addition, there were *comales* now made of iron instead of clay; ornate wooden *molinillos*, or chocolate beaters, bean mashers, newly designed specifically to prepare refried beans, and other Spanish kitchen tools made of metal, including pots and pans.

The mixing of the cuisines really began when Hernán Cortés and his men ran out of their own provisions and had to rely on the Indians for food. The conquistadors soon learned to eat corn, beans, turkey, and chocolate. Later, while the wealthy and influential Spanish immigrants were, to some extent, able to maintain their European culinary traditions, those of lesser means had no choice but to integrate many Indian foods with their own cuisine, particularly tortillas, tamales, atoles, beans, and chiles. In so doing they filled their tacos and tamales, not as the Indians did with beans and squash but with beef, pork, chicken, lamb, and goat meat.

From the beginning a major difference between the Spanish and Indians was the amount they ate and their attitude toward food in general. According to Janet Long in *La Nueva España*, the Spanish were amazed to find that the average Indian ate but a fraction of what was consumed by the average conquistador. (Long 1997, 6) Even as late as 1843, Martín Gonzáles de la Vara quotes an American businessman who was surprised at how little the average Indian ate, allowing that an Englishman would eat more at one sitting than an entire Indian family in a day. (González de la Vara 1996, 39)

But while the Indians were Spartan in their attitude toward food and other aspects of life, the Spanish ate in what might be called a gluttonous manner whenever they had the opportunity. This was certainly evident in the banquet hosted by Cortés to celebrate his victory over the Aztecs. Huge quantities of pork, imported from Cuba, were eaten, and the soldiers behaved so badly in comparison to the Indians that Bernal Díaz del Castillo said he was ashamed. (Fernández and Ruiz Naufal 1993, 110) Because Spanish soldiers for the most part lived frugally—though not due to religious conviction as did the Indians but out of necessity—when they had the opportunity they would binge. In contrast to the soldiers, the Spanish members of the religious orders, especially in the early days of New Spain, lived a much more Spartan existence. Their lives were regimented, and their dining habits designed to avoid overindulgence. The Indians quickly noticed this similarity to their own ascetic ways, and were predisposed to treat the clergy with respect. Consequently, it was not the boisterous conquistadors but the humble Spanish friars, monks, and nuns who gained the confidence of the Indians, facilitating pacification and eventually conversion of the Indians to Christianity. (Long 1997, 12, 13)

Over time, the mixing of Indian and Spanish cuisines continued, although both the Indians and the Spanish were at first reluctant to abandon their valued culinary traditions. The Spaniards were accustomed to bread, meat, and wine and the Indians to tortillas, vegetables, and *pulque*. In some cases the rejection of a food went beyond issues of taste and familiarity. A notable example of this occurred when the Spanish forbade the Indians to utilize amaranth, which they called *bledo*, because of its use as a sacrament in the worship of their pagan gods. The Spanish even ridiculed it by coining a saying, *"no vale un bledo"* ("it's not worth amaranth"), which is still in use. Through this and similar actions, the Indians quickly learned they were no longer masters of their own world.

Although originally interested in eating only familiar foods, many Spanish soldiers, clergy, and administrators came to accept tortillas, tamales, chile sauces, and the other tastes of New Spain. To the Spanish *olla podrido* or *cocido (stew)*, based on European meats and seasonings, ingredients from the Indian *pipián* (fricassees) were added, including fresh and dried chiles, tomatoes, *tomatillos*, pumpkin seeds, and squash. In Spain, the cooking fats of choice were olive oil and butter, but in New Spain the use of pork lard came to predominate and to be a signature of the cuisine, especially with dishes like tamales and *gorditas*. As time passed, many Spanish ingredients were not only imported into New Spain but were eventually produced there with great success. Some of the corn-based foods improved by Spanish ingredients, such as meat, cheese and milk, were tamales, enchiladas, *tostadas*, *gorditas*, *picadas*, *memelas*, *peneques*, and *atoles*. These foods came to be called *antojitos mexicanos*, literally "little Mexican whims." In fact, they became the backbone of mestizo and Indian cuisine. And in spite of the important Spanish additions of lard, meat, and cheese, so vital were the basic pre-Hispanic dishes that they have retained dominance over this aspect of the cuisine to this day. In fact, outside of Mexico it is *antojitos mexicanos* that are by far the best-known form of Mexican cooking.

Initially Spanish women had little effect on the creation of the new cuisine. Between 1520 and 1539, only 845 women were listed as passengers on ships from Spain, and most of them came in 1535 and 1536. However, by the beginning of the seventeenth century, 10,118 women had immigrated. Newly arrived women were at first interested in maintaining their European culinary traditions, but they also eventually began mixing Indian ingredients into their recipes. Of the women immigrants, 58 percent were from the Province of Andalucia, where there was a great Moorish influence on the culture, including the cooking. (Taibo I 1992, 70) Although the dishes of these women undoubtedly required ingredients that were unavailable, the resulting adaptations probably had a strong Moorish quality to them.

However, Janet Long postulates that, considering the pretensions of many new arrivals from Spain, it is doubtful that many women immigrants spent a great deal of time in the kitchen. (Long 1997, 45) Therefore, at least directly after the conquest, Spanish soldiers probably had their meals prepared for them almost exclusively by Indian women, either in the capacity of spouses or servants. And as children were born of these alliances, they were brought up around kitchens where there was a combination of Spanish and Indian culinary customs, and it was through them that the cuisine we now think of as Mexican developed.

As the Spanish established towns, they planned them to have a central plaza, or *zócalo*, with a market located nearby. And in the public markets the newly introduced foods such as meat, garlic, cheese, rice, onions, and lard began to appear side by side with Indian tomatoes, corn, beans, squash, chiles, and tortillas, encouraging further mixing of the two cuisines through trial and error. Janet Long and others speculate that in addition to the cooking taking place in homes and haciendas some of the first experiments in mixing ingredients of the cultures were performed by cooks in market food stalls, who had easy access to both sets of ingredients. This was taking place at the same time that Indian cooks working with Spaniards in the convents and haciendas were mixing the two sets of ingredients together in their own ways. (Long 1997, 52)

In addition to the European influence on Mexican cooking, there was also African influence. The writer Ignacio Taibo notes that the Spanish brought African slaves to Mexico and that in 1570 there were 30,000 people of African heritage in the country. (Taibo I 1992, 72) And many of the African women worked in Spanish kitchens, where, through their skills, their rank in society could be elevated. In fact, it was considered a status symbol to have an African cook. These women are credited with adding some of their own favorite foods to the culinary mix, including plantains and coconut.

In sixteenth-century Europe, culinary practices and medical philosophy were intertwined, and this view was brought to Mexico. In 1570, Felipe II of Spain sent Francisco Hernández to study the medicinal uses of the plants in New Spain. One result of this emphasis on plants as medicine was that, included in the recipes of the day, were many native and imported foods intended to cure ailments. For example, *jícama* was eaten in the belief that it would help alleviate the symptoms of scurvy; tamarind water was used to combat fevers; honey, sugar, pepper, egg, and ginger were utilized to treat skin problems; and chocolate was consumed as a cure for constipation. In addition, certain foods were thought to facilitate general well-being, including veal, kid, and chicken; while others, such as beef and rabbit, were thought to produce the opposite result. (Long 1997, 11)

During the sixteenth century, efficient food distribution was made difficult in rural areas by Mexico's poor system of roads. The principal reason for the problem was that the Indians had never used the wheel, possibly because they did not have the draft animals that would have made this tool truly useful. When the conquistadors arrived, they found only footpaths.

Near urban areas there was greater access to a variety of food products. Mexico City's basic needs were met by food-producing haciendas. In addition, shiploads of goods from Spain arrived at Veracruz, where they were sorted and transported to Mexico City. Also from 1571 to 1734, the famous *Nao*, Galleon of Manila, sailed between the Orient and Acapulco, bringing such products as rice, cloves, saffron, mango, tamarind, cinnamon, nutmeg, silk, tea, and porcelain. (Farga 1980, 86) All these commodities were eventually distributed by the famous *arrieros*, or mule drivers, from whose cooking several famous dishes were named. These men drove teams of four to five mules in groups that numbered up to fifty mules, each carrying around 250 pounds of merchandise. (Long 1997, 33)

To convert the Indians to Christianity, the Spanish sent a veritable army of priests, monks, and nuns, most belonging to the Franciscan, Dominican, and Agustinian orders. Because of the Spanish custom of primogeniture, in which the eldest son received the family title and inheritance, the younger brothers of leading families, for lack of another option, often entered the church and through political clout secured prestigious positions. In addition, for girls from upper class families the vows and convent life were sometimes the only alternative to marriage. Consequently, many monks, nuns, and clerics came from influential families and were not only well educated but accustomed to the finer things of life. Thus monasteries and convents in Mexico became centers of learning and culture in addition to religious institutions. Moreover, except for a few, these convents did not adhere strictly to vows of poverty but prided themselves on their cultural refinement and intellectualism.

The friars created huge refectories, and due to their ethic of self-sufficiency they produced much of the food served in them. Because the friars and nuns grew much of their own food, particularly fruits, which they planted both in their courtyards and in adjoining fields, and because one of the few earthly pleasures allowed them was the enjoyment of food, religious establishments soon became culinary centers. They also made contributions in the development of new irrigation systems and growing techniques.

In some convents everyone performed kitchen chores, which meant that the cooking was done by intelligent, well-educated, and creative individuals, in combination with Indian servants. The result was often superb, inventive cookery. So good were some of these recipes that the convents sold them to the public to get additional income for the work of the order.

In many convents of that time, communal life was not strictly observed, so many of the religious had their own small kitchens and servants to help them prepare meals, which they ate in solitude. This practice became so prevalent that a scandal ensued, and by the late eighteenth century the Spanish Crown decreed a common life, resulting in the construction of some of the grandest convent kitchens. (Long 1997, 47) But whether or not life in convents was communal, the services of Indian women were used in the kitchen. Consequently, it was Indian women working with Spanish nuns in convents, for the owners of grand haciendas, or for Spanish soldiers who were central to the fusion of the cuisines. These women put their own stamp on dishes requested by their Spanish employers, husbands, and lovers.

Those who lived in the convents were responsible for the creation of numerous dishes. It was there that old Spanish recipes were adapted to New World ingredients, and where they were offered to dignitaries, who spread their fame. Many convent recipes were also written down and passed around or were eventually spread by the children who were educated there. (Long 1997, 14–15) Cooks in convents were particularly instrumental in the creation of sweets. One of the reasons for this was that much of the religious art required the use of egg yolks for making tempera colors, which left large quantities of egg whites, only some of which were used in the gilding process. The nuns were also responsible for incorporating the New World foods like pumpkin, sweet potato, and fruits into the traditional, sugar-based confections of Spanish cooking.

While much of the credit given to the convents for their culinary innovation is undoubtedly deserved, in *Brevísima historia de la comida mexicana*, Jesús Flores y Escalante raises the possibility that much of what was said to originate in the convents might actually have come from the popular cuisine. (Flores y Escalante 1994, 77)

The most popular drinks in New Spain were *pulque, mezcal*, and various *aguardientes*, including probably the best-known one, *chinguirito*. Of the various drinks, *pulque* was by far the most popular, and was sold in the plazas from numerous open-air stands. According to Janet Long, besides being the least expensive it was also the only native alcoholic beverage approved throughout the country because it was deemed to be more beneficial than harmful. Before the conquest *pulque* had been used primarily in religious ceremonies, and in moderation. However, after the conquest the restrictions against the abuse of *pulque* that had been instituted by the

Aztecs, including the death penalty, were no longer in force, and the number of religious celebrations grew, resulting in increased misuse of this alcoholic beverage. (Long 1997, 19)

The cultivation of sugarcane in New Spain and mastery of distillation resulted in the production of Mexico's version of *aguardiente*. Much higher in alcohol content than *pulque*, the popularity of *aguardiente* only aggravated the problems of alcoholism. Janet Long relates that a popular expression of the time, *hacer la mañana* (make the day), referred to drinking *aguardiente* at breakfast. Besides drinking it straight, the people often combined *aguardiente* with various juices and flavorings to create mixed drinks, including one made with milk, eggs, and cinnamon, which Janet Long suggests was the precursor to *rompope*, Mexico's version of eggnog. (Long 1997, 18) Eventually, *aguardiente* was banned, and penalties were imposed for possessing it, including whipping—all of which simply created a thriving black market for it.

Although wine was by far the favorite beverage in Spain, the wine exported to New Spain was frequently of poor quality and expensive. Wine of good quality was usually reserved for fancy banquets and Communion, while ordinary varieties were often combined with fruit juices and spices to make them palatable. To this day these *ponches* (punches) are favorite regional beverages throughout Mexico.

Almost immediately after the conquest inns and restaurants were established. The first *mesón*, or inn, in Mexico City was licensed in 1525 to Pedro Hernández Paniagua. Shortly afterward another was registered to Jerónimo Ade Alderete, a brother of one of Cortés's officials. (Farga 1980, 47)

> Terms describing public places offering hospitality during the colonial period included: *Albergue*, a place of hospitality or shelter; *Bodegón*, a shop where plain food was prepared and dispensed; *Cantina*, a bar or pub where drinks were served; *Figón*, a place where food was prepared and sold at low prices; *Fonda*, places

where food was served in the cities; *Hostería,* a place offering food and lodging; *Hospedería,* rooms for guests in the convents; *Parador,* a place to rest along the highways; *Posada,* a public place; *Taberna,* a shop where alcoholic beverages were sold; *Venta,* a place along the highways that provided food and/or lodging. (Farga 1980, 50, 51)

French Court Influence & Culinary Invention in the Seventeenth Century

In Mexico, the seventeenth century is considered the baroque period, which separated the colonial and national periods. Actually, this era extended from the mid-sixteenth to the mid-eighteenth century, reaching its peak about the middle of the seventeenth century.

Popular historian Ignacio Taibo reports that by the middle of the seventeenth century New Spain had a total population of 3,800,000 made up of 200,000 Caucasians, 150,000 mestizos, 30,000 people of African heritage, 20,000 mulattos, and 3,400,000 Indians. This last number is notable because at the time of the conquest it was estimated that there were approximately 20 million Indians. So, if the numbers are correct, about 16.5 million Indians had perished, some in the initial battles but most through diseases brought by the invaders. (Taibo I 1992, 111)

During this period the economy collapsed, and much farmland was destroyed by rapidly growing herds of cattle. This caused widespread famine. However, in spite of the economic disasters, and because of Mexico's bountiful natural resources, including cheap Indian labor, the Spanish settlers were still able to lead a far more genteel life than they could have in Spain. And as all *nouveau riche*, they lived extravagantly, expressing their new wealth in baroque architecture, dress, and cooking. In fact, the viceroys and other top administrators lived in such exaggerated opulence that their political enemies sent word of the excesses back to Spain, resulting in laws against such extravagances. However, the laws were either ignored or new administrators would quickly adopt the spendthrift habits of their predecessors. This baroque era was, as Irving A. Leonard declares, a time "whose anachronistic spirit deliberately strove to conceal substance behind an elaborate facade of intricately ornate design." (Leonard 1959, viii)

This behavior is exemplified by Archbishop Fray García Guerra, the first archbishop of the baroque era who later became viceroy. After becoming viceroy, he diverted funds that had been raised to build a convent in order to construct a bullring within the viceregal palace. He then decreed that bullfights take place each Friday, beginning on Good Friday. Ironically, an earthquake that killed several spectators occurred during this first event—perhaps a reflection on his corrupt behavior.

With regard to cooking, Ignacio Taibo calls this period the "century of the *mole*," Mexico's most famous—and baroque—dish. In fact, *mole poblano*, with its thirty or so ingredients, is the perfect culinary expression of this age of excess. It is thought that Sor Andrea de la Asunción of the Dominican convent of Santa Rosa invented *mole poblano*. The traditional story of the invention of this dish is that when this acclaimed cook was given the responsibility of preparing a meal for a visiting dignitary and prayed for inspiration she was guided to add nearly all the ingredients in the huge convent kitchen to a more ordinary stew.

However, according to another version of this story, the recipe was from an Indian woman working with Sor Andrea who came from a long line of renowned cooks. She was thought to be a direct descendant of a woman who had been captured in a raid by the Aztecs and who had been marked for sacrifice. Before the ritual her cooking skills were recognized, and she was spared. She later cooked for Emperor Montezuma. Her descendant, who had been selected to cook in the convent of Santa Rosa, delighted in the new ingredients with which she worked and often hid cinnamon, anise, sesame seeds, and other exotic substances under her blouse, which she would secretly mix with chiles, tomatoes, and chocolate late at night.

Early in the morning of the banquet for the viceroy, Sor Andrea instructed her assistant to make a stew, a recipe which her family had prepared for generations in Spain. Having complete confidence in the Indian woman, and not feeling well, Sor Andrea then retired to rest. The talented young cook was troubled, knowing in her heart that, while the stew she had been asked to prepare was excellent, it was not nearly as superb as the one she had perfected during her late-night experiments. So she decided to make her own creation. All day long while she sang the prayers of her people her *mano* flew over the *metate*, and the perfectly ground ingredients were put into a huge painted *olla*. When, just before the dinner was to be served, Sor Andrea, dressed in her finest habit, came to the kitchen, looked into the pot, and discovered what had happened, she scolded the girl. But in reply the young woman merely dipped a wooden spoon into the bubbling stew and handed it to the nun. As Sor Andrea gingerly tasted the sauce, her face broke into a smile and she patted her servant on the cheek. After initial trepidation, the viceroy's reaction to the sensual concoction of chiles, spices, and chocolate was boundless joy. And so might have been born the dish which three centuries later is still the most revered in Mexican cooking.

During the seventeenth century, the Spanish ruling class regarded the French court as a model of gracious living. French cooking was spread by cookbooks and European-trained chefs; Mexican foods were prepared with French techniques and ingredients; and, regardless of origin, favorite dishes were given French names.

The following description by Irving A. Leonard of early Mexico City reflects how life of the Spanish upper class was influenced by the model of the French court:

The transplanted Spaniard, like his kinsmen at home, lived much of his life in the streets, enjoying the continuous jostle and animation of bustling activity and of endless throngs. At almost any hour of the day gilded coaches of the gentry, attended by brocaded lackeys, passed by. Thomas Gage alleged that in 1625 there were some fifteen thousand of these vehicles, whose trimmings of gold, silver, and Chinese silk outshone anything that the Court of Madrid had to offer. In this busy traffic mingled sedan chairs, whose bejeweled occupants swung rhythmically to the trotting pace of the uniformed bearers, squeaking carts with ponderous, solid wheels, haughty riders on horseback with silver studded saddles on gay yellow blankets, and raucously braying donkeys laden with faggots, charcoal, chicken coops, and strings of red-clay pottery. Weaving about these vehicles, mounts, and beasts of burden were a throng of pedestrians representing the whole spectrum of a society of class, caste, and race. Clergymen and friars in black, brown, and grey habits of plain cloth strode among the crowd as ladies in bright *basquiñas* or petticoats, their faces plastered with powder, lipstick, and artificial beauty spots, picked their way over the cobblestones or rutted surface in satin high-heeled *chapines* or slippers, followed by pages holding parasols over their mistresses. Lordly gentlemen strutted under large plumed hats, displaying silver or pearl-hilted swords as insignia of their rank. With an easy disdain they ignored the submissive, ragged Indians in rough sandals and dirty *sarapes*; the garrulous *léperos*, or beggars, even more ragged and bare, who wandered aimlessly about reciting incoherent ballads, whining out their ills, or muttering prayers; the old hags with wrinkled faces hardly visible under their *rebozos*, or shawls, counting the beads of a rosary, or patting *tortillas* with rhythmic precision, or mutely vending pitiful wares spread out on straw mats; and the cursing muleteers guiding their docile but occasionally obdurate animals through this maze. (Leonard 1959, 76–77)

Regional Culinary Variations & Hospitality in the Eighteenth Century

During the eighteenth century, under the Spanish Bourbons Mexico achieved economic prosperity in mining, agriculture, and industry. To accomplish such changes, the country was reorganized, unfair laws were amended, and more honest officials were appointed. In this period the baroque style reached its height with the even more ornate churrigueresque architecture, then, around the middle of the century, was superseded by the far more restrained neoclassical style. Using food as a metaphor to describe these periods, Ignacio Taibo characterizes *mole poblano* as the baroque, *chiles en nogada* as the churrigueresque, and roast veal in its own juices as the neoclassic. (Taibo I 1992, 117)

In 1766, Flanders-born Don Carlos de Croix arrived in Mexico as viceroy of New Spain. Although he is best remembered for the heavy-handed methods he used in performing his duties, including putting down Indian rebellions and expelling the Jesuits from Mexico, he imposed French court customs on Mexican upper-class society.

Since De Croix was well versed in the social and eating habits of the French court, his cooks introduced the rich sauces, elaborate pastries, and techniques of French court cooking to the society of Mexico City. And regardless of laws and threatened punishment from Spain, eighteenth-century upper-class Mexicans maintained their extravagant lifestyle.

The French Revolution further increased French influence on Mexican cooking, since many chefs formerly employed by the French aristocracy opened restaurants in Mexico, sharing their cuisine with the public.

In New Spain, great disparity between the lifestyles of various classes continued. While life for the upper classes was often one big fiesta with political banquets, bullfights, and cultural events, the lower classes lived on the fringes of society. Their precarious economic situation was exacerbated by crop failures caused by weather and insects. In 1785, an unusual freeze destroyed the corn crop in the Valley of Mexico, resulting in the death of 30,000 people. (Taibo I 1992, 129) And between 1767 and 1770 a plague of crop-eating insects (probably grasshoppers) hit Tabasco, creating famine in the area. (Taibo I 1992, 130) Such inequities among the classes prompted Alexander von Humboldt, the German naturalist, following his visit to Mexico in 1803, to call it the "country of inequality." (Long 1997, 49)

Other important influences on Mexican cuisine that served to make people aware of regional variations were the *ferias*, or fairs. During much of its early history, Mexico's various governments imposed severe taxes on commercial transactions, including those involving food. In response to this, tax-free *ferias* were established that became huge regional market-places and distribution centers. The serving of food, usually regional dishes dispensed from small stalls, was an integral part of these *ferias*. The most important fair was established at Jalapa, Veracruz, in 1720. In describing this fair, Taibo notes that it had the advantage of being ideally located to take advantage of the cargos of European goods newly arrived from Spain. For example, it was there that *bacalao*, dried Spanish-style fish, Spain's traditional Christmas meal, cooked with tomatoes, chiles, olives, and capers, was first prepared. (Taibo I 1992, 133) The combination of these ingredients undoubtedly inspired one of Mexico's most important regional dishes, Red Snapper Veracruz Style.

Probably the second most important *feria* was at Acapulco, where the Manila galleons delivered their cargos of goods from the Orient. Also of importance were the fairs of San Juan de los Lagos and Aguascalientes.

The *ferias* were ideal vehicles for spreading regional cooking throughout the country. As they proliferated, they became much like our county fairs, places where typical crafts and food were shared with visitors and where merchants resold goods they had purchased in various parts of the country.

As in all cultures, what types of foods various people ate was determined by a combination of social class and location. Those living in Mexico City, Puebla, or along main trade routes, in addition to local produce had access to food imported from Europe and other regions of Mexico. In these areas the upper class had the option of dining on a wide variety of foods, from simple Indian *antojitos* to the most extravagant banquet dishes. By contrast, those living in areas further away from the major trade routes, regardless of wealth, were more restricted to regional cuisines. This meant that in major cities the Spanish and *Criollos* (Mexican-born Spanish) ate whatever they wanted, including many European-based court dishes, while rich provincials, ordinary mestizos, and Indians consumed more traditional corn-based dishes.

Another important influence on cooking in the eighteenth century was the development of stoves that gave cooks more control, allowing them to prepare different dishes simultaneously, thus increasing the potential for culinary innovation.

By all accounts the first inns, which were designed to accommodate travelers with livestock, were inferior places. Either attached to them or separate were eating places called *fondas* or *figones* (chop houses). Most of the meals were made in large *cazuelas* (cooking pots) and included rice, beans, and various stews. It was not until after independence from Spain that Mexico was opened to foreign businessmen, like innkeepers and hoteliers from France and Italy, whose expertise revolutionized the hospitality industry.

However, despite their shortcomings, the early *fondas* became associated with the notion of reasonably priced regional meals and had a positive impact on the development of regional cuisines.

Similar *fondas* can still be found today at any marketplace in any Mexican city. Most markets have a special area for *fondas*, often little more than permanent stalls built of brick and covered with colorful tiles, with a stove and counters which hold the *cazuelas*. Such *fondas* are part of the special community that is the Mexican market and offer some of the best places to sample regional cooking.

THE RISE OF HACIENDAS & CULINARY TRANSFORMATIONS THROUGH TECHNOLOGY IN THE NINETEENTH CENTURY

B y the beginning of the nineteenth century, Spain's power in the world declined. Native-born *criollos* chaffed under the rule of the Spanish, with whom they had increasingly less in common. The logical consequence was the War of Independence of 1818 to 1821 in which Mexico gained independence.

Unfortunately, the war was not the solution to Mexico's problems; it was more the beginning. Independence from Spain was followed by hardship, as well as political and military chaos. Between 1833 and 1855, there were thirty-three presidential inaugurations. Antonio López de Santa Ana became president eleven times. There were scores of minor insurrections; a war with the United States (1864 to 1867) that resulted in the loss of over half the country's territory; and the rise to power of Porfirio Díaz (1876). As T. R. Fehrenbach said:

> By 1840 Mexico was less a civilized country than it had been. For a generation, Mexico had fed off material and intellectual capital stored up under the crown, without replenishing either. (Fehrenbach 1985, 386)

During this era, Mexico was torn apart numerous times, a process that traumatized many of the privileged, who wanted nothing more than to imitate the affectations of the French court, and wreaked havoc with the lives of the more humble mestizos and Indians, whose ambitions often did not go much beyond staying alive.

All aspects of society and culture were affected by this upheaval, including cooking. According to Taibo, the nineteenth century was such a difficult time for Mexico that cooking did not evolve significantly. (Taibo I 1992, 137) However, in some ways this time of trial was critical in the development of both the country and its cuisine. Many of Mexico's most renowned dishes are served primarily at fiestas and special occasions. While it would seem there was little to celebrate during the nineteenth century, in Mexico being alive and well is often cause for celebration, and fiestas continued, affecting the creation and refinement of various dishes.

For example, directly following General Agustín de Iturbide's drafting of the Treaty of Córdoba, which ended the War of Independence, *chiles en nogada* was invented and became an instant sensation.

As with *mole poblana*, the margarita, *nachos*, and *chimichangas*, there is more than one version of the origin of *chiles en nogada*. According to one version, three prominent young ladies in Puebla created the dish on August 28, 1822, to honor their boyfriends, who had returned from service with Iturbide's army. Another version contends that it was first prepared by some women on August 21, 1821, in Puebla for Iturbide himself, who following the peace accord became emperor. Of the two stories, based on an analysis of circumstances and the fact that the date 1821 came too soon after the destructive war, Taibo accepts the former account as being most probable. (Taibo I 1992, 142–43) But other people have told me that the rapid rise to popularity of this dish is best explained by its having been served to Emperor Iturbide, and perhaps that dates were somehow mixed up and that he was presented with it on the inauguration occurring in 1822. Whatever the truth, *chiles en nogada* has remained an important dish in Mexican cuisine.

Chiles en nogada, related to the much plainer and more familiar *chile relleno*, consists of a *chile poblano* stuffed with a mixture of ground pork, fruits, and nuts. The chile is sometimes prepared *capeado*, fried with an egg batter, and sometimes without being fried. It is covered with a rich sauce of ground walnuts, soft cheese, and cream, and garnished with pomegranate seeds. This famous dish, which is customarily made in August when the *poblano* chiles, walnuts, and pomegranates are at their best, is time-consuming to prepare because among other steps it requires peeling each walnut that goes into the sauce to maintain its pure white color. In *El universo de la cocina mexicana*, María Stoopen notes that this dish incorporates elements of all the sources of Mexico's culinary heritage: Indian, Arab, Oriental, and Spanish. (Stoopen 1988, 26) Its presentation in the green, white, and red of the Mexican flag symbolizes the values of religion, union, and independence.

During the nineteenth century, the esteem in which French cooking had been held for so many years reached its apex with the installation of Emperor Maximilian. Some historians credit the beginning of the French intervention to the Pastry War. During the upheavals of the mid-century, Mexico was forced to rely on Europe for economic survival, and the people grew to resent their dependence. There were riots and reprisals against foreigners in the capital, and since there was no reliable recourse within Mexico, the expatriate victims turned to their homelands for help. In one case, a French baker whose shop was destroyed by carousing Mexican army officers in 1828 petitioned France for assistance. Ultimately, in 1838 the French attacked the port of Veracruz, and Mexico was forced into a financial settlement it could ill afford. By the time he ascended to the throne in 1864, Maximilian served to cement the centuries-long fascination of the Mexican upper class with all things French, while at the same time creating more political upheaval.

Maximilian brought with him a Hungarian chef named Tudos and a veritable army of assistant cooks, who produced lavish meals in the French style. For example, a list of foods from an 1865 banquet included the following: *lomos* (pork loin) *a la parisiense, truchas* (trout) *a la genovesa, pasteles* (cakes) de Estrasburgo, *coliflores* (cauliflower) *a la francesa,* and *pollos* (chicken) *con trufas* (truffles). (Taibo I 1992, 151)

Focusing on a magazine article of the period that commented on the craze for French food during the nineteenth century, Taibo notes that what used to be called *fondas* were now called *restaurantes*, what once were called *mesones* and *posadas* came to be called *hoteles*, what used to be called *dulcerías* and *pastelerías* were now called *confiterías* and *patiserías*, and what once was the traditional *caldo* (soup) with chickpeas, strips of green chile, and lime juice was now called consommé. (Taibo I 1992, 147)

At the same time that these luxuries were being enjoyed by the privileged, the common people, including soldiers, were trying to survive on tortillas and beans, and horses and mules disappeared daily as the hungry population used any available source of meat. However, in modest dwellings and markets, the stronger and more basic aspects of Mexican cooking were evolving. Yet despite this evolution of ethnic cooking it was not until the early twentieth century that regional cuisines began to mix.

Because of Mexico's poor road conditions and the ever-present danger of highway robbery, particularly during the chaos following independence from Spain, the country was divided into regions, and did not at first develop as a true national entity. It was not until the time of Porfirio Díaz (1876 to 1911) that a national highway system was established, and it was not until the early 1900s, when the railroad finally provided a national transportation system for goods, that the country's regional cuisines were brought closer together.

Martín González de la Vara describes the various regions as: the northwest, including the Californias, Sonora, and Sinaloa; the north-central, including Zacatecas, Durango, Chihuahua, and New Mexico; the northeast, including Texas, Coahuila, San Luís Potosí, Nuevo León, and Tamaulipas; the west, including Jalisco, Colima, and Michoacán; the central and gulf zone, including Guanajuato, México, Hidalgo, Morelos, Querétero, Puebla, Veracruz, and Tabasco; the south, including Guerrero,

Oaxaca, and Chiapas; and the Peninsula of Yucatán. (González de la Vara 1997, 27) Not surprisingly, these areas correspond fairly closely (with the exceptions of Upper California, New Mexico, and Texas) to many of Mexico's current culinary regions.

While court life in Mexico City, which was influenced by European fads, dominates historical accounts, the vast majority of the people—mestizos and Indians—lived on small farms far from the capital and were less impacted by political upheavals. They produced and ate relatively small amounts of corn, beans, squash, and chiles, as well as Old World meats and cheeses. In the process of living their daily lives, they were continuing to develop the corn/tortilla-based cuisine of pre-Hispanic Mexico into one that would one day rank with the world's greatest. In recognition of this, sociologists during the reign of Porfirio Díaz classified Mexico as "the culture of corn." (González de la Vara 1997, 22) And throughout the entire process, chile, once used to spice up a bland diet, became, after corn, the most noteworthy element in the cuisine.

While rural Mexicans, even those with considerable wealth, did not have the same access to foods as city dwellers, haciendas, many of them far from any city, became communities in themselves, producing commodities such as beef, *pulque*, cotton, wheat, and sugar, and providing a unique lifestyle for both owners and employees. The most famous haciendas were oriented around the production of *pulque*. The golden age of these enterprises was between 1890 and 1910, during the reign of Porfirio Díaz, when thousands of acres were planted with maguey, and a multitude of Indian workers produced hundreds of thousands of liters of *pulque* for the enjoyment of the lower classes and profit of the aristocracy. (González de la Vara 1997, 20)

The houses of the haciendas were huge, and the wives of the peons provided a large domestic workforce that performed every imaginable household chore, including cooking. Most of the servants worked for not much more than room and board, the latter consisting of supplies of foodstuffs, both those produced by the hacienda and by the workers themselves on small plots they rented from their employers. The kitchens were on the same grand scale as the houses themselves, and although the food prepared in them was more simple than that in upper-class city homes, it was abundant and ever present. There were always people in the kitchen, gossiping and snacking. Typically, meals consisted of broiled meats, stews, beans, tortillas, squash, and other vegetables.

In addition to the large haciendas, there were many small ranchers whose lifestyle depended on the region of the country and how much land they had. In northern Mexico, most of the activities revolved around raising cattle, sheep, and goats. But the lucky (or clever) ranchers whose property ran along riverbanks had the added advantage of irrigated fertile land on which to grow a wide variety of fruits, nuts, and vegetables. In addition to the stock raised for meat, they kept cows or goats from which milk, butter, and cheese were obtained.

Another cultural group that contributed to the mixing of cuisines was the Chinese. Just as in the western United States, a significant number of Chinese immigrated to Mexico to work on the railroads. Most of these people went to northern Mexico, particularly to the Baja California cities of Tijuana, Ensenada, and Mexicali. These newcomers stuck close together to protect themselves and their culture. In Mexico City, the Chinese established *cafés de chinos*, which began catering to the bohemian set. However, unlike in the United States, Chinese food was not readily accepted by the population, except to some extent in northern Mexico, where the *fondas chinas* were patronized for their cleanliness and low prices. Soon these Chinese modified their recipes to include corn and chiles, adding to culinary variations. (Taibo I 1992, 177)

Perhaps the most notable aspect of Mexican society during the latter part of the nineteenth century was a liberalization that profoundly changed centuries-old traditions and mores. Until the second half of the century, it was not common for friends and family to meet for meals in restaurants. Instead, they usually went to each other's homes or met at religious celebrations and at the Sunday evening promenades, where young men and women would parade around the plazas. And prior to the revolution most places of hospitality consisted of the *fondas* and similar enterprises, which were known for cheap food rather than decor, and which were often not considered suitable for ladies.

However, during the reign of Maximilian and later, foreigners, Italians and French predominantly, who saw the opportunity presented by the lack of first-class facilities, came to Mexico to open hotels, cafés, and restaurants. Also the appeal of the traditional paseos and festivals began to wane, especially in the capital among the upper classes. The resulting need for places where people could go to eat and amuse themselves was filled by new, European-managed establishments. In addition to serving snacks and pastries, some of the cafés began to present live entertainment, while others added private rooms, booths, large banquet halls, and installed marble tables and silver services bearing the prestigious monogram of Maximilian. These were considered sophisticated establishments where the gentry could entertain themselves. (Rabell Jara 1996)

For the growing middle class, which in 1895 was estimated to be about 6 percent of the population (Rabell Jara 1996, 36), Mexico had been a place of discipline based on conformance to religious strictures. And women's social activities were limited to school, religious, and family functions. Cafés and *cantinas*, where only those of like mind and disposition congregated, provided a place where women temporarily escaped from such restrictions. Only the theaters competed with cafés in popularity among women. (Rabell Jara 1996, 34)

Further evidence of the growing liberalism, particularly among the affluent, are the names of ice cream concoctions of the time; described by René

Rabell Jara as "sinful," they included "Maiden's Love," "Depth of Hell," and "Clergyman's Love," and were served at places like the Café de Progreso and the Tívoli Fulcheri. (Rabell Jara 1996, 42)

Also during the nineteenth century the establishment of breweries led to the expansion of *cantinas*, especially in northern Mexico. In reaction to this trend, competition developed between the traditional *tequila* and the new *cerveza*, which Taibo notes was resolved with the invention of the *submarino*, which consisted of a shot glass of tequila submerged in a large mug of beer. (Taibo I 1992, 179)

Since the arrival of the Spanish, Mexican society had had a problem with alcohol, one which reached serious proportions toward the end of the nineteenth century. In 1864, there were officially 51 *cantinas* in Mexico City; by 1885, the number had grown to 817; by the beginning of the twentieth century, there were 946 *pulquerías*, one for every 340 inhabitants, 3 for each meat market, and 28 for every bakery. (Rabell Jara 1996, 25) To deal with this situation, authorities devised many laws and educational programs. For example, some places selling alcoholic beverages were not allowed to have chairs, so the clientele would have to stand and presumably get tired and leave; others were not permitted to have windows, which served to hide their existence; and new vagrancy laws were passed to keep the drunks off the streets. The principal result was that more and more *cantinas* and *vinaterías* (establishments selling wine) operated outside the law, although the anti-alcohol environment ushered in the era of cocktail bars, which were considered more acceptable because the alcohol in cocktails was diluted with other ingredients. At least one of these laws, which required *cantinas* to serve food as well as alcohol, did have a positive effect. To this day, such places are known to serve some of the best *botanas* (appetizers) in the country.

By the end of the nineteenth century, the development of cafés, *cantinas*, and other such establishments, as well as the increase of Indian street vendors selling such items as tacos, had discouraged dining at home, where for most of the nineteenth-century kitchens were often unpleasant and inefficient. Because of the lack of refrigeration, fresh food was purchased daily, much of it from street vendors, while cooking was done with wood and charcoal.

At the end of the century development of gas and electric stoves and the icebox, as well as the train and automobile, began to transform cooking methods and culinary customs. Around 1860, the first mechanized tortilla machines were introduced, although they did not immediately become popular. Among the poor, the entire process of making tortillas from the nixtamalization of corn through cooking the tortilla remained the prime activity of housewives. Most of these people lived in dwellings with scarcely more than one room, and existed on tortillas and beans with an occasional treat of beef or pork. (González de la Vara 1997, 39)

Another new development of the late nineteenth century that reflected changing customs was that Mexican foods, including hot sauces, tortillas, chocolate, and *pulque*, began to appear at banquets of the rich, who had previously taken no interest in Mexican foods. Martín González de la Vara asserts that this culinary ambivalence reflected a paradoxical aspect of the upper classes that while they tried to appear cosmopolitan, they were actually quite traditional. (González de la Vara 1997, 36)

Observation of a nineteenth-century wealthy family indicates both the large quantity of food eaten and the range of foods of both European and Mexican origin. Firsthand reports indicate the following was a typical schedule of meals for a wealthy family during the mid-nineteenth century. Around 8 A.M. family members would, in their own rooms, have a cup of chocolate with some sweet bread. At about 10 A.M. they would have a hot breakfast consisting of broiled or stewed meat, eggs, and refried beans. The main meal, beginning around 3 P.M., would include a bowl of soup, a *sopa seca* of rice or pasta, followed by the main course, which might be a combination of beef, mutton, a little pork, bacon, chicken, small *chorizos*, cabbage, green beans, pears, plantains, celery, cilantro, and parsley, all cooked at the same time, but with the vegetables and meats being served on different platters from which the diners could help themselves. This main course was followed by a small serving of meat or fish in a strong broth, then a dessert and various sweets. After the main *comida* there would be a siesta, and about 6 P.M. chocolate, or in the summer ice or gelatin of fruits, would be served. A supper of broiled meat, salad, beans, and a dessert was served about 10 P.M., after which the family would go to sleep. (González de la Vara 1997, 32)

Nearly every historian writing about Mexico's colonial era remarks that the upper classes, with their lives of leisure and huge banquets including fatty foods, were anything but thin in stark contrast to the Indians, whose ascetic customs and hard work kept them slender. The attitude of the upper classes toward eating was undoubtedly influenced by the European belief that to be thin implied either sickness or the inability to obtain food.

Tradition & Innovation in Twentieth-Century Mexican Cuisine

In 1901, oil was found in Mexico in the state of San Luís Potosí, a discovery that was to revolutionize both transportation and cooking through the development of motor vehicles to replace mule teams and stoves to replace wood-fired hearths. These innovations occurred at the same time that Porfirio Díaz was bringing a semblance of order and prosperity to the country. The ruling class again turned to France for culinary inspiration, resulting in a new wave of French chefs coming to Mexico. Once again, while the upper class was prosperous the lower classes remained impoverished, creating dissatisfaction that culminated in the Mexican Revolution, from 1911 until 1925.

After the revolution, Mexico was again open to foreign influences, particularly through tourism, resulting in improved transportation and hotels, as well as increased importation of food luxury items, including cheese, liquor, hams, truffles, salmon, and caviar. (Farga 1980, 204)

As in other parts of the world, technology transformed eating and cooking customs in Mexico. By 1904, electricity was common in the most important Mexican cities (Carreño King 1997, 6), paving the way for electrical appliances, including water heaters, refrigerators, stoves, hot plates, blenders, pressure cookers, mixers, and washing machines. But it was not until the 1950s that Mexican kitchens were nearly universally equipped with modern conveniences, many of them imported from the United States. The stove, both electric and gas, replaced the wood-fired hearth; the blender replaced the *molcajete*; and the refrigerator made the daily trips to the market unnecessary.

During the first decade of the twentieth century, machines to make tortillas, which had been invented around 1860, began to appear in *tortillerías* throughout the country, thus freeing people from the most time-consuming task in the Mexican kitchen. Modern technology also encouraged the establishment of bakeries, which made breads and pastries available that had taken many hours to prepare.

The difference between the development of *tortillerías* and bakeries highlights aspects of Mexican culture. The tortilla represented Indian Mexico, and while considered to be "common" was nevertheless the most important food item in the country. In accordance, *tortillerías* were located around the markets and in lower-class *barrios*. They were and are purely functional spaces with concrete floors, plain masonry walls, and little or no decoration. On the other hand, bakeries were viewed as part of Mexico's European heritage and consequently were located in open, well-lighted, often upscale facilities in the better areas of town.

In addition to labor-saving appliances, new technology brought a plethora of prepared foods like powdered chocolate, gelatin desserts, packaged cookies, biscuits, and frozen dinners. Moreover, Mexico's version of fast-food outlets proliferated, including hole-in-the-wall outlets featuring rotisserie-cooked chicken, and stalls selling what Tania Carreño King calls vitamin T: tamales, tortas, and tacos. All these developments decreased the work related to preparing the daily meals. (Carreño King 1997, 44)

Technology also precipitated other social changes. First, it had a profound effect on the changing role of women in the society. Traditionally, the role of women in Mexico was to provide food and comfort for their husbands, and care and education for their children. Their domain was the home, all aspects of which were their responsibility. In fact, women were rarely seen outside the home. Men, on the other hand, had the responsibility of providing money and protection that allowed the home to exist, and their domain was outside the household. While the cafés which sprang up in the nineteenth century allowed women to take a more active part in public life, they were nearly always accompanied by their husbands and families. Because of time-saving technology and the Mexican Revolution, when they proved themselves by serving as soldiers, women began to participate more in the outside world, assuming many of the tasks formerly assigned solely to men. By 1953, when women were permitted to vote, the process accelerated. To this day, the café is a preferred place for women to socialize with each other—to discuss both the day's business and the latest gossip.

The changing roles of family members have ultimately altered mealtime traditions. Traditionally, the entire family shared the day's main meal. However, since husbands and wives now frequently both work, sometimes in very different locations, the family often grabs a quick lunch on the run and then gathers for a light supper around 8:00 P.M. Nowadays, Sunday is the only day of the week when families have the traditional mid-afternoon *comida corrida*.

Ignacio Taibo discusses how modern life has necessitated the institution of *la cocina económica*, small neighborhood restaurants specializing in inexpensive versions of the *comida corrida*, the traditional four-course main meal. This institution, which developed from the *fondas*, began in the late nineteenth century and continues today. These places, usually with just a few tables, are normally clean, and often provide excellent, although fairly ordinary food. The usual offering consists of soup, rice, a stew served with beans, tortillas, or *bolillos* (rolls), and a simple dessert. (Taibo I 1992, 199) As a result of such neighborhood restaurants, many more families of modest means now eat meals outside the home.

During the presidency of Miguel Alemán (1946 to 1952) economic prosperity created a demand for new restaurants. Thus, in the late 1950s the Zona Rosa became Mexico City's Fifth Avenue, the place where people went to dine in luxury and to be seen. However, this area has become a bit seedy lately, so the most popular dining areas are the Polanco and Condesa Districts. Moreover, during the 1950s fine restaurants, including Prendes, were established around the historic center of the city, and cooking schools were founded to teach housewives proper food preparation and etiquette for entertaining, much of it related to the French tradition.

Until the 1980s, imported foods were the hallmark of class, and traditional Mexican foods were reserved for holiday fiestas and home use. Then creative chefs began to experiment with the traditional cuisine, mixing its various elements, applying new techniques, and placing a new emphasis on visual presentation. The results were popular with the public, and by the mid-1990s this new style called *nueva cocina mexicana* was well on its way to becoming part of the cuisine.

Part II

RECIPES

CHAPTER 4
NEW COOKING FROM MEXICO

Nueva cocina mexicana cuisine is growing so rapidly that no single book could chronicle its development. However, this section attempts to provide a "feel" for the cuisine, and in the process present some delicious recipes.

Nueva cocina mexicana differs from other styles of nouvelle and fusion cooking in that its ingredients and techniques come, for the most part, from various aspects of Mexican cooking rather than from a combination of other cuisines. Historically, Mexican cuisine developed on two levels simultaneously, with "peasant" and "court" cooking evolving separately. In *nueva cocina mexicana*, these two paths merge, with dishes combining these aspects in various ways. *Nueva cocina mexicana* involves primarily two types of integration: a mixing of traditional ingredients, techniques, and recipes; and incorporation of the predominantly French and Spanish-based Mexican "court" cooking into traditional cooking.

Authorities on Mexican cooking have described *nueva cocina mexicana* in a variety of ways. For example, it has been characterized as follows:

> Rooted in ancestral customs that have been adapted to different circumstances over the centuries, Mexican cuisine continues at the end of the millennium, but with greater emphasis on finding a place where the arts, the food, the customs of the country and the world merge and mix, producing universal symphonies that conform to domestic traditions. This cuisine is ecumenical in that traditional Mexican ingredients are served on porcelain, fine china is used with artisan plates, glass with crystal, linen with openwork and lace. (Fernández and Ruiz Naufal 1993, 25)

> Whereas an informal meal or a supper between friends is gracefully complemented by clay dishes from Michoacán or talavera from Puebla, the *nueva cocina mexicana*, which mixes crepes with *huitlacoche*, quail with white *mole*, shrimp with tamarind sauce, squash blossoms with artichokes, salmon with sauce of *epazote*, mangos, and strawberries, is appropriately served…on porcelain of Limoge, Sèvres, Meissen, Bavaria, Rosenthal, Herend, Royal Doulton, Buen Retiro, or Noritake. In crystal from Baccarat, Saint Louis, Lalique, Val Saint Lambert Venecia y Bohemia, the fine wines of the world are served, including some from Mexico; meanwhile, pieces of Christofle, Alex, Albers Art Noveau, Tiffany, or Sheffield compete equally with Mexican pieces designed by Spratling or Tane. (Fernández and Ruiz Naufal 1993, 42)

Ignacio Taibo's comments on this cuisine emphasize both its innovation and its reliance on traditional aspects of Mexican cuisine:

> New ways, new words, old concepts with a new twist, ancient recipes that are reborn in the present time, which requires the modification of some formulas and the discarding of others. Ultimately, the new Mexican cooking is born, propelled by the other new cuisines….
> And that means that it is born knowing what others have

learned through trial and error, and because of that its birth was delayed, but, on the other hand, it came into the world with undisputed wisdom....

Those who for a long time denied that the national cuisine could compete with that of other gastronomically important countries have to cede before the reality that is being imposed. Here one can dine well with a different and delicious cuisine, a national food that does not have to be based upon chiles as it was before.

However, Taibo cautions that it is too soon to be certain of the ultimate impact *nueva cocina mexicana* will have on the overall evolution of Mexican cuisine:

The new Mexican cuisine is now with us, but it arrived after we saw how a similar adventure in elegance and exquisiteness fared in Europe, and because of that voices are already raised in alarm.

The restoration is among us but we must wait—let it repose—before we can really know what will be the ultimate impact of so many new recipes. (Taibo I 1992, 213–14)

In presenting recipes of *nueva cocina mexicana*, I have attempted to avoid the pitfalls sometimes associated with writing about or giving demonstrations of food preparation, such as taking cooking too seriously and relying on theatrical presentations like that described by Jean-François Revel in *Culture and Cuisine:*

As for branches of fennel, it is a veritable farce that we witness in the so-called "great fish restaurants" of Paris every time we see uniformed maîtres d'hôtel making desperate efforts to control a fire that they themselves have just lighted by putting a match to a heap of hay piled up under the wrinkled flanks of some hapless sea-creature whose skin thus chars to a cinder while its flesh remains ice-cold.

On the other hand, as Revel goes on to state, cuisine and food presentation that is not periodically infused with creativity becomes stagnant and uninteresting:

> [T]he difficulty lies in discovering, behind the verbal façade of fancy cuisines, the popular, anonymous, peasant or "bourgeois" cuisine, made up of tricks and little secrets that only evolve very slowly, in silence, and that no individual in particular has invented. It is above all this latter cuisine, the average cuisine, the gastronomical art of the "depths" that is responsible for there being countries where one "eats well" and others where one "eats badly." But by itself, cuisine that is merely practical, traditional family cooking does not suffice either. If it is not stimulated by the innovation, the reflection, and indeed the extravagance of a handful of artists, popular cuisine itself becomes atrophied, dull and uninteresting. The gastronomical serial written by the centuries has as its "plot" the constant battle between the good amateur cook and the thinking chef, a lover's quarrel that, as in all good adventure novels, ends, after many a stormy scene, with a marriage. (Revel 1982, 14)

In presenting the following recipes, I have attempted to sustain a balance between traditional views and innovation—something that has not been difficult because at its best *nueva cocina mexicana* combines the elegance of Mexican "court" cooking with traditional Mexican cuisine—maintaining the earthy, soul-nurturing appeal that has made Mexican cuisine one of the world's greatest culinary achievements.

New Cooking Recipes

THE SALAD:

4 cups fresh spinach, stemmed
   and washed

1 cup thinly sliced red onions

THE DRESSING:

4 ounces bulk chorizo

1 tablespoon minced white part
   of green onion

1 tablespoon minced garlic

½ cup olive oil

2 tablespoons cider vinegar

1 teaspoon sugar

¼ teaspoon salt

Freshly ground black pepper to
   taste

½ cup crumbled goat cheese

❈ SPINACH SALAD WITH GOAT CHEESE & CHORIZO
❈❈

■ This recipe was adapted from "Spinach and Goat Cheese with Warm *Andouille* Dressing" presented in *Emeril's New Orleans Cooking,* by Emeril Lagasse and Jessie Tirsch. ■

To make the salad, combine the spinach and onions in a large bowl.

To make the dressing, sauté the chorizo in a skillet over medium-high heat for 1½ minutes. Add the onion and garlic and sauté until the chorizo is thoroughly cooked, about 1 minute. Add the olive oil and vinegar, cook for 1 minute, and remove from the heat. Stir in the sugar, salt, and pepper, and immediately toss with the salad. Place the tossed salad on 4 serving plates and top with the goat cheese. Serves 4.

❈ CILANTRO DRESSING FOR SALAD
❈❈

1 cup corn oil

½ cup rice vinegar

1 teaspoon lime juice

4 cloves garlic, coarsely chopped

⅓ cup onion, chopped

1 tablespoon Worcestershire
   sauce

1 teaspoon sugar

½ teaspoon lemon pepper

1 bunch cilantro, washed, dried,
   and coarsely chopped

1 egg

■ This delicious dressing is a house specialty at Saltillo's La Canasta Restaurant. It has the tartness but not the bite of green goddess—and something more. Its only drawback is that, to obtain the proper thick, creamy consistency, it must be made at least one day before using and refrigerated overnight. However, it is well worth the effort. It is important to use corn oil; the one time I used canola oil instead of corn oil the dressing separated. Also, note that the original recipe calls for 2 tablespoons Knorr powdered chicken broth instead of Worcestershire sauce; I prefer the latter. Serve the dressing with tossed mixed salad greens, garnished with garlic croutons, and a little cooked crabmeat or shrimp, if you wish. This dressing is also used on the delicious *nueva cocina mexicana*-style sandwich *Torta de queso y chile* and is good as a mayonnaise substitute with most other sandwiches. ■

Combine all the ingredients in a blender and blend for 1 minute. Place the dressing in the refrigerator and chill for 8 hours or overnight. Serve on any tossed green salad. Makes about 2 to 2½ cups.

❈ Vampire Salad

■ This excellent variation on the *sangrita* and tequila theme was inspired by a recipe in *Gran libro de la cocina mexicana* by Alicia and Jorge De'Angeli. ■

To make the dressing, whisk together all the ingredients except the olive oil until well combined. Little by little whisk in the olive oil, and reserve the dressing.

Combine and chill all the salad ingredients. Five minutes before serving combine the dressing with the vegetables. Serves 4.

THE DRESSING:

1½ tablespoons orange juice

1 teaspoon grenadine

Heaping ¼ teaspoon salt

Scant ¼ teaspoon ancho chile powder

2 teaspoons tequila

1½ teaspoons lime juice

3½ tablespoons olive oil

THE SALAD:

1½ cups cooked or canned garbanzos, drained and rinsed

2 cups chopped zucchini, steamed until just soft

½ cup cooked or frozen corn kernels, thawed

1 cup sliced nopalitos, cooked until soft and rinsed, or canned nopalitos, rinsed

1 cup sliced mushrooms, steamed until just soft

2 tomatoes, chopped

4 cups chopped romaine lettuce

½ cup shredded añejo or cotija cheese

❊ Green Salad with
❊ ❊ Pumpkin Seed & Walnut Dressing

THE DRESSING:

2 tablespoons roasted pumpkin
    seed oil

2 tablespoons walnut oil

1 tablespoon cider vinegar

¼ teaspoon salt

¼ teaspoon black pepper

THE SALAD:

¼ cup raw pumpkin seeds

¼ cup pine nuts

1 head butter lettuce, cut into
    pieces

1 medium tomato, cut in half
    and sliced

2 green onions, chopped

1 apple, cut into ⅛-inch slices,
    about ½ inch wide by 1 inch
    long, and drizzled with lime
    juice

2 ounces cotija or añejo
    cheese, grated

2 ounces panela cheese, grated

■ This delicious and elegant salad is made with dark green, fragrant, roasted pumpkin seed oil and walnut oil, both of which can be found in specialty food and better grocery stores. ■

To make the dressing, whisk together the dressing ingredients.

To make the salad, toast the pumpkin seeds by placing them in a medium-sized skillet over medium heat and cooking, stirring frequently, until they have popped (do not allow them to scorch). Just before the seeds are done, add the pine nuts and continue cooking until they just begin to brown.

Combine the lettuce, tomato, and green onions. Toss with the dressing, and place the salad on 4 serving plates. Garnish the salad with the pumpkin seeds, pine nuts, apple slices, and grated cheeses. Serves 4.

✳ Shrimp with Chipotle Remoulade Sauce

■ This recipe was adapted from one by Emeril Lagasse, whose cooking is very similar to that of many practitioners of *nueva cocina mexicana*. It adds a much-needed change to the traditional shrimp cocktail. ■

To make the remoulade, place all ingredients in a food processor fitted with a steel blade and process for 1 minute.

To prepare the shrimp, clean and devein them, leaving the tails intact. Then place them in a large quantity of boiling water over high heat and cook them, checking them frequently, by cutting into them with a small, sharp knife, until they are just cooked through. Immediately immerse the shrimp in ice water, and place them in the refrigerator until they are thoroughly chilled.

To serve, slice the cucumber and jícama into thin pieces and place them on a large serving plate to form a bed for the shrimp. When the shrimp are chilled, dry and place them on the plate and decorate with carved radishes. Serve with the sauce. Serves 4.

THE CHIPOTLE REMOULADE:

2 tablespoons fresh lime juice

3 tablespoons olive oil

3 tablespoons canola oil

¼ cup chopped onion

¼ cup chopped celery

I tablespoon chopped garlic

2 medium, canned chipotle chiles, seeded and chopped, or to taste

I½ tablespoons Dijon mustard

I½ tablespoons American yellow mustard

I½ tablespoons catsup

⅓ cup loosely packed, chopped cilantro

½ teaspoon salt

¼ teaspoon black pepper

THE SHRIMP & GARNISH:

I pound large (approximately 20/pound) shrimp

I large cucumber

I small jícama

I–4 carved radishes

✳ CREAM OF PECAN SOUP

1½ tablespoons butter

¾ cup minced onion

6 tablespoons unsalted tomato sauce

3½ ounces pecan bits (a little over ¾ cup), ground to a paste

3 cups unsalted chicken broth

¾ teaspoon salt

⅓ cup cream

1 teaspoon ground nutmeg

■ The state of Chihuahua grows large quantities of pecans. It is also filled with talented cooks, and over the years they have done about everything possible with their nuts. This rich and elegant recipe, which I adapted from one in the Mexico Desconocido's *Guía Gastronomía* series, is unquestionably one of the best. For good results, it is very important to grind the nuts to a paste in a spice or coffee grinder and not to omit the nutmeg. ■

Melt the butter in a pot over medium heat, add the onion and cook, stirring often, until it is soft but has not browned. Add the tomato sauce and continue cooking for 2 minutes. Then add the pecan paste, and stir it into the onions and tomato sauce. Stir or whisk in the chicken broth a little at a time, the way you would add liquid to a roux, making sure each addition is well incorporated before adding more. Bring the soup to a boil, turn down the heat, and simmer for 10 minutes. If you used salted tomato sauce and/or broth, add salt to taste. If you used unsalted sauce and broth, add the ¾ teaspoon salt and cook 1 minute. Then add the cream, bring the soup back to a simmer, and serve it with a dusting of nutmeg on top. Serves 4 to 6.

SOUP TLAPAN STYLE

PAMBACITOS

TAMALES

NEW WORLD INGREDIENTS

CAZUELITAS

DRINKS

GELATINA DE CAJETA

SALMON PIBIL

RICES AND BEANS

GREEN POZOLE

✳ PORK RIND SOUP

■ Despite the somewhat unappealing English translation of this recipe, it is delicious. One night my friend Elena Hannan called from Mexico City to say she had just tried a soup that she thought was exquisite and would try to get the recipe. I paid attention because Elena, who has lived most of her life in Mexico, knows a great deal about Mexican food. A few weeks later when the recipe arrived, I eagerly tried it and was well rewarded, as I hope you will be. The recipe, to which I have made some alterations and additions, is from the Calle de la Barraca, a member of the Barraca Orraca restaurant chain which serves some excellent fare, both traditional and *nueva cocina mexicana. Chicharrones,* called pork rinds, can be purchased throughout the United States in the snack section. ■

Place the pork rinds in a food processor fitted with a steel blade, process until thoroughly ground, and reserve. Place the broiled tomatoes in a blender with the roasted garlic. Heat a small skillet over medium heat, add the butter, and sauté the onions until they are soft and beginning to turn golden. Then scrape the onions into the blender and add the chiles. Blend the contents for 1 minute, then strain through the fine blade of a food mill. Place the blended, strained ingredients in a pot, add the cilantro and broth, then whisk in the processed pork rinds. Bring the mixture to a boil, then remove it from the heat and allow it to cool slightly. Blend the mixture in batches for 1 minute (being mindful of the fact that, if the blender is too full, hot ingredients have a tendency to overflow) and return it to the pot. Add the cream, salt, and pepper, bring the soup to a boil, and simmer for 15 minutes. Ladle the soup into 4 bowls, add a dollop of the crème fraîche, sprinkle on a little of the chile powder, and serve. Serves 4.

100 grams (about 4 ounces) pork rinds

4 medium tomatoes, broiled

4 cloves roasted garlic

1 tablespoon butter

1½ cups chopped onions

2 small to medium canned chiptole chiles, or to taste

¼ cup loosely packed, chopped cilantro

6 cups chicken broth

1 cup whipping cream

¼ cup crème fraîche or 3 tablespoons sour cream mixed with 1 tablespoon whipping cream

Salt and pepper to taste

1 teaspoon ancho chile powder

 LETTUCE SOUP

8 cups finely chopped romaine
   lettuce

2 cups water

2 tablespoons butter

½ cup minced onion

2 teaspoons minced serrano
   chile

2 cloves garlic, minced

5 cups chicken broth

1 cup evaporated milk

2 tablespoons lime juice

½ teaspoon ground nutmeg

1½ teaspoons salt

½ teaspoon ground black
   pepper

½ cup garlic-flavored croutons

■ This recipe was inspired by a soup served at the famous Villa Montaña resort on the outskirts of Morelia, a frequent honeymoon destination and weekend getaway for people in Mexico City. I made several changes to the original recipe, and the result is both beautiful and delicious. ■

Put the lettuce in a pot, add the water, bring to a boil, and barely simmer, covered, for 15 minutes. Meanwhile, melt 1 tablespoon of the butter in a small skillet over medium heat, and sauté the onion and chile until the onion is soft but not browned. Add the garlic and cook 1 more minute, then spoon the onion and garlic into a blender. Add the lettuce and its cooking water to the blender, plus 2 cups of the chicken broth, and blend until the lettuce is very finely chopped but not completely puréed. Pour the contents of the blender into a large pot, add the remaining chicken broth, 1 tablespoon butter, the evaporated milk, lime juice, nutmeg, salt, and pepper, bring to a boil, and simmer for 15 minutes, uncovered. Serve the soup immediately, garnished with the croutons. Serves 4.

LENTIL SOUP

■ The name of this soup is deceiving in its simplicity, as a glance at the list of ingredients, which show strong Moorish roots, will make evident. The coconut milk and spice mixture make it very much like an East Indian curry soup. ■

Cook and purée the lentils, and poach and shred the chicken breast. Melt the butter in a pot over medium heat, add the bacon, and cook until it begins to brown. Add the onion and sauté until it just begins to turn golden. Next add the garlic and ginger and cook 1 more minute. Then add the saffron, coriander, cumin, cinnamon, pepper, and chile powder, and cook for another minute. Stir in the lentil purée, then add the chicken broth, little by little. Next stir in the tomato purée, the lime juice, and bay leaves and simmer the soup for 10 minutes. Then add the shredded chicken, simmer for 2 minutes, add the salt, then add the coconut milk. Heat the soup until almost boiling, remove the bay leaves, and serve. Serves 4.

1 cup lentils, simmered until tender, then puréed with 1 cup of their cooking liquid

1 boneless chicken breast (2 pieces), poached until just tender and shredded

4 tablespoons butter

2 tablespoons minced bacon

1½ cups finely chopped onion

3 cloves garlic, minced

2 teaspoons minced, fresh ginger

¼ teaspoon saffron

2 tablespoons ground coriander seed

½ teaspoon ground cumin

½ teaspoon ground cinnamon

½ teaspoon ground black pepper

1 teaspoon ancho chile powder

5 cups unsalted chicken broth

½ cup tomato purée

2 tablespoons lime juice

2 bay leaves

1½–2 teaspoons salt, or to taste

1 cup canned coconut milk

✳ CREAM OF AVOCADO & TEQUILA SOUP

1 pound (about 2 large) avocados, weighed whole

1 cup freshly squeezed orange juice

¼ teaspoon grated orange peel

2½ tablespoons tequila

2 small serrano chiles, stemmed, seeded, and minced

Heaping ½ teaspoon salt

3 tablespoons fresh cilantro, minced

3 cups unsalted chicken broth

4 cilantro leaves

½ teaspoon ground cumin

½ teaspoon paprika

■ *Crema de aguacate*, in one form or another, is a staple of *nueva cocina mexicana* chefs, and most versions contain cream in liberal amounts, but this one contains none at all, even though it is creamy in both taste and texture. The recipe was adapted from one in *Gran libro de la cocina mexicana* by Alicia and Jorge De'Angeli, and it certainly has the least calories of any I have tried. The creamy avocado with the fruity overtones of orange and maguey from the tequila are tantalizingly delicious, and I do not believe it is possible to find a recipe of this quality that is any easier to prepare. ■

Chill all the ingredients except the salt, cumin, and paprika in the refrigerator for several hours before preparing the soup. Cut the avocados in half around the seeds, scoop out the meat, and put it in a blender. Add the orange juice, orange peel, tequila, *serrano* chiles, salt, and cilantro, and blend until puréed. Add the chicken broth and blend until well combined. Ladle the soup into small bowls or cups. Place a cilantro leaf in the center of each cup or bowl, sprinkle a little cumin on one side and some paprika on the other side, and serve. The soup can be refrigerated for 2 to 3 hours before serving. Serves 4.

❊ WILD MUSHROOM SOUP

■ This is a fine soup kissed by the flavor of a variety of mushrooms and made special by the addition of *epazote*. The more different kinds of mushrooms you use (fresh or dried and rehydrated) the better it will be. ■

Broil the tomatoes as close to the heat element as possible until they are soft and the skins are blackened, and place them in a blender. Soak the dried tomatoes in hot water for ½ hour, and place them in the blender. Add 1 cup of the chicken broth to the blender, and blend for 1 minute. Strain the mixture through the fine blade of a food mill and reserve.

Heat the oil over medium heat, add the onions and green onions and sauté for 3 minutes. Add the mushrooms and sauté for 5 minutes. Add the tomato mixture, the remaining 5 cups broth, and the remaining ingredients except the cheese and croutons, and cook at a low simmer for 20 minutes. Remove the chiles and bay leaves. Place two of the cheese strips in each of 4 serving bowls, ladle in the soup, and top with the croutons. Serve immediately. Serves 4.

12 medium tomatoes

3 tablespoons chopped, dried sundried tomatoes

6 cups chicken broth

3 tablespoons olive oil

1¾ cups sliced onion

2 green onions, minced

1 pound mushrooms (brown, Portabello, shiitake, oyster, etc., fresh or dried and rehydrated in warm water)

½ teaspoon marjoram

2 tablespoons minced, fresh parsley

2 guajillo chiles, seeds and stems removed

½ heaping teaspoon salt

½ heaping teaspoon sugar

2 bay leaves

8 strips of queso fresco, ¼ inch by ½ inch (or substitue Monterey Jack)

1 cup croutons

✳ THREE CHILES SAUCE

4 habanero chiles, stemmed

4 serrano chiles, stemmed

4 jalapeño chiles, stemmed

6 tablespoons orange juice

2 tablespoons lime juice

2 tablespoons rice vinegar

½ heaping teaspoon salt

■ This sauce was inspired by one from *Guía Gastronomía* entitled *Salsa Tamulada* from the Yucatán. The recipe called for 20 *habanero* chiles, by far the world's hottest, and even after "curing" the sauce in the orange juice, lime juice, and vinegar overnight it was too hot. Consequently, I tried the recipe with a combination of *habaneros, jalapeños,* and *serranos,* and although the sauce was still too hot immediately after being made, after a night in the refrigerator with the juices and vinegar, which "cook" out some of the heat in the way they "cook" *cebiche,* it was tolerable. This sauce has a terrific flavor. The scorched chiles blend perfectly with the tart liquid and salt, and, used sparingly, the sauce goes beautifully with charbroiled fish and chicken. Of course, some people delight in partaking of sauces that could be classified as chemical weapons. If you know someone like this, give them the sauce directly after making it. ■

Place the chiles on a baking sheet as close to the broiler as possible and broil them until they are well charred, 15 to 20 minutes. Meanwhile, mix together the juices and vinegar. Allow the chiles to cool, then slit them and remove as many of the seeds and veins as possible. (If you are sensitive to chiles, you should wear rubber gloves.) Chop the chiles and place them in a *molcajete,* or mortar and pestle. Add the salt and a little of the juices, and grind the chiles, adding the remaining liquid, little by little, until they are well mashed. You can also give the sauce a few whirls in a food processor, but the texture will not be quite right. Place the sauce in the refrigerator for at least 3 hours or overnight. Makes enough for a small bowl.

 CHIPOTLE SAUCE

■ This is one of the best sauces that I have ever served with broiled meats and *tacos al carbón*. Be sure to broil the tomatoes until their juices have carmelized. ■

Simmer the *chipotles* in water to cover until they are very soft, about 20 minutes. Cool the chiles, remove the seeds, and coarsely chop them.

Place the tomatoes on a baking sheet as close to the broiler as possible and broil until they are blackened and their juices have caramelized, about 20 to 25 minutes. Dip the garlic cloves in the oil and place them on the baking sheet next to the tomatoes for the last 5 minutes of broiling. Place the *chipotles*, 1 broiled tomato, the garlic, lime juice, and Worcestershire sauce in a blender and blend for 1 minute. Place the remaining tomatoes in a food processor fitted with a steel blade, pour the contents of the blender onto them, add the green onion, cilantro, and salt, and process, pulsing for 1 second at a time until the ingredients are just mixed but not puréed. Makes 1 to 1½ cups.

2 dried chipotle peppers, stemmed

3 medium-sized tomatoes

2 cloves garlic

1 teaspoon cooking oil

1 teaspoon lime juice

¼ teaspoon Worcestershire sauce

1 green onion, minced

2 tablespoons minced cilantro

½ teaspoon salt

❋ FRIED CHEESE

THE GREEN SAUCE:

½ pound tomatillos, husked, stemmed, and finely chopped

¼ cup finely chopped onion

¼ cup finely chopped lettuce

1 Anaheim chile, stemmed, seeded, skinned, and finely chopped

2 teaspoons sugar

¼ teaspoon salt

1 tablespoon water

THE RED SAUCE:

3 ancho chiles (about 50 grams), stemmed and seeded

1 clove garlic

¼ teaspoon dried marjoram

¼ teaspoon dried oregano

1¼ cups water

¼ teaspoon cinnamon

½ tablespoon rice vinegar

2 tablespoons orange juice

½ teaspoon sugar

¼ teaspoon salt

■ One of my favorite restaurants is Los Parados de Tony Vega in Chihuahua City. It is an old-fashioned northern Mexican steak house that, despite being well established, has some delicious *nueva cocina mexicana* twists to some of its offerings. On my first visit to the restaurant, I enjoyed the *Queso frito* appetizer, which is deep-fried cheese served with red and green sauces. The waiter told me essentially what was in the sauces, and I was able to recreate the dish successfully. When the restaurant's recipe was included in the Mexico Desconocido's *Guía Gastronomía* series, I was pleased to find that my version of the recipe was very close to the original. The following version is a mixture of both. I have substituted *queso* Oaxaca for the original Chihuahua cheese made by the Mennonites because the *queso* Chihuahua sold in this country is a poor rendition. ■

To make the green sauce, place all the ingredients in a small saucepan and bring them to a simmer over medium-high heat. Turn the heat down and simmer until the *tomatillos* are soft, 5 to 6 minutes.

To make the red sauce, place the chiles, garlic, marjoram, and oregano in a small saucepan with the water. Bring to a boil over medium-high heat, cover, turn the heat down to a simmer, and cook for 15 minutes. Then put the mixture in a blender, add the remaining ingredients, and blend for 1 minute.

Dip the cheese slices in the beaten eggs and immediately roll them in the bread crumbs without draining off the egg. Repeat the process, making sure the cheese is well covered with bread crumbs, and refrigerate for at least 1 hour.

Heat ½ inch oil in a skillet over medium heat until a drop of water evaporates immediately upon contact. Fry the cheese on both sides until it is golden brown and starts to ooze out of the bread crumbs, but do not allow it to scorch. Drain the cheese on paper towels and place 2 pieces on each of 4 serving plates. Cover half of each piece of cheese with the *tomatillo* sauce and half with the *ancho* sauce. Garnish with the toasted sesame seeds and serve. Serves 4.

THE CHEESE:

8 slices Oaxaca cheese, about ½ inch thick, 1½ inches wide, and 4–4½ inches long

2 eggs, beaten

Toasted bread crumbs

Cooking oil

2 tablespoons sesame seeds, toasted to a golden brown in a dry skillet over medium heat

❋ CHEESE & CHILE SANDWICH

■ This delicious sandwich is a Mexican version of the French *croque monsieur*, and is appropriate for a snack, light lunch, or cut into smaller pieces for cocktail party fare. ■

Heat a griddle or very large skillet over low heat.

Brush one side of each slice of bread liberally with the dressing. On 4 of them place slices of cheese and some of the chile, then cover with the remaining slices of bread. Brush the top of 1 of the sandwiches with butter or olive oil and invert it on the griddle. When the bottom side of the sandwich is golden brown, brush the uncooked side with more butter or oil, turn the sandwich, and continue cooking until both sides are a crisp golden brown and the cheese has melted. Repeat the procedure for the other sandwiches. Serve immediately. This can also be served as an *antojito*. Serves 4.

8 slices French bread, trimmed of crusts

8 ounces Oaxaca cheese, sliced

2 poblano chiles, roasted, peeled, stemmed, and seeded

⅔ cup cilantro dressing (p. 92)

Melted butter or olive oil

✳ Mushroom, Squash & Carrot Medley

2 tablespoons butter or olive oil

¼ cup minced onions

1 tablespoon minced serrano chiles

2 large Portobello mushrooms, finely diced

1 medium zucchini, finely diced

1 carrot, cut into julienne strips

½ teaspoon dried thyme

¼ teaspoon dried marjoram

1 teaspoon sugar

Juice of ½ lime

Heaping ¼ teaspoon salt

¼ teaspoon ground black pepper

■ This is an excellent vegetable dish that goes well with almost anything, and because of the meat-like taste and texture of the mushrooms, stands on its own as a vegetarian entrée. ■

Heat the butter or olive oil in a skillet over medium-high heat, add the onions, and cook, stirring frequently, until they are soft but not browned. Add the remaining ingredients and continue cooking, stirring often, until the vegetables are just soft. Serves 4.

❋ ROASTED RATATOUILLE A LA MEXICANA

■ This is a terrific recipe adapted from one in the April 1997 issue of *Gourmet* magazine that is easy to prepare and low in fat. It goes particularly well with roasted or charbroiled fowl and fish. ■

Preheat the oven to 450 degrees. Mix all the ingredients except the raisins, lime zest, and lime juice, and place them in a large, lightly oiled ovenproof skillet or baking dish. Roast the vegetables, stirring occasionally, until tender and golden brown, about 20 minutes. Stir in the raisins and roast 3 minutes more. Place the roasted vegetables in a bowl, toss with the lime zest and juice, and serve immediately. Serves 4.

1 medium zucchini, sliced into ½- to ¾-inch pieces

1 red bell pepper, cut into ¾-inch pieces

1 small poblano chile, cut into ½-inch pieces

1 red onion, cut into ¾-inch pieces

1 small eggplant (about 1 pound), cut into ¾-inch pieces

½ cup frozen corn kernels, thawed

2 tablespoons olive oil

Scant ½ teaspoon salt

¼ teaspoon black pepper

¼ cup golden raisins

2 teaspoons grated lime zest

2 teaspoons lime juice

✳ Black Beans with Spanish Cheese

1 recipe Black Beans (p.206)

½ teaspoon ground cumin

2 tablespoons lard or olive oil

Heaping ½ cup Oaxaca or asadero cheese

Heaping ½ cup Spanish manchego cheese

■ This recipe derives its *nueva cocina mexicana* designation from the fact that it replaces pinto beans with black beans in the famous Sonoran dish *frijoles maneados* and adds Spanish *manchego* cheese to the more traditional *asadero*. This is my favorite version of *frijoles refritos*, or refried beans, and it is appropriate for nearly any occasion at which you would serve them. They are particularly good with broiled meats and poultry, with *antojitos mexicanos,* and with fried eggs. These beans can be made the traditional way with a bean masher, but using a food processor saves a lot of effort and produces a smoother result. ■

Drain the liquid from the Black Beans and reserve it. If you are using a food processor, place the beans, and the ingredients cooked with them, including the *ancho* chile, and the cumin in a food processor fitted with a steel blade. Process the beans, adding enough liquid to produce a medium-thick purée. Heat a skillet over medium to medium high heat, add the lard or olive oil, and when it is very hot add the bean purée (if you used the food processor) or the whole beans, cooked vegetables, and cumin. If you are using the processed beans, add the cheese and stir it into the beans, then continue stirring the mixture until it is heated through and thick enough to hold its shape when served. If you are using the whole beans, add about ½ cup of the reserved bean broth and mash them with a bean masher or back of a large spoon until they are puréed. Add the cheese and continue cooking and stirring as with the processed beans. Serves 4.

❊ ANCHO CHILE RICE

■ Mexican cuisine has some of the world's greatest rice dishes, many of them relatively unknown, such as this dish. A terrific change from *arroz mexicana* and *arroz blanco*, it goes particularly well with charbroiled meats. ■

Place the chiles in a saucepan, cover with water, bring to a boil, then cook at a bare simmer, uncovered, for 15 minutes. Remove the pot from the heat, cover it and allow the chiles to soak for an additional 10 to 15 minutes. Drain the chiles, put them in a blender, add the garlic and ⅓ cup of water, and blend for at least 1 minute, starting at low speed and gradually turning to high speed, and reserve the resulting purée. In a separate container, mix together the chicken broth, milk, and salt. Melt the ½ tablespoon butter in a small skillet over medium to medium low heat, add the almonds and cook, stirring often, until they are golden brown, but not burned. Reserve the almonds.

Heat the olive oil and 1 tablespoon butter in a large pot or Dutch oven over medium heat, add the rice and onions and cook, stirring frequently, for 5 to 6 minutes. The rice and onions should be starting to turn golden. Turn the heat to between medium and medium high, stir in the chile paste from the blender and continue cooking, stirring every 30 seconds, until almost all of the moisture has evaporated and the rice no longer sticks together, about 7 to 10 minutes. Add the broth and milk mixture, and the oregano and thyme, stirring to mix well. Bring the liquid to a boil, cover the pot, turn the heat to very low, and simmer for 20 minutes. Turn off the heat, stir the reserved toasted almonds into the rice, replace the top, and allow the rice to continue steaming for 15 minutes. Serve the rice garnished with a dollop of sour cream and the avocado slices. Serves 6 to 8.

4 medium to large ancho chiles, stemmed and seeded

4 cloves garlic, chopped

⅓ cup water

1¾ cups chicken broth

⅓ cup plus ¼ cup milk

1¼ teaspoons salt

½ tablespoon butter

⅓ cup blanched, slivered almonds

3½ tablespoons olive oil

1 tablespoon butter

1½ cups long grain rice

⅓ cup finely chopped onion

1 teaspoon dried oregano

1 teaspoon dried thyme

½ cup sour cream

One avocado, peeled and sliced

✳ Saffron-Chipotle-Roasted
✳✳ Garlic Mashed Potatoes

2 small or 1 large head garlic

1 teaspoon olive oil

2 pounds russet potatoes,
   peeled

½ cup half-and-half

Pinch saffron

2–3 teaspoons sauce from
   canned chipotle chiles

½ heaping teaspoon salt

2½ tablespoons butter, cut into
   bits

2 tablespoons fresh parsley
   minced

½ cup loosely packed, grated
   Spanish manchego cheese

■ These are the best mashed potatoes I have ever eaten. They go perfectly with many *nueva cocina mexicana* dishes, especially Filet with Red Onion, Wine, and Port Sauce (p. 118). ■

Preheat the oven to 400 degrees. Brush the garlic head(s) with olive oil, wrap in a small piece of aluminum foil, and place in the preheated oven until very soft and beginning to caramelize, about 45 minutes. Remove the garlic from the foil, and allow it to cool.

Cut the potatoes into 2- to 2½-inch pieces and place in a pot. Cover the potatoes with water, bring them to a boil, and simmer them until they can be easily pierced by a fork or pointed knife. Do not overcook or they will be soggy. While the potatoes are cooking, mix together the half-and-half and saffron and heat until the mixture is hot but not boiling, then remove from the heat. Add the *chipotle* sauce, salt, butter, and parsley, stir until the butter has melted, and reserve.

When the potatoes are done, pour off all the water. Either mash the potatoes in the hot pot with a potato masher, adding the warm half-and-half mixture and cheese as you do so, or sieve them through a potato ricer back into the pan and stir in the liquid and cheese. The former method will result in a slightly chunky, earthy texture, while the latter will produce a smooth, more refined one. Serve the potatoes immediately, or keep them in a covered double boiler over simmering water for up to 30 minutes. Serves 4.

�֎ PROVINCIAL VEGETABLES

■ I am always on the lookout for vegetable dishes that can stand on their own. The reason for this is that vegetarian cooking is both healthy and appealing. When I am serving vegetables with a meat entrée, I want them to be more than just an afterthought. This dish, inspired by the traditional peasant French rendition, fits all the criteria. When served alone, I suggest you use more mushrooms and add shitake mushrooms because of their ability to substitute in both taste and texture for meat. ■

Preheat your oven to 350 degrees. To make the base, heat a skillet over medium heat, add the oil and onions, and mix well. Add the remaining ingredients except the garlic and cook, lowering the heat, if necessary to keep the ingredients from scorching, until the onions are soft and beginning to turn golden. Then add the garlic and sauté for 1 minute. Transfer the onion mixture to a baking dish with a bottom of about 65 square inches. (To use a larger dish, prepare the base in greater quantity in proportion to the size of your dish.)

To prepare the casserole, place the zucchini, yellow squash, mushrooms, and tomatoes on top of the onion mixture in the baking dish in whatever order you like. Whisk together the mustard, olive oil and chile powder, and with a pastry or basting brush, brush it on top of the vegetables. Sprinkle salt and pepper to taste. Place the vegetables in the oven and bake for 1 hour or until they are golden brown. Serve immediately. Serves 4.

THE BASE:

1½ tablespoons olive oil

2 medium to large yellow onions (2–3 cups)

½ teaspoon ancho chile powder

½ teaspoon marjoram

½ teaspoon thyme

¼ teaspoon salt

Kernels from 1 ear of corn

1 large clove garlic, minced

THE CASSEROLE:

1 large zucchini, cut into ½-inch (or just slightly thinner) rounds

1 large yellow squash cut into ½-inch (or just slightly thinner) rounds

3 large button mushrooms, cut into ½-inch (or just slightly thinner) rounds

2 large Roma tomatoes, cut into ½-inch (or just slightly thinner) rounds

1½ tablespoons grainy French-style mustard

1½ tablespoons olive oil

¼ teaspoon ancho chile powder

Salt and pepper to taste

✳ ROASTED ANCHO POTATOES

¾ **pound russet potatoes, cut into ¼-inch strips as for French fries**

¾ **cup water**

1½ **tablespoons olive oil**

¾ **teaspoon ancho chile powder**

Salt to taste

■ It is a little-known fact that in some parts of Mexico, most notably the state of Nuevo León, French fries are commonly served with both entrée dishes and as *antojitos mexicanos*. These roast potatoes are an excellent substitute for French fries, and much lower in fat. In fact, this is one of the best potato dishes I have ever tried and one of the easiest to prepare. They go well with all broiled meats. ■

A half-hour before you begin cooking, cut and rinse the potatoes thoroughly, place them in a bowl, and cover them with cold water. In another container, mix together the ¾ cup water, olive oil, and chile powder and reserve.

Preheat the oven to 435 degrees. When you are ready to cook the potatoes, lightly oil an 11- to 11½-inch skillet (measured at the bottom) that can be placed directly into the oven, and add the potatoes and bring the liquid to a boil as quickly as possible, then place the skillet into the oven and allow the potatoes to cook for 30 minutes. Remove the potatoes, and using a spatula and kitchen tongs, carefully turn the potatoes and replace the skillet in the oven. Continue cooking until the potatoes are crisp and golden brown, between 5 and 10 minutes. Remove the potatoes, salt to taste, and serve. Serves 4.

❋ Puréed Spinach, Squash & Avocado

■ One of the greatest challenges facing any cook is producing a vegetable that matches the quality of the best entrées. This one, although quite simple, often receives as much praise as anything else on the plate. And it is easy to make with a food processor and microwave oven. ■

Thaw the spinach, then using a towel squeeze out as much liquid as possible. Using a food processor, grate the zucchini. Change from the grater to a steel knife, add the reserved spinach to the zucchini, then add the olive oil, cream, and cheese. Process the mixture until it is puréed, then put it into a medium-sized dish appropriate for use in a microwave. Cook on high for 2½ to 3½ minutes, depending on the power of your microwave, add salt and pepper to taste, and reserve. Just before you are ready to serve, scoop the avocado into the bowl of the food processor and add the lime juice. Heat the spinach-zucchini mixture in the microwave until it is steaming hot, then spoon it into the food processor on top of the avocado. Pulse the food processor until the avocado is mixed with the remaining ingredients and serve. Serves 4.

2 10-ounce packages frozen spinach

1 large zucchini

2 tablespoons olive oil

2 tablespoons whipping cream

½ cup grated añejo or cotija cheese

Salt and pepper to taste

2 small or 1 medium to large avocado, seeded, skinned, and chopped

1 tablespoon lime juice

Squash & Cactus in Adobo Sauce

THE ONIONS:

1 tablespoon plus 1 teaspoon cooking oil

1½ cups sliced onions

2½ tablespoons vinegar

½ teaspoon dried thyme

½ teaspoon dried marjoram

½ teaspoon dried oregano

¼ teaspoon salt

THE NOPALITOS & SQUASH:

2 large ancho chiles, stemmed, seeded, deveined, and torn into several pieces

⅓–¼ pound fresh or canned nopalitos, cut into ⅛-inch–¼-inch strips, and between 2 and 3 inches long

⅔–¾ pound zucchini, cut into ¼-inch strips between 2 and 3 inches long

1 tablespoon olive oil

1 clove garlic, minced

5 teaspoons vinegar

2 teaspoons brown sugar

1 teaspoon salt

The reserved onions

½ cup grated cotija or añejo cheese

■ *Adobo* refers to food which has been covered with a chile-based seasoning paste, usually meat or poultry. I adapted this recipe from one in *De manteles largos* by Alicia and Jorge De'Angeli. It is an excellent vegetable accompaniment that is served at room temperature. Heated and stuffed into steaming corn tortillas, it makes fine tacos. It is particularly appropriate for anyone not certain of their reaction to *nopalitos* (cactus paddles), and in fact can be made without them, as in the original recipe. While canned *nopalitos* may be used, fresh ones are preferable; however, I have included instructions for both. ■

Heat a small skillet over medium heat, add the cooking oil, then the onions. Turn the heat to medium low and cook the onions, stirring frequently, until they begin to soften, about 5 minutes. Pour the onions into a bowl with the vinegar, thyme, marjoram, oregano, salt, and refrigerate.

Place the chiles in a bowl, cover with boiling water, and allow to rehydrate for 20 minutes. If you are using fresh *nopalitos*, make sure all the spines have been removed. Cut around the cactus about ⅛ inch from the edge and discard the tough woody outer portion. Slice the cactus and place it in simmering water for 10 minutes. Remove the cactus to a strainer and rinse under cold water, rubbing it to remove as much of the sticky juices as possible. Dry and reserve the cactus.

To produce squash which is tender but not totally limp, immerse it for about 15 seconds in boiling water, then immediately put it into a pan of ice water to stop the cooking process. When the squash is cool, remove and dry it.

To make the *adobo* seasoning paste, first remove the chiles from the soaking water and pat them dry with a towel. Heat a small skillet over medium-low heat, add the olive oil, garlic, vinegar, sugar, salt, and chiles and cook the mixture for 5 minutes. Transfer the contents of the skillet to a blender and blend to a thick paste, adding just enough water to allow the blender to work properly. Mix the zucchini and *nopalitos* together in a nonreactive bowl, then add the *adobo* paste and mix well. Chill the mixture overnight.

To serve, spoon some of the seasoned zucchini and *nopalitos* onto a serving plate, top with some onion, and sprinkle the cheese over it. Serves 4.

❋ CORN & SQUASH CASSEROLE

THE CORN & SQUASH:

5–6 ears corn

2 tablespoons butter

⅓ cup minced onion

4 cups zucchini or yellow squash, chopped into ⅓-inch squares

½ teaspoon dried thyme

1 tablespoon minced fresh parsley

½ tablespoon lime juice

THE SAUCE & GARNISH:

1 poblano chile, peeled, seeded, and chopped

⅔ cup milk

1 tablespoon butter

1 tablespoon flour

½ cup milk

Pinch ground nutmeg

¾ teaspoon salt

¼ teaspoon finely ground black pepper

1 ounce Spanish manchego cheese, grated

1 ounce asadero or Oaxaca cheese, grated

1 ounce añejo or cotija cheese, grated

■ I adapted this delicious casserole dish from a recipe in *La cocina del maíz* by Patricia van Rhijn Armida. It is one of the few *nueva cocina mexicana* dishes that uses a sauce thickened with flour, in this case a typical white sauce made with butter, flour, and milk, but with the notable addition of puréed corn and *poblano* chiles, which make it special. It can be prepared a day or two ahead and reheated just before serving. ■

Using a sharp knife, slice the kernels from the corn and reserve. There should be about 3¼ cups. Heat a large skillet over medium to low heat, add the butter, and when it has melted add the onion and sauté until it just begins to soften. Add 2½ cups of the reserved corn, squash, and the remaining ingredients except those for the sauce and garnish, and cook, stirring often, until the vegetables just begin to soften. Remove the skillet from the heat and reserve while you prepare the sauce.

Preheat the oven to 350 degrees. Place the remaining ¾ cup corn kernels in a blender with the chile and ⅔ cup milk, and blend to a purée, about 30 seconds at high speed. Strain the purée through the coarse blade of a food mill and reserve.

Melt the butter in a saucepan over medium heat, add the flour, and cook until it just begins to brown. Remove the saucepan from the heat, and, little by little, stir or whisk in the ½ cup milk. Replace the saucepan on the burner, add the nutmeg, salt, and pepper and cook, stirring constantly, until the mixture thickens. Add the strained corn-chile purée and simmer until the mixture thickens.

To complete the dish, stir the sauce into the cooked vegetables and spoon the mixture into a medium-sized casserole dish. Combine the cheeses and sprinkle over the dish, place it in the oven, and bake, uncovered, for 20 minutes. If, at the end of the baking the top is not browned, place it under the broiler until it just begins to turn golden. Serves 4.

✳ GREEN CHILE POZOLE

■ This *nueva cocina mexicana* version of pozole, which is practically the state dish of Jalisco, is the best I have ever tried. It can be made with any combination of charbroiled meats, including pork, beef, lamb, or veal. Shredded meat from either *barbacoa* or *cochinita pibil* also works well. When I am cooking over the fire, I often put on extra pieces of meat, then chop and freeze them for this purpose. If you are using shredded, cooked meat as from *barbacoa*, use as is; chop other meats coarsely in a food processor to the consistency of "chile grind." ■

Heat the olive oil in a pot over medium-high to high heat, add the meat, cook for about 2 minutes, then remove and reserve it. Add the zucchinis to the pot (with a little more oil, if necessary) and cook until just beginning to brown, then remove them and reserve. Turn the heat to medium, add the onion (with a little more oil, if necessary) and cook until it is golden brown. Add the garlic and *poblano* chiles and cook 1 more minute. Add the broth, the reserved meat, the cumin, oregano, pozole, vinegar, and salt, and simmer, covered, for 30 minutes. Remove the top from the pot and continue simmering for an additional 15 minutes. Add the reserved zucchinis, the tomatoes, and olives, and cook for 5 minutes. Spoon the pozole into 4 soup bowls, top with the cheese and lettuce, and serve with the lime wedges. Serves 4.

2 tablespoons olive oil

1 pound charbroiled or smoked meat or a combination of meats

2 large zucchinis, minced

1 medium onion, minced

4 cloves garlic, minced

4 medium poblano chiles, roasted, peeled, stemmed, seeded, and minced

6 cups chicken broth

½ teaspoon ground cumin

½ teaspoon dried oregano

4 cups cooked pozole (hominy) made from dried hominy or canned hominy, drained and rinsed

1 tablespoon rice vinegar

½ teaspoon salt

2 Roma tomatoes, minced

¼ cup chopped black olives

1 cup jalapeño Monterey Jack cheese

2 cups finely shredded lettuce

Lime wedges

❊ Filet with Red Onion, Wine & Port Sauce

THE SAUCE:

3 cups thinly sliced red onion

3 large cloves garlic, coarsely chopped

1 teaspoon dried thyme

1 tablespoon chopped fresh parsley

4 medium-sized mushrooms, chopped

1½ cups dry red wine

½ cup port wine

1 large canned chipotle chile

2 cups beef broth

3 tablespoons unsalted butter

Salt to taste

THE STEAK:

4 pieces tenderloin, ½–1 pound each

Salt and pepper to taste

■ In recent years tenderloin steak, roasted whole, has become a popular dinner party dish. After roasting, the filet is usually sliced into fairly thin pieces and served with or without sauce. However, for many years a dish that is similar to this has been prepared in various parts of northern Mexico. There the filet is cut into ½- to 1-pound chunks, broiled over hot coals until crusty on the outside, mouthwateringly tender on the inside, and served whole. The following *nueva cocina mexicana* version of this traditional dish is perhaps my favorite steak dish. It has all the gusto of a real steak meal with a lot more refinement, far less fat than a T-bone, and the sauce is very easy to prepare. When served with Saffron-*Chipotle*-Roasted Garlic Mashed Potatoes (p. 110) it is a nearly perfect comfort food. ■

Note that tenderloins taper from a wide end to a very thin tail. For smaller-sized steaks, cut them from the small end and for larger ones from the middle. If you cut them from the large end, they will take longer to cook and will be nearly round rather than elongated, causing them to roll around on the plate while being cut. If made with chicken rather than beef broth, the sauce is also delicious with veal and chicken. It can be made several days ahead of time and refrigerated.

To make the sauce, place all the ingredients except the broth, butter, and salt in a large saucepan, bring to a boil, and simmer until the mixture is reduced by half. Add the broth and reduce by half again. Strain out and discard the onions and mushrooms, and return the liquid to the pot. There should be about 1½ cups of liquid. Continue reducing again until there is just over ⅓ cup remaining. Then remove the sauce from the heat until just before you are ready to serve. At that time return it to a simmer, remove from the heat, and stir in the butter and salt to taste. If the sauce has been prepared in advance and refrigerated, when you are ready to serve, heat it until it is close to simmering.

Prepare a hardwood or charcoal fire. Salt and pepper the steaks and broil them at 6 to 8 inches from the coals until they are done as you like, about 18 to 28 minutes, depending on the size of the steaks and distance from the fire. When properly cooked, the steaks should be crusty but not burned on the outside. Complete the sauce and spoon a tablespoon or so over each steak. Serve with Roasted *Ancho* Potatoes (p. 112) or with Saffron-*Chipotle*-Roasted Garlic Mashed Potatoes (p. 110). Serves 4.

✳ TENDERLOIN STEAK WITH ANCHO-PORT SAUCE

1½ tablespoons olive oil

1 pound white onions, cut into
 ¼-inch slices

1 teaspoon sugar

1 teaspoon ancho chile
 powder

¼ teaspoon ground black
 pepper

¼ teaspoon dried oregano

¼ teaspoon dried thyme

3 tablespoons port wine

1 tablespoon butter

¼ teaspoon salt or to taste

1 tablespoon minced parsley

4 tenderloin steaks, 6–8 ounces
 each

■ This delicious steak, which is a combination of continental and Mexican cooking, goes particularly well with Roasted *Ancho* Potatoes (p. 112). ■

Light a fire of hardwood or hardwood charcoal, and while it is burning to coals prepare the onions. Heat a large skillet over medium heat, add the olive oil then the onions and mix well with the oil. Add the sugar, chile powder, pepper, oregano, and thyme, and cook, turning occasionally, until the onions are soft and golden, about 20 minutes. Turn the heat to very low while you broil the steaks. When they are done as you like, turn the heat back to medium, add the port, butter, salt, and parsley and continue cooking for 1 minute. Place the cooked steaks on 4 serving plates, top with the onions, and serve with Roasted *Ancho* Potatoes. Serves 4.

❋ Filet Mignon with Creamy Chipotle Sauce

■ When I was living in Switzerland, one of my favorite dishes was a filet mignon in a spicy cream sauce that I found on trips to northern Italy. I was never able to duplicate it until some years ago I found it in *Northern Italian Cooking* by Biba Caggiano. Last year when I was asked to do a cooking demonstration for some women from Mexico City who were taking English lessons in San Antonio, I was desperate to do something that would be both new and fit into their entertainment recipe repertoires. Adding a smoky *chipotle* chile to this already rich and spicy sauce turned out to be very successful!. ■

Combine the catsup, mustard, Worcestershire sauce, *chipotle*, and cream in a bowl.

Heat a skillet over medium-high heat, add 1 tablespoon of the butter and 1 tablespoon of the olive oil and sauté the meat for 1 or 2 minutes on each side or until it is lightly browned. Then turn the heat to medium and remove the meat. Add a little more butter and olive oil, if necessary, and sauté the green onions and garlic until soft, about 1 minute. Add the brandy and stir to deglaze the pan, with caution.

Add the cream mixture, mix well, and return the meat to the skillet. Continue to cook over medium heat, turning once or twice, until the meat is done as you wish. Place the meat on 4 serving plates, add the salt and pepper, and spoon the sauce over the meat. Serves 4.

2 tablespoons Heinz catsup

3 tablespoons Dijon mustard

4 drops Worcestershire sauce

1 canned chipotle chile, stemmed, deveined, and minced plus some liquid from the can

½ cup heavy cream

2 tablespoons butter

2 tablespoons olive oil

4 filet mignons ¾–1 inch thick

2 green onions, minced

2 cloves garlic, minced

⅓ cup brandy

Salt and pepper to taste

✳ TENDERLOIN STEAK WITH
✳ ✳ ANCHO-CHIPOTLE-PASILLA SAUCE

THE SAUCE:

1 ancho chile

1 chipotle chile

1 pasilla chile

1 tablespoon olive oil

1⅓ cups chopped white onion

2 cloves garlic, chopped

1 tablespoon brandy

**¼ cup loosely packed minced
   cilantro**

2 tablespoons olive oil

¾ cup beef broth

Heaping ¼ teaspoon salt

¾ teaspoon brown sugar

THE STEAK:

4 6–8-ounce tenderloin steaks

Juice of 1 large lime

Salt and pepper

1 tablespoon olive oil

**½ cup grated Oaxaca cheese,
   or substitute provolone or
   mozzarella**

**⅓ cup grated cotija or añejo
   cheese**

■ This steak is a real favorite. The crunchy texture of the meat's exterior contrasts beautifully with the tender interior, and the earthy taste of three of Mexico's most distinctive chiles is sublime. Although this dish is not as hot as one might imagine, since the piquance is cut by the cheeses, it can be a bit warm. It is, however, the subtle heat so dear to the real chile afficionado, rather than the biting fire craved by the *jalapeño* contest/tequila-shooter set. ■

Toast the chiles briefly in a hot skillet. Stem, seed, and devein them, then cover them with hot water and allow them to soak for about 20 minutes. Drain the chiles and put them in a blender.

Put 1 tablespoon olive oil into a skillet over medium heat, add the onion, and allow it to cook until it is golden brown, adjusting the heat as necessary to prevent scorching. Add the garlic and let it cook 1 to 2 minutes, but do not allow it to scorch. Place the contents of the skillet into a blender with the chiles and add the brandy and cilantro. Blend the mixture for 2 minutes. You will probably have to add some water for the machine to work properly, but do not add any more than is absolutely necessary. Scoop out and reserve the resulting paste.

Put the 2 tablespoons olive oil in a saucepan over medium-high heat, and when it is just beginning to smoke add the chile paste. Cook the paste, stirring constantly to incorporate it into the oil, then continue cooking until it is very thick, about 2 to 4 minutes. Turn the heat to medium, stir in the broth, little by little. Add the salt and sugar and simmer until the mixture is the consistency of a medium thick sauce.

Sprinkle the steaks with the lime juice, then salt and pepper them to taste. Heat a skillet over medium-high heat, add the olive oil, then sear the steaks on one side. Turn the steaks and sear them on the other side, then continue cooking until they are done as you like them, lowering the heat as necessary—they should be brown and crusty on both sides but not burned. When the steaks are done, put each on an ovenproof serving plate. While the skillet is still hot, pour the sauce into it and stir to incorporate any brown bits and juices from the meat. Sprinkle some of the Oaxaca cheese on each steak, spoon the sauce over them, then top them with some of the *cotija* or *añejo* cheese. Place the plates under the broiler for about 1 minute, then serve. These steaks go very well with Roasted *Ancho* Potatoes (p. 112). Serves 4.

✳ SÁBANAS STUFFED WITH MUSHROOMS & HUITLACOCHE

THE PASILLA SAUCE & STUFFING:

I head garlic

Olive oil

4 pasilla chiles, stemmed

1½ tablespoons butter

2 teaspoons brandy

Heaping ¼ teaspoon sugar

Heaping ¼ teaspoon salt

⅓ cup beef broth

2 tablespoons butter

¼ cup minced onions

3 cups finely diced Portobello
mushrooms

½ cup diced huitlacoche, or
substitute an additional ½
cup mushrooms

¾ cup finely diced, peeled, and
seeded tomatoes

½ teaspoon dried thyme

½ tablespoon lime juice

Additional salt to taste

THE TOMATILLO SAUCE:

I pound tomatillos, peeled

2 serrano chiles

2 tablespoons butter

½ teaspoon sugar

½ teaspoon salt

½ teaspoon dried oregano

■ In Spanish, *sábana* means sheet, and that is exactly what these tenderloin steaks resemble, a sheet less than ⅛ inch thick and about 9 inches by 7 inches in size. This cut was popularized in Mexico City's Loredo restaurants, established by José Inés Loredo, who invented the Steak *Tampiqueña*. The way the meat is placed on a colorful combination of *tomatillo* sauce and thin refried beans was inspired by the similar treatment of a *sábana* stuffed with *chicharrones* at Mexico City's Los Alcatraces restaurant. The restaurant featured (it has since closed) dishes developed by some of Mexico's premier cooks, and that recipe came from one of the best, Lula Beltrán. Preparing this dish takes a little organization, but the unique flavor and visual effect make it well worth the effort. The sauce, beans, and mushroom stuffing can be prepared a day ahead and reheated before serving, minimizing the need for last-minute preparation. If you cannot find *huitlacoche*, just add more mushrooms. ■

Preheat the oven to 350 degrees. Drizzle the head of garlic with a little olive oil, wrap it in aluminum foil, and place it in the oven for 45 minutes. Remove the garlic and allow it to cool. Slice off the end of the garlic head and squeeze out the roasted purée.

To prepare the *pasilla* sauce, in a skillet over medium heat, toast the chiles for about 30 seconds on each side, then rinse them under cold water, tear them into pieces, and place them in a blender. Cover the chiles with very hot water and allow them to rehydrate for about 20 minutes. Pour off all but ⅔ cup of the water and blend the chiles to a purée at high speed, about 1 minute. Strain the chiles into a bowl through the fine blade of a food mill. Heat a saucepan over medium heat and add the 1½ tablespoons butter. When the butter has melted and the foam subsided, add the chile purée and cook, stirring constantly, for about 1 minute. Add 1 tablespoon of the garlic purée, the brandy, sugar, ¼ teaspoon salt, and beef broth. Combine well and simmer until the sauce is thick enough to hold its shape but not so thick that it becomes pasty, about 10 minutes. Reserve the sauce until you are ready to finish preparing the stuffing.

Melt the 2 tablespoons butter in a skillet over medium-high heat, and when the foam has subsided add the onions and cook, stirring often, for 1 minute. Add the mushrooms, *huitlacoche*, tomatoes, and thyme and cook until the mushrooms are soft and most of the liquid has evaporated, about 5 minutes. Reduce the heat to medium, add the reserved *pasilla* sauce, and cook, stirring frequently, until the mixture is quite thick, about 5 minutes. Add the lime juice and salt to taste. The stuffing can be prepared a day in advance and kept refrigerated.

Place the *tomatillos* and the chiles in a saucepan, cover with water, bring to a boil, and simmer until the *tomatillos* are very tender but not falling apart, about 5 to 10 minutes. Drain off the water, place the *tomatillos* and chiles in a blender and blend for 30 seconds at high speed. Strain the sauce through the fine blade of a food mill. Then melt 2 tablespoons butter over medium heat in a saucepan and when the foam has subsided add the *tomatillo*-chile purée and the remaining *tomatillo* sauce ingredients. Simmer the sauce until it is thick enough to coat the back of a spoon, about 15 minutes, and reserve.

Combine the beans, *epazote* leaves, and water to cover in a pot, bring to a boil, and simmer, partially covered until the beans are very tender, about 1 hour, adding additional water if necessary. Discard the *epazote* leaves, place the beans in a blender, and blend to a purée, adding enough cooking liquid to make a fairly thin mixture, about 30 seconds at high speed. Heat a skillet over medium-high heat, add the lard or oil, then add the puréed beans, salt, and cumin and cook, stirring constantly, until the mixture just begins to thicken. The mixture should be quite thin, but do not become concerned if it becomes too thick. You can remedy this by adding a little water to thin it.

½ cup chicken broth

THE BEANS:

¾ cup black beans, picked over and rinsed

2–3 epazote leaves

Water to cover and cook the beans

2 tablespoons lard or cooking oil

Salt to taste

¼ teaspoon ground cumin

THE STEAK:

1 ounce Spanish manchego cheese, grated

1 ounce asadero or Oaxaca cheese, grated

1 ounce añejo cheese or queso enchilada, grated

4 4½-ounce pieces filet mignon

Salt and pepper

Combine the cheeses in a bowl and refrigerate until ready to use.

Make sure your meat is from the heart of the tenderloin, that is, the center portion which comes in 1 piece. Lay a piece of plastic wrap, about 12 inches by 12 inches, on a chopping block and place 1 steak in the center. Top with another piece of plastic wrap of the same size. Using a meat pounder, carefully pound the meat until it is flattened and about ⅓ inch thick. Remove the top layer of plastic wrap, fold the meat into a slightly oval package, and replace it on the plastic wrap, folded side down. Replace the top layer of plastic and continue pounding the meat, from the center out to avoid shredding the edges, until it is about ¼ inch thick. Turn the meat over and continue pounding until it is no more than ⅛ inch thick, at which point it should be about 9 to 10 inches by 7 to 8 inches in size. Tear off a sheet of wax paper a little larger than the meat and spray or brush it lightly with cooking oil. Remove the top layer of plastic wrap and carefully turn it over and place the meat on the wax paper. Remove the remaining layer of plastic wrap, spray or brush the meat with oil, and cover it with another piece of wax paper. When you have formed all the steaks, place them in the refrigerator until you are ready to complete the dish.

Just before you are ready to cook the meat do the following:

Place 4 serving plates in an oven preheated to a very low temperature. You want them to be warm but not so hot that they will burn your hands. Heat a large (at least 11- to 12-inch) skillet over medium-high heat. Reheat the *tomatillo* sauce, the stuffing, and the bean purée. I like to use a microwave to keep the beans and stuffing from scorching, and because it can be done so quickly. Remove the top layer of wax paper from the steaks and salt and pepper them.

Spoon a layer of *tomatillo* sauce over half of each warmed serving plate. When the pan is hot, spray a thin coating of oil onto it. Pick up one of the steaks and quickly invert it onto the hot pan, removing the remaining wax paper as soon as the meat hits the pan. Obviously the meat will cook very quickly; the objective is to just sear it on one side, about 20 seconds, then turn it using a large spatula (tongs will tear the thin meat), and repeat the process. Place the cooked meat onto a serving plate, spoon ¼ of the stuffing onto the side that is on top of the *tomatillo* sauce, sprinkle on about 3 tablespoons of the cheese mixture, and turn over the other side as if you were folding a taco. The folded package should be sitting directly on top of the *tomatillo* sauce. Prepare the remaining steaks in the same fashion. Spoon a thin layer of bean purée over the rest of the serving plates and serve. Serves 4.

❋ Filet Mignon with Pasilla-Shiitake Sauce

2 pasilla chiles

⅔ medium onion, cut into ½-inch slices

3 cloves garlic, peeled

4 green onions, chopped, with white and green portions kept separate

12 Roma tomatoes

½ cup loosely packed cilantro

1 canned chipotle chile

1½ teaspoons brown sugar

¾ teaspoon balsamic vinegar

1½ teaspoons brandy

Cooking oil

4 corn tortillas

Olive oil

4 fresh shiitake mushrooms

4 6-ounce tenderloin steaks, trimmed of fat

1 tablespoon butter

4 slices smoked provolone cheese

■ Toast the *pasilla* chiles by placing them on an ungreased skillet over medium heat for a few seconds on each side, but do not allow them to burn. When the chiles are cool enough to handle, remove the stems, veins, and seeds, and put the chiles in a blender. ■

Place the onion, garlic, and white portions of the green onions in a medium-sized, ovenproof, iron skillet or pie pan, then put the whole tomatoes on top of them. Place the pan about 2 inches under the broiler and broil until the tomatoes are well blackened and soft, about 15 to 20 minutes. Add the contents of the pan to the blender, along with the cilantro, green portions of the onions, and the *chipotle* chile. Pulse the mixture until it is just chopped, then allow it to sit for 15 minutes to soften the toasted chiles. Pulse the mixture again until it is well chopped and combined but still chunky. Do not purée it. Pour the sauce into a bowl and stir in the brown sugar, vinegar, and brandy, and reserve.

Pour about ⅛ inch cooking oil into a skillet that is just large enough to accommodate the tortillas. Heat it until a drop of water sputters immediately on contact, then fry the tortillas, keeping them as flat as possible and turning once, until they are just beginning to harden. You do not want them to be at all crisp, just slightly stiff. This will take just a few seconds on each side if your oil is the right temperature. Drain and reserve the tortillas.

Heat a medium-sized skillet over medium-high heat, add just enough olive oil to barely film the pan, and sear the mushrooms until they begin to brown. Remove the mushrooms, chop them coarsely, and reserve. Sear the steaks in the same manner until a brown crust has formed on both sides. Remove the steaks to a small plate.

Turn the heat to medium, then add the butter to the pan, scraping up any brown bits from the steaks and mushrooms. Immediately stir in the reserved sauce and the chopped mushrooms and add the steaks, including any juice from them. Continue cooking for 2 to 3 minutes on each side or a total of 4 to 6 minutes (for rare to medium rare). Place 1 of the fried tortillas on each plate, then place 1 steak on each tortilla. Top each steak with a slice of cheese, then with the sauce. Place the plates under the broiler until the cheese has just melted, about 1 to 2 minutes. Serve with Mexican Rice (p. 208). Serves 4.

❊ Steak Café de Tacuba

THE ENCHILADA SAUCE:

2 tablespoons poblano chile, peeled, seeded, and minced

2 tablespoons tightly packed spinach, washed and minced

2 cups whipping cream

3 tablespoons butter

¼ teaspoon salt or to taste

THE ENCHILADAS:

Cooking oil

4 corn tortillas

4 ounces Spanish manchego cheese, grated

THE STEAK:

2 tenderloin steaks, about 2½ inches thick and weighing 9–10 ounces each

Juice of 1 lime

Salt and pepper to taste

THE ASSEMBLY & GARNISH:

2 cups green beans, cut into 2-inch lengths

½ cup carrots, peeled and cut into small, thin slices, about 1 inch long, ¼ inch wide, and ⅛ inch thick

¼ cup sliced onion

■ Whenever I arrive in Mexico City, it is never more than an hour or two before I go to the Café de Tacuba* in the historic center of the city and order the following dish. The restaurant, decorated with fine art, has the feel of a turn-of-the-century eatery and is always filled with people from all walks of life—customers who can afford no more than to share a *tamal* and a cup of coffee and others stylishly dressed being served the following dish. As with the Steak *Tampiqueña*, deciding whether this qualifies as a *nueva cocina mexicana* dish was a difficult choice. In spite of the fact that this entrée has been served in the restaurant for many years, since I have not encountered it elsewhere, I have called it a *nueva* dish.

I included a recipe for the enchilada that is served with the steak in *La cocina de la frontera* under the name *Enchiladas con crema*. As in the restaurant this enchilada is not filled with chicken (or much of anything else). ■

Put the chile, spinach, and 1 cup whipping cream in a blender and blend until the vegetables are puréed. Melt the butter in a saucepan over medium heat, stir in the contents of the blender, the remaining 1 cup of whipping cream, and the salt. Simmer the sauce until it begins to thicken, then remove it from the burner.

Heat about ½ inch cooking oil in a small skillet over medium heat until a drop of water vaporizes immediately on contact. Using kitchen tongs, place a tortilla in the oil for just a few seconds, turn it, and cook a few more seconds, but do not allow it to stiffen. Remove the tortilla from the skillet and drain on paper towels, then fry the remaining tortillas in the same manner. To form the enchiladas, roll the softened tortillas very loosely, place 1 on each of 4 ovenproof serving plates, and reserve until you are about to cook the steaks. About the time you put the steaks on to cook, pour a liberal amount of sauce over each folded tortilla, top with the cheese, and place closely under the broiler until the cheese begins to brown. Remove the plates and place a piece of cooked steak beside each enchilada.

This steak is cut in the Mexican fashion, which means that it is cut in somewhat the same way a chef slices the peel from an orange in 1 piece. Place 1 steak on a chopping board on its side (see diagram with Steak *Tampiqueña,* p. 225). If you are right handed, place the knife on the top of the steak about ¼ inch from the right edge and carefully slice downward until you are about ¼ inch from the bottom. Turn the steak a half turn to the left and again cut down to within ¼ inch from the bottom, making sure that the strip you are removing stays in 1 piece and is about ¼ inch thick and about 2½ inches wide. The result will be 1 long thin strip about 12 to 14 inches long. Cut the strip into 2 portions, and, using a meat pounder or edge of a cleaver, lightly pound it to remove any irregularities resulting from the slicing. Prepare the remaining steak in the same way. With just a little practice you will be able to do this quickly and accurately. Sprinkle some lime juice over the steaks, salt and pepper them to taste, and reserve.

To cook the steaks, place a little lard or cooking oil on a griddle or skillet over medium-high to high heat, and pan-broil the steaks about 1½ to 2 minutes on each side or as you like.

Steam the vegetables until they are soft and reserve. You do not have to reheat the vegetables prior to serving as the original dish serves them close to room temperature.

When the steaks are nearly done, place the enchiladas under the broiler and heat until the cheese on top begins to brown. If you are serving 4, it is best to heat them in a baking dish or pizza pan and transfer them to serving plates. If you are serving just 2 and have ovenproof plates, put the plates themselves under the broiler. In either case, place a cooked steak next to the enchilada, add a portion of the steamed vegetables, and serve. Serves 4.

* I recently learned that the Café de Tacuba has been damaged by fire and may or may not be restored.

THE FILLING:

½ *pound boneless lamb with some fat (or ground lamb)*

½ *tablespoon serrano chiles, minced*

½ *tablespoon cilantro, minced*

½ *tablespoon garlic, minced*

1 *tablespoon olive oil*

½ *tablespoon fresh mint, minced*

¼ *cup pine nuts*

½ *tablespoon fresh parsley, minced*

½ *teaspoon fresh rosemary, minced*

¼ *teaspoon salt*

¼ *teaspoon ancho chile powder*

THE LEAVES:

12 *large grape leaves, either preserved or fresh*

3–4 *large hoja santa leaves*

THE SAUCE:

½ *cup white tequila*

2 *teaspoons lime juice*

1 *teaspoon garlic, minced*

½ *teaspoon salt*

1 *teaspoon serrano chile, minced*

2 *teaspoons Cross & Blackwell mint sauce*

1 *tablespoon onion, minced*

Pepper to taste

¼ *cup heavy cream*

6 *tablespoons butter, cut into small pieces*

Ancho chile powder (optional)

Mint leaves (optional)

■ This delicious recipe of Middle Eastern origin can be made with prepared ground lamb, or it can be ground easily in a food processor. ■

Cut the lamb into ½-inch pieces and place it in a freezer for 15 minutes. Remove the lamb from the freezer and put it in the bowl of a food processor fitted with a steel blade. Add the remaining filling ingredients and, using about 20 to 30 pulses, grind the meat to the consistency of hamburger. (If you are using ground lamb, mix it well with the other ingredients.)

If the grape leaves are preserved, rinse and dry them. If you are using fresh leaves, simmer them in water to cover for 2 minutes, allow them to cool, and dry them.

Cut the *hoja santa* leaves, which have an anise-like flavor, to roughly the same size as the grape leaves. (If you cannot find *hoja santa* leaves, simply omit them.) Place a grape leaf on a flat work surface, then place 2 pieces of *hoja santa* on top of it. Put 1 to 2 tablespoons of the filling on the leaves, fold over the ends, and roll up like a tiny burrito. Place 3 stuffed leaves on each of 4 shish kebab skewers and grill over a moderate fire of mesquite coals.

Place all the sauce ingredients except the cream, butter, and chile powder in a saucepan and bring the mixture to a boil over medium-high heat. Stir in the cream and continue boiling for 4½ to 5 minutes or until the mixture begins to thicken. Remove the sauce from the heat and stir in the butter.

To serve, spoon some sauce on each of 4 serving plates and top with 3 grape leaves. Garnish with a mint leaf and sprinkle some *ancho* chile powder on the sauce, if desired. Serves 4.

✳ Lamb & Bulgur Salpicón

■ In traditional Mexican cooking, *salpicón* is a main-course salad whose main ingredient is shredded meat, beef in the north and pork in the south. This *nueva cocina mexicana* version utilizes bulgur (a familiar ingredient in the Middle Eastern dish tabouli), lamb, and mint from Mexico's Moorish heritage to make a delicious luncheon dish or cocktail fare. ■

Place the lamb in a pot, cover with water, bring to a boil, then simmer, partially covered, until tender, about 1¼ hours. Drain the meat, and when it is cool shred it, either by hand or using the plastic blade in a food processor, and reserve.

Bring the 1½ cups water to a boil in a medium-sized pot, add the bulgur, cover, and simmer for 3 minutes. Turn off the heat and allow the bulgur to steam for ½ hour. Remove the top from the pot and allow the bulgur to cool, then refrigerate it until chilled, about 1 hour.

To make the dressing, whisk all the dressing ingredients together.

Place the lamb and cooked bulgur in a large salad bowl, add the remaining salad ingredients, except the lettuce, and toss to mix well. Add the dressing and refrigerate until ready to serve, but not longer than 2 hours. To serve, mound the salad onto plates over a bed of lettuce. Serves 4.

THE SALAD:

¾ pound very lean lamb, cut into ¾-inch pieces

1½ cups water

1 cup bulgur (cracked Arab-style wheat)

1 cup minced fresh parsley

½ cup minced fresh mint leaves

1½ cups tomato, seeded and minced

2 green onions, minced

½ cup minced fresh cilantro

1 cup pine nuts

1½ cups panela cheese, grated

2 medium avocados, skinned and chopped

1 small head lettuce for garnish

THE DRESSING:

¼ cup plus 3 tablespoons lime juice

1½ tablespoons liquid from a can of chipotle chiles en adobo

¾ teaspoon salt

4 cloves garlic, minced

¼ cup plus 3 tablespoons olive oil

❋ Lamb Chimichanga with Mint Cream Sauce

THE DRIED MEAT:

¾ *pound very lean lamb, sliced thin*

Lime juice

Salt

THE FILLING:

1 tablespoon olive oil

1–1¼ cups dried, processed lamb

¼ cup minced onion

¼ cup finely chopped, peeled, and seeded poblano chile

⅓ cup finely chopped tomato

¼ cup pine nuts

1 tablespoon garlic water (made by blending 1 clove of chopped garlic in 1 tablespoon water)

½ tablespoon lime juice

¼ cup water

3 tablespoons grated Spanish manchego cheese

THE FLOUR TORTILLAS:

1 cup all-purpose flour

¼ teaspoon salt

1 tablespoon lard, or substitute vegetable shortening

1 tablespoon butter

¼ cup or more water

■ This version of the famous Sonoran specialty is an excellent example of *nueva cocina mexicana*. It takes a traditional form, a filling of dried beef wrapped in a paper-thin flour tortilla that is deep-fried and topped with a simple red or green chile sauce, and changes it by substituting lamb and pine nuts for the beef and introducing a tart, creamy, green chile sauce with minty color and taste overtones that goes perfectly with the lamb and its golden crispy wrappings. This recipe is time-consuming because of the need to make the dried lamb and the special thin, Sonora-style tortillas that are not usually available in stores. However, the lamb can be prepared several days in advance, and the tortillas can be made a day ahead, making the final preparation reasonably quick and easy. ■

To prepare the dried meat, place the meat between sheets of plastic wrap and, using a meat pounder, pound the meat as thin as possible. Place the meat in a nonreactive bowl, mix the lime juice and salt together, and toss it with the meat until it is well coated. Allow the meat to marinate for ½ hour. Place the meat in an electric food dehydrator and dry it at 145 degrees for 2½ to 3 hours or until it is fairly dry but still slightly flexible. Slice the meat into small pieces, place it in a food processor fitted with a steel blade, and process until the meat is shredded and fluffly in texture. Reserve the prepared meat.

Heat a small skillet over medium heat, add the oil then add the lamb and toss it until it is thoroughly coated with the oil. Add the onion, chile, tomato, pine nuts, garlic water, and lime juice and continue cooking until the onion is soft, about 5 minutes. Add the water and continue to cook, stirring often until most of the liquid has evaporated, about 5 minutes. Allow the filling to cool, mix in the cheese, and reserve.

To make the tortillas, mix the flour and salt together in a bowl. Heat the lard or shortening, butter, and water together until the lard and butter are just melted. Allow the mixture to cool slightly then stir it into the flour and salt, adding additional water, if necessary, to make a soft dough. Wrap the dough in a slightly moistened towel and allow it to rest for 15 minutes. Divide the dough into 4 equal pieces, roll them into balls, cover with the towel, and allow them to rest for at least 15 minutes. Sprinkle a little flour on your work surface, place 1 of the balls of dough on it, and flatten it slightly with your hand. Roll the ball into a thin circle of 8 to 9 inches. The following technique works well for me: with a rolling pin, roll the dough from the middle up to the top edge, then roll to the bottom edge. Give the dough about a ⅓ turn then repeat the rolling process, being careful to roll straight up and down, not at an angle. Give the dough another ⅓ turn and roll again. Turn the dough over, sprinkle a little more flour on the surface, and repeat the process, rolling and turning the dough 3 more times. When the dough is about as thin as you can get it, stretch it a little more by hand. If necessary, allow the dough to relax a little. The tortillas should be nearly paper thin and 8 to 9 inches in diameter.

To cook the tortillas, heat a large skillet or griddle over medium heat. Place a tortilla on the hot surface and cook until it puffs, about 45 seconds. Turn the tortilla and cook for another 30 to 45 seconds. If the pan is at the correct temperature, the tortilla should be done. If not, continue cooking until it is just done. It is better to use heat that is too low than too high because these very thin tortillas can easily be overcooked, which will make them dry and inflexible. Wrap the cooked tortilla in a towel and allow it to steam while you cook the remaining tortillas.

Heat a deep fryer to 350 degrees. To prepare the sauce, place the vodka, lime juice, crème de menthe, garlic, onion, and salt in a small saucepan. Place the cream, goat's milk, parsley, cilantro, and chile in a blender and blend until the mixture is just puréed, about 15 seconds.

THE SAUCE & FINAL PREPARATION:

½ cup plus 1 tablespoon vodka

2 tablespoons lime juice

1½ tablespoons crème de menthe

½ tablespoon minced garlic

½ tablespoon minced onion

¾ teaspoon salt

¼ cup plus 2 tablespoons cream

3 tablespoons evaporated goat's milk

1 tablespoon chopped parsley

½ tablespoon chopped cilantro

Heaping ⅓ cup poblano chile, peeled, seeded, and chopped

6 tablespoons butter

THE GARNISH:

¼ cup Spanish manchego cheese

At this point prepare the chimichangas. Using either a griddle, or a microwave, which is easier, heat the tortillas until they are soft and flexible. Place ¼ of the filling slightly off center toward yourself. Fold the 2 sides of the tortilla, to your right and left, partially over a portion of the filling; then, beginning at the side closest to you, roll the tortilla into a burrito. Secure the package in two or three places with toothpicks, and fry it until it is crisp and golden brown. Drain the cooked chimichangas on paper towels and place them in a 250-degree oven to keep them warm.

To complete the sauce, bring the mixture in the saucepan to a boil over medium-high heat, add the mixture in the blender, and boil, stirring nearly constantly until the sauce has thickened, about 3 to 4 minutes. Add the butter to the sauce, remove the pan from the heat, and whisk or stir in the butter until it is completely incorporated into the sauce. Spoon a little of the sauce onto each serving plate, place a chimichanga on top of it, then spoon the remaining sauce over the tops of the chimichangas. Garnish with the cheese and serve. Serves 4, more if served as an *antojito*.

LAMB CARNITAS

■ *Carnitas* are one of Mexico's most important dishes. Traditionally, chunks of pork are simmered in lard to cover at fairly low heat until they are crisp and crunchy, and are then eaten with guacamole and corn tortillas. Around Mexico City and in some parts of northern Mexico, a much less fatty version is prepared. In that version, leaner, smaller chunks of pork are simmered slowly in water to cover and then, when it has boiled away, the pork is fried crisp in the fat which has been rendered from the pork. This latter method is used here, but lamb is used instead of pork and a combination of water and fruit juices rather than simply water, creating a delicious filling for tacos that is very easy to prepare. ■

Place the lamb in a very large (11- to 12-inch), lightly greased skillet. Add the juices and enough water to liberally cover the meat. Bring the liquids to a boil, skim off and discard the scum that rises to the surface, then add the remaining ingredients, except the cilantro, and a little more water, if necessary. Turn the heat down to a simmer, and cook the meat until nearly all the liquid has evaporated. Turn the heat to medium high, add the cilantro, and continue to cook the meat in the fat in the pan, stirring often, until it is brown and crispy. Serve with guacamole, salsa, and hot tortillas. Serves 4.

2½ **pounds lamb from the leg, cut into ½-inch pieces with most of the fat removed**

½ **cup fresh orange juice**

½ **cup pineapple juice**

½ **tablespoon lime juice**

Water

½ **tablespoon cider vinegar**

2 **tablespoons olive oil**

1 **teaspoon dried oregano**

1 **teaspoon dried mint flakes**

½ **teaspoon salt**

¼ **cup loosely packed, minced cilantro**

THE LAMB:

4 loin lamb chops

THE MINT-PINE NUT BUTTER:

1 tablespoon pine nuts

2 tablespoons butter

½ teaspoon dried mint flakes

1 clove garlic, minced

Scant ¼ teaspoon Cross &
    Blackwell mint sauce

¾ teaspoon lime juice

1 large serrano chile, seeded
    and minced

Pinch salt

Pinch ground black pepper

THE SAUCE:

2½ tablespoons mescal

1½ tablespoons pineapple juice

1 teaspoon lime juice

½ teaspoon minced garlic

¼ teaspoon salt

½ teaspoon minced serrano chile

1 teaspoon Cross & Blackwell
    mint sauce

½ tablespoon minced onion

¾ teaspoon dried mint flakes

Pinch black pepper

2 tablespoons heavy cream

3 tablespoons mango butter (see
    Broiled Red Snapper and
    Shrimp with Avocado and
    Mango Butters, p. 156)

LAMB CHOPS WITH MESCAL-MANGO SAUCE

■ This dish is delicious with just the flavored butter, but with the mescal sauce on which the grilled chops are placed it is really special. ■

To make the mint-pine nut butter, toast the pine nuts in a small skillet over medium heat until they just begin to brown, allow them to cool, then chop them finely. Place the nuts in a small bowl, add the remaining ingredients, and mix to a paste. Place the butter mixture in the refrigerator until ready to use.

Prepare a charbroiler with either hardwood or hardwood charcoal. While the material is burning into coals, prepare the sauce up until the boiling stage. When the coals are ready, broil the chops, making sure they do not burn, until they are done to preference. Meanwhile, finish the sauce.

Place all the sauce ingredients except the cream and mango butter in a small saucepan. When the lamb chops are nearly done, bring the liquid to a boil, timing it so that it reaches this stage just before the lamb chops are ready to be removed. Add the cream and simmer briskly over medium-high heat for about 4½ minutes. During this time remove the lamb chops from the fire. Remove the pan from the heat, and stir in the mango butter. Spoon some of the sauce onto each of 4 serving plates, top with broiled lamb chops, and garnish them with equal amounts of the flavored butter. Serves 4.

✺ VEAL WITH TEQUILA CREAM SAUCE

■ This dish, the sauce for which is adapted from one by Emeril Lagasse, that goes beautifully with veal scallops, produces a result that might be described as a slightly richer version of the Italian classic veal piccata. It is very easy to prepare. ■

Sprinkle the veal with the lime juice and salt and sift some flour over just the top of each piece. Press the flour into the meat then shake it to remove any excess. Place the meat in the refrigerator until you are ready to complete the preparation.

To prepare the sauce, place the minced chile, green onion, parsley, cilantro, tequila, lime juice, and salt in a small bowl, mix well, and reserve until you are ready to cook the dish.

To cook the meat, heat a skillet or sauté pan over medium-high to high heat, and add 2 tablespoons of the olive oil. When the oil just begins to smoke, place ½ of the meat in the pan, floured side down, and sauté it until it is golden brown, about 1–2 minutes. Turn the meat and continue cooking until it is just cooked through, about 30 seconds. Place the cooked meat on 2 serving plates, add the remaining 2 tablespoons oil to the pan, and cook the remaining meat in the same manner.

When the meat has been cooked and placed on the plates, turn the heat to medium to medium high, stir the cream into the sauce mixture, and pour it into the pan. Cook the sauce, stirring constantly until it has been reduced and is fairly thick, about 1 to 3 minutes. Place the butter in the pan and immediately remove it from the heat, continuing to stir until the butter is melted and the sauce is thick and glossy. Pour the sauce over the meat and serve with steamed broccoli or squash and white rice. Serves 4.

THE VEAL & SAUCE:

1 pound veal scallops, cut or pounded to between ⅛ and ¼ inch thick

2 tablespoons lime juice

Salt to taste

Flour for dredging

1 tablespoon minced serrano chiles, seeds removed

1 tablespoon minced green onion

2 teaspoons minced parsley

2 teaspoons minced cilantro

½ cup silver tequila

1 tablespoon lime juice

½ teaspoon salt

¼ cup olive oil

⅓ cup whipping cream

6 tablespoons butter at room temperature

✳ PORK TENDERLOIN WITH APPLE-CHIPOTLE SAUCE

THE MARINADE & PORK:

½ cup apple juice

6 tablespoons soy sauce

¼ cup honey

½ tablespoon minced garlic

1 tablespoon minced ginger-root

½ tablespoon dry mustard

⅛ teaspoon Worcestershire sauce

¼ cup dark rum

2 pounds pork tenderloin

THE SAUCE:

½ cup apple jelly

1 canned chipotle chile, minced

1 teaspoon liquid from chipotle can

½ teaspoon dried thyme

Pinch grated nutmeg

1½ tablespoons lime juice

■ This dish, which I adapted from a recipe in *Gourmet* magazine that was designed for pork chops, is one of the best recipes I have ever tried. The flavors are simply magnificent, and it has the added advantage of being quite low in fat and ideal for advance preparation. In fact, the entire dish can be prepared ahead and, if the tenderloin is heated slowly to just the right temperature in a microwave, it loses very little in quality. ■

Mix together the marinade ingredients and marinate the pork for at least 6 hours or overnight.

Remove the pork from the marinade and reserve. Place the marinade in a saucepan, add the apple jelly, chile, chile juice, and thyme and bring to a boil. Turn the heat down so that the sauce continues cooking at a brisk simmer, and cook it until it is reduced slightly. Spoon out about 3 tablespoons of the sauce and reserve it. Continue to reduce the sauce until it measures just over 1 cup, and remove it from the heat.

Broil the marinated tenderloin over a wood fire until it is cooked through. It should be about 145 degrees. Just before removing it from the fire, brush the pork with the reserved sauce. While the pork is cooking, simmer the sauce until it is heated through, and add the nutmeg and lime juice. When the pork is done, allow it to rest for a few minutes, then slice it into 12 pieces, about 1¼ to 1½ inches thick. Spoon some of the sauce onto each of 4 serving plates, and place 3 pieces of the pork on each one. Serve the pork with steamed broccoli, a roasted half onion, and/or rice. Serves 4.

❋ PORK LOIN VAMPIRO

■ In Mexico, the most popular way of drinking tequila is straight with a chaser of *sangrita*, which is a combination of orange juice, grenadine, chile powder, and sometimes tomato juice. When the tequila is mixed directly with the *sangrita* and topped with soda water, the resulting concoction is called a *vampiro*. I had been experimenting with using *sangrita* as a sauce for food with only moderate success when I discovered a recipe for pork loin cooked in a sauce similar to *sangrita* in *La cocina de Laura*, by Laura B. de Caraza Campos. I tried it and loved it, especially the ease of preparation, which makes it perfect for entertaining. Here it is with some minor changes for adaptation to ingredients available in this country. Warning: this dish is quite hot, especially if you use 4 rather than 3 chiles (as does the original recipe); however, judicious use of the sauce should make it tolerable to all but people most averse to hot foods. ■

Preheat the oven to 350 degrees. Tear the chiles into pieces, place them in a bowl, cover them with boiling water, and allow them to rehydrate and soften for 20 minutes. Drain the chiles and place them in a blender. Add the orange juice and lime juice and blend for 1 minute. Strain the mixture through the fine blade of a food mill, then add the grenadine, tequila, salt, thyme, and onion, and reserve.

Salt and pepper the pork. In a heavy, ovenproof Dutch oven, heat the oil over medium-high heat until it is very hot but not quite smoking. Add the pork and cook it, turning as necessary, until it is golden brown on all sides, about 4 minutes. Remove the pork to a plate and the pot from the heat and allow it to cool briefly. Add the chile mixture to the pot, stirring well to incorporate any caramelized pieces of pork and its juices. Put the pork back in the pot and heat until the sauce just begins to bubble lightly, but do not bring it to a complete boil. Place the pot in the preheated oven and

3–4 medium ancho chiles, stemmed, seeded, and deveined

2 cups freshly squeezed orange juice

3 tablespoons lime juice

¼ cup grenadine

½ cup tequila

1 teaspoon salt

1 teaspoon dried thyme

1 cup sliced white onion

1 3-pound boneless pork loin (the kind with 2 loins tied together)

Salt and pepper to taste

2 tablespoons lard or olive oil

bake for 1½ hours (about 30 minutes per pound) or until the pork reaches an internal temperature of between 145 and 150 degrees, spooning some of the sauce over it every 15 minutes. Remove the pork from the pot to a chopping block and allow it to rest for 5 minutes, then slice it into servings (I like to make them about ¾ inch thick). While the meat is resting, you can reduce the sauce if it is too thin.

Spoon some sauce onto each of 4 serving plates and top with a slice of pork. White rice goes well with this dish. Serves 4.

 SPIT-ROASTED PORK WITH FRUIT SAUCE

THE MARINADE & MEAT:

1 large ancho chile, stemmed, seeded, and torn into small pieces

1 large pasilla chile, stemmed, seeded, and torn into small pieces

2 cloves garlic

1 teaspoon oregano

3 ounces canned mango juice

3 ounces canned peach juice

2½ tablespoons lime juice

½ teaspoon salt

¼ teaspoon ground black pepper

■ It is best to prepare this dish on a covered barbecue fitted with a rotisserie, but it can also be successfully made over an ordinary kettle-style barbecue. Using a barbecue with a top and dampers to regulate the heat is important because with devices lacking a cover you must prepare coals in another receptacle and add them to the fire periodically. The sweet marinade and sauce combine beautifully with the flavor of smoke and chiles. It can also be made with any combination of fruit juices with only subtle changes in the result. ■

To make the marinade, combine all the marinade ingredients in a blender, and blend until the chiles are roughly chopped. Allow the chiles to absorb the liquid for 20 minutes, then blend again for 1 minute. Put the meat in a nonreactive bowl, cover with the marinade, and place in the refrigerator to marinate for 2 to 3 hours. After marinating, remove the meat and reserve as much of the marinade as possible. There should be around ¾ cup. Mix 3 tablespoons of the marinade with 1 tablespoon cooking oil, and use this mixture to baste the meat as it cooks.

To prepare the meat, start a fire of hardwood or hardwood charcoal, preferably in a barbecue with a cover and/or rotisserie attachment. When the fire has burned to grey coals, roast the meat at from 8 to 12 inches from the coals for about 50 minutes to 1 hour or until it reaches an internal temperature of 145 to 150 degrees, basting at least every 10 minutes. While the meat is cooking, make the sauce.

Heat a small saucepan over medium-high heat, and add the 1 tablespoon butter. Just as the oil begins to smoke add the reserved marinade and cook it, stirring often, until it begins to thicken, about 1 to 2 minutes. Add the chicken broth, bring to a boil, then simmer briskly until the sauce is reduced to 1¼ cups, about 10 minutes. Remove about ¼ cup of the sauce to a separate container and mix in the cornstarch-water mixture, then add it to the rest of the sauce. Continue simmering the sauce until it has thickened to the point where it will just hold its shape when poured on a plate.

When the meat has finished cooking, remove it from the fire and allow it to sit for 10 minutes while you either complete or reheat the sauce. Then pour the accumulated pan juices into the sauce and mix well. Ladle some of the sauce onto each of 4 serving plates, slice the meat into thick steaks, and place on the sauce. Serve with a guacamole cup, garnished with deep-fried, julienned sweet potato, steamed squash, and/or white rice. Serves 4.

1¾ pounds boneless pork loin roast in 1 piece (not 2 tied together)

1 tablespoon cooking oil

THE SAUCE:

1 tablespoon butter

¾ cup reserved marinade

1⅓ cups chicken broth

¾ teaspoon cornstarch diluted in 1 teaspoon water

❊ Northern Turkey Mole

4 ancho chiles

⅓ cup pineapple juice

Scant ½ teaspoon whole cumin

2 tablespoons sesame seeds

½ teaspoon whole cloves

2 inches stick cinnamon

¼ cup lard or cooking oil plus 1 tablespoon

1 cup zucchini, diced into ⅓-inch pieces

1½ pounds turkey breast meat, chopped into ½- to ¾-inch pieces

¾ cup finely chopped onions

2 cloves garlic, minced

1 teaspoon oregano

1 tablespoon brown sugar

1 tablespoon cider vinegar

1 teaspoon salt or to taste

1 cup chopped fresh pineapple, or substitute unsweetened canned pineapple

2 tablespoons coarsely chopped Mexican chocolate, or substitute bittersweet chocolate

■ This dish has much to recommend it. It is quite similar to the famous northern wedding dish *asado de boda*, except that it uses turkey instead of pork and adds squash and sesame seeds. Due to the use of very lean turkey and because the cooking oil that is specified can be reduced in half without a substantial loss of quality, this makes an excellent low-fat entrée. And because of its simplicity it is an ideal dish to serve when one wants to capture the feel of the more complex *moles* without all the work. ■

Heat a skillet over medium heat, and toast the chiles until they just become soft and fragrant. Do not allow them to burn or the sauce will be bitter. When the chiles are cool enough to handle, rinse them under cold water, remove the stems and seeds, and place them in a blender. Add about 4 cups hot water, and allow the chiles to rehydrate for 20 minutes. Drain off the liquid, then add back 2¾ cups of water. Add the pineapple juice and blend the mixture for 2 minutes or until completely puréed.

Heat a small skillet over medium heat and toast the cumin, sesame seeds, cloves, and cinnamon, stirring almost continuously, until the sesame seeds begin to turn golden. Place the toasted spices in a spice or coffee grinder and grind to a powder.

Heat a 3- to 4-quart pot or Dutch oven over medium heat, add the lard or oil, and when it just begins to smoke add the zucchini. Cook the zucchini, stirring constantly, until it has browned, then remove it to a bowl and reserve. Unless your pot is very large it is best to brown the turkey in 2 batches. Reheat the pot over medium-high to high heat, add 2 tablespoons of the lard or oil, and when it begins to smoke add about ½ the turkey. Allow the turkey to sizzle for about 15 to 20 seconds, then, using a large spoon, turn it, and allow it to cook for another 15 to 20 seconds. Continue cooking the turkey, turning constantly as in stir-frying, until it is just browned.

Then remove from the pot to a bowl and reserve. Cook the remaining turkey in the same way, then remove it and reserve it with the first batch of turkey.

Turn the heat to medium, add the onions, and a little more oil, if necessary, and cook until the onions are golden, about 5 minutes. Add the garlic and cook 1 more minute. Replace the browned turkey in the pot, and add the contents of the blender, the oregano, the sugar, vinegar, and salt. Bring the liquid to a boil, turn down the heat, cover, and simmer for 40 minutes.

When the 40 minutes are up, add the pineapple to the pot, bring to a boil, and continue cooking at a brisk simmer until the sauce has thickened, about 15 minutes. Add the reserved zucchini and cook 1 or 2 minutes, then add the chocolate and continue cooking until it has melted and is well combined, about 1 to 2 minutes.

Serve the turkey with white rice. A nice way of doing this is to spoon rice into a lightly greased, 5-inch, round mold. Invert the mold onto the center of a serving plate, tap, and remove the mold, which will leave a ring of rice on the plate. Spoon some of the mole into the center of the rice ring. Do the same thing with the other plates and serve. Serves 4.

STUFFED CHICKEN BREASTS IN TOMATILLO-TEQUILA SAUCE

THE FILLING & CHICKEN:

1 pasilla chile, seeded, stemmed, and torn into pieces

1 tablespoon butter

2 tablespoons minced onion

1 clove garlic, minced

2 tablespoons almonds

¼ cup mushrooms, finely chopped

¼ cup huitlacoche, finely chopped

¼ cup peeled, seeded, and chopped tomato (about ½ medium tomato)

2 tablespoons chopped black olives

¼ teaspoon dried thyme

2 cups lightly packed fresh spinach leaves, finely chopped

Pinch salt or to taste

3 tablespoons whipping cream

½ teaspoon lime juice, or to taste

1 ounce Spanish manchego cheese, grated

1 ounce asadero cheese, grated

■ This recipe is delicious as well as being a fine example of *nueva cocina mexicana*. If you do not wish to use the *huitlacoche*, omit it and double the amount of mushrooms. Much of the success of this dish depends on how well the filling is wrapped in the chicken, which in turn depends a great deal on the size of the breasts, and how evenly, in terms of both thickness and shape, they are pounded. Make sure the breast halves are about 8 ounces each as smaller ones will give you much less room for error. ■

Place the chile in a blender, cover with hot water, and allow it to soak for 20 minutes. Heat the butter in a skillet over medium heat and sauté the onion until soft but not browned. Add the garlic and continue cooking for 1 minute. Add the almonds and continue cooking until they begin to turn golden. Add the mushrooms, *huitlacoche*, tomato, olives, and thyme, and sauté until the mushrooms become soft. Add the spinach and continue cooking for 3 minutes, then add the salt.

Meanwhile, strain the water from the chile in the blender and discard. Add the cream and blend for 1 minute, adding a little more cream if necessary, until the mixture becomes a paste. Using a small spatula or spoon, transfer as much of the *pasilla* cream as you can from the blender into the skillet with the other ingredients, and continue cooking until most of the liquid has evaporated and the mixture is quite thick, 5 to 10 minutes. Stir in the lime juice. Remove the mixture to a bowl and allow it to cool, then add the cheeses, stirring to combine well.

Place each breast between sheets of plastic wrap, and, using a meat pounder or heavy cleaver, pound each one to about ⅛ inch thick, keeping them as round as possible. When you are pounding, make sure the breasts stay between plastic wrap, and begin the process from the middle outward to prevent the edges from shredding. Also do not hurry until you have got the hang of it, which should not take long. Place equal portions of the filling just off center of each pounded breast, fold over the sides, and roll up like a burrito, securing them with toothpicks.

Place the *tomatillos* and chile in a small saucepan, cover with water, bring to a boil, and simmer until the *tomatillos* and chile are soft, 5 to 10 minutes. Remove the *tomatillos* and chile from the pan, place in a blender, and blend until puréed, about 30 seconds. Strain the *tomatillo* mixture through the fine blade of a food mill, and place ¼ cup in a small saucepan. Add the tequila, salt, and lime juice and bring the liquid to a boil. Add the cream, and simmer the sauce briskly for about 4 minutes or until it thickens. You can do this partially beforehand then complete it just prior to serving if you wish. Remove the sauce from the heat, stir in the butter, and reserve.

To cook the stuffed chicken:

Melt 1½ tablespoons butter in a skillet over medium heat, add the rolled chicken breasts, and sauté them until they are golden on all sides and heated through. To serve, place a stuffed breast on each of 4 serving plates and top with the sauce. This dish goes well with white rice. Serves 4.

1 ounce cotija or añejo cheese, grated

4 ½ chicken breasts, about ½ pound each

THE SAUCE:

6–8 ounces tomatillos, husked

1 small serrano chile

¼ cup tequila

¼ teaspoon salt

1 teaspoon lime juice

3 tablespoons whipping cream

3 tablespoons butter

❊ CHICKEN BREAST WITH
❊ ❊ POBLANO-SQUASH BLOSSOM SAUCE

4 boneless, skinless ½ chicken breasts

Salt and pepper to taste

2 tablespoons olive oil

1½ tablespoons butter

3 tablespoons minced onion

1 clove garlic, minced

1 cup (about 4 medium) poblano chiles, peeled, seeded, and finely chopped

¼ teaspoon dried thyme

¼ teaspoon dried marjoram

¼ teaspoon dried oregano

3 tablespoons dry or moderately sweet white wine

½ cup sour cream

¼ cup heavy whipping cream

Pinch saffron

1½ cups chopped fresh squash blossoms or 1 small can of squash blossoms, coarsely chopped

½ teaspoon salt

¼ teaspoon black pepper

■ This is the best version I have found of a dish that is often served in restaurants featuring *nueva cocina mexicana*. The dish can be made with fresh or canned squash blossoms, but the fresh ones are far better. Although it is also good without squash blossoms, it is much more interesting with them. ■

Salt and pepper the chicken breasts to taste. Heat a skillet over medium-high heat, add the olive oil, then sauté the chicken breasts until they are golden brown and just cooked through, turning down the heat if necessary. Place the breasts on a warm plate and cover them with a tent of foil to keep them warm while you prepare the sauce.

Turn the heat to medium, pour off the excess olive oil, add the butter, and when it is melted add the onion and garlic, and cook for 1 to 2 minutes or until the onion begins to soften. Next, add the *poblano* chiles, thyme, marjoram, and oregano and cook another 1 to 2 minutes. Then add the wine and stir to deglaze the pan. When most of the wine has evaporated, add the remaining ingredients and simmer the sauce until the squash blossoms are cooked through, about 2 minutes. Place the chicken breasts on each of 4 serving plates, spoon some sauce over them, and serve. Serves 4.

❊ ROAST DUCK WITH ANCHO-CHERRY SAUCE

■ This dish can also be made with chicken, Cornish game hen, or guinea hen. If you want to go to the extra trouble, it is especially delicious when the duck is spit-roasted over hardwood coals. ■

Preheat the oven to 350 degrees. Salt and pepper the ducklings and roast them until golden brown, 1 hour to 1¼ hours, then slice them in half lengthwise and serve on the sauce.

Toast the chiles, remove the stems, veins, and most of the seeds, place the chiles in a blender, and add the cherries. Heat 1½ cups of the broth until nearly boiling, add it to the blender, and allow the chiles and cherries to rehydrate for 20 minutes. Blend the mixture at high speed for 2 minutes and strain through the small disk of a food mill.

Heat the oil in a saucepan over medium-high heat, add the strained chile mixture, and cook, stirring constantly, until it begins to thicken, about 2 minutes. Reduce the heat, add the remaining ½ cup broth, the vinegar, bay leaf, marjoram, thyme, and salt, and simmer the mixture until it is thick enough to coat a spoon. Pour some sauce on each of 4 serving plates and top with a half roast duck. Serves 4.

THE DUCK:

2 ducklings

Salt and pepper to taste

THE SAUCE:

2 ancho chiles

¼ cup pitted, dried cherries

2 cloves garlic, minced

2 cups chicken broth or water

2 tablespoons cooking oil

1 teaspoon cider vinegar

1 bay leaf

¼ teaspoon dried marjoram

¼ teaspoon dried thyme

½ teaspoon salt or to taste

1 tablespoon achiote seeds

¼ teaspoon cumin seeds

1 teaspoon dried oregano

¼ teaspoon ground allspice

1 teaspoon ground ancho chile

½ teaspoon ground cinnamon

¼ teaspoon ground cloves

½ teaspoon salt

1 tablespoon cider vinegar

2 tablespoons orange juice

**1 4½- to 5-pound duck
(to serve 2)**

THE STUFFING:

**4 ancho chiles, stemmed and
seeded**

1 teaspoon achiote seeds

½ tablespoon dried oregano

½ teaspoon whole cumin seeds

**Heaping ¼ teaspoon ground
allspice**

Heaping ¼ teaspoon salt

¼ cup fresh orange juice

1 tablespoon lime juice

**3½ tablespoons pumpkin seed oil,
or substitute cooking oil**

**1 pound mushrooms, stemmed
and minced**

½ cup crushed, canned pineapple

**⅓ cup dried mango, minced, or
substitute another dried fruit
such as apricot**

**1 14½-ounce can unsalted
tomatoes, drained and puréed**

MAYAN DUCK

■ The stuffing for this dish is based on a modified version of *chilmole* or *recado negro*, perhaps the most interesting of the many seasoning pastes found in the Yucatán. In Mexican cooking, the chiles are usually toasted briefly to soften them and bring out their flavor, but these are placed on a dry griddle until they are nearly black. When making traditional *chilmole*, cooks often sprinkle the chiles with grain alcohol, which enhances the charring and produces an even darker color. But for this dish they are only cooked until they begin to blacken. The exterior of the duck is rubbed with yet another *recado* made savory with cinnamon, cloves, and allspice. ■

To prepare the duck, place all the ingredients except the vinegar, orange juice, and duckling in a spice or coffee grinder, grind to a powder, and transfer the powder to a small bowl. Add the juices and mix to a watery paste, using a little more orange juice, if necessary. Rub the paste into the outside of the duck, making sure the breast and legs are well coated. Place the duck in the refrigerator until ready to stuff.

To make the stuffing, toast the chiles on an ungreased skillet over medium heat until they begin to blacken and become crisp. They will still be somewhat flexible, but after they have cooled for a couple of minutes they will be completely dry and brittle. If, after cooling, they are still damp and flexible, toast them a little longer. Tear the chiles into small pieces and grind them in a spice or coffee grinder with the achiote seeds, oregano, cumin, allspice, and salt. Mix the orange and lime juice and stir it into the ground spices until a thick, slightly runny paste is formed. This should take most of the juices. Reserve the paste.

Sauté the mushrooms in the pumpkin seed oil over medium-high heat until most of the moisture has evaporated. Turn the heat to medium low, add the remaining ingredients, including the reserved seasoning paste, and cook, stirring constantly, until the mixture is about the consistency of mincemeat, about 20 to 25 minutes. Turn down the heat as necessary to keep the stuffing from burning. Remove the stuffing from the heat, and when it has cooled stuff and truss the duck.

Preheat the oven to 350 degrees, then place the duck on a rack in a roasting pan, breast side up, and roast for about 20 minutes per pound. While the duck is roasting, prepare the sauce.

Melt the butter in a saucepan over medium heat and sauté the onion and chile until the onion is soft but not browned. Add the remaining ingredients and bring to a boil, turning the heat to medium high, and cook the sauce until it is reduced to ¾ cup.

When the duck is done, remove it from the oven and allow it to rest for 3 to 5 minutes. Carve the duck and serve it with some sauce spooned over the top and the stuffing on the side. Serves 2.

Kernels from 2 medium ears of corn, grated while on the cob

¼ cup pumpkin seeds, browned in ½ teaspoon oil and crushed in a molcajete

⅓ cup loosely packed, fresh minced cilantro

1 tablespoon honey

THE SAUCE:

1 tablespoon butter

⅓ cup minced onion

1 large serrano chile, preferably fully ripe (red), minced

½ cup crema de membrillo liquor, or substitute peach brandy

½ cup chicken broth

1 cup mango juice

1 tablespoon lime juice

¼ teaspoon rubbed sage

¼ teaspoon dried thyme

¼ teaspoon dried marjoram

½ teaspoon paprika

2 tablespoons finely chopped, loosely packed cilantro

Heaping ¼ teaspoon salt or to taste

❋ Red Snapper Veracruz Style

4 red snapper filets of 6–8
ounces each

1 stick unsalted butter

½ cup peeled, finely chopped
granny smith apple

¼ cup roasted, peeled, finely
chopped red bell pepper

¼ cup peeled, finely chopped
celery

1½ tablespoons peeled, pithed
and finely chopped lime

1½ tablespoons capers

½ cup peeled, seeded, finely
chopped roma tomatoes

¼ cup finely chopped green,
Spanish olives

2 tablespoons minced fresh
parsley

2 tablespoons minced fresh
cilantro

1 tablespoon plus 1 teaspoon
catsup

⅓ cup aged sherry vinegar

Salt and ground pepper, to
taste

■ This is a rich and delicious *nueva cocina* version of this tradi-tional seafood dish. ■

Cut the butter into 1 tablespoon-sized pieces and melt in a small saucepan over medium heat until it has turned a nutty golden brown. Remove from the heat and reserve. Place the remaining ingredients, except the vinegar, salt, and pepper, in a small bowl and reserve.

To cook the fish, salt and pepper it on both sides. Heat a skillet over medium high heat, add 3 tablespoons clarified butter and sauté the fish until it is cooked through and brown on the outside. Place on serving plates and keep warm.

Place the vinegar in a small saucepan over medium heat, bring to a simmer and reduce until it is almost syrupy. Add the browned but-ter and the reserved ingredients in the bowl and cook until they are just hot. Add salt and pepper to taste and spoon over the fish. Serve with white rice. Serves 4.

✼ Sea Bass or Tuna a la Margarita

■ It was inevitable that someone would invent a dish based on the ingredients in the famous cocktail, and I have seen several. This one is a credit to its namesake. It uses the ingredients for the Margarita in much the way that compound butters are used, with a delicious result that requires little last-minute preparation. It works equally well with sea bass or yellowfin tuna. With sea bass, I like to use a regular iron skillet for baking since it produces a crusty, golden texture on the surfaces of the fish. With tuna, I prefer to use a ridged iron grill pan, which provides much of the flavor and appearance of grilling. ■

To make the sauce, combine all the ingredients except the carrots and butter in a small saucepan and bring to a boil. Add the carrots and blanch them for about 1 minute. They should still be fairly crisp and infused with the flavors of the sauce. Continue simmering until the mixture is reduced to about ⅓ cup. The sauce can be prepared to this point then kept 1 or 2 hours unrefrigerated or 1 or 2 days refrigerated.

To prepare the fish, first preheat the oven to 350 degrees. The fish will be first seared in a skillet on top of the stove, then put in the oven to finish cooking, so select a skillet that can be placed in the oven.

Salt and pepper the sea bass or tuna on one side. Place the olive oil in a skillet or lightly oil a ridged grill pan and place over medium-high heat. When the pan is very hot but not smoking, add the fish. Allow the fish to cook for 2½ minutes, or until the bottom of the sea bass is golden brown and crisp, or the tuna is seared and crisp, without turning. Turn the fish and place the skillet or grill pan in the preheated oven. Bake the sea bass for 13 minutes or until it is cooked through and flaky. Bake the tuna for about 8 minutes for medium rare. In either case, remove the fish to serving plates.

To finish the sauce, bring it to a boil and simmer until it is reduced to 3 tablespoons. Then remove it from the heat and whisk in the butter. Spoon about 1 tablespoon of the sauce over each piece of fish, garnish with the blanched carrots and parsley, and serve with the lime wedges and orange slices to one side of the fish. Serves 4.

THE SAUCE & GARNISH:

¼ cup white tequila

¼ cup lime juice

3 tablespoons triple sec

1 serrano chile, stemmed, seeded, and minced

Heaping ¼ teaspoon salt

½ cup carrots, cut into julienne strips

1½ tablespoons butter

THE FISH:

4 boneless sea bass steaks, 6–8 ounces and 1¼ inches thick, or 4 yellowfin tuna steaks, 6–8 ounces and 1¼ to 1½ inches thick

Salt and pepper to taste

1 tablespoon olive oil

1 tablespoon minced fresh parsley

4 lime wedges

4 ¼-inch orange slices

❊ SALMON PIBIL

THE SAUCE:

1 habanero or Scotch bonnet chile

⅓ cup onion, minced

2 green onions, minced

¾ cup orange juice

¼ cup lime juice

¾ teaspoon salt

THE RECADO:

1 tablespoon annato seeds

1 teaspoon dried oregano

¼ teaspoon cumin seeds

1 teaspoon coriander seeds

2 cloves

12 peppercorns

⅛ teaspoon ground allspice

¼ teaspoon salt

⅛ teaspoon ground cinnamon

5 cloves garlic, minced

3 tablespoons sour orange juice, or substitute a mixture of 2 tablespoons orange juice and 1 tablespoon lime juice

1¾–2 pounds salmon filet

1 banana leaf (optional)

■ This dish combines the traditional ingredients and ancient pit cooking of the Yucatán with salmon, which was cooked in a similar way by Indians of the Pacific Northwest, who, however, did not have access to exotic seasonings. In the Yucatán, seasoning pastes called *recados*, which usually contain the deep red seeds of the annato tree, are used in the same manner as *adobo* pastes in other parts of Mexico. ■

To make the sauce, broil the chile until it begins to char, then remove the seeds, mince, combine it with the remaining ingredients, and refrigerate for at least 3 hours.

In a spice or coffee grinder, grind the annato seeds, oregano, cumin seeds, coriander seeds, cloves, and peppercorns to a fine powder. Mix in the allspice, salt, and cinnamon. In a *molcajete* or rough-sided Japanese mortar and pestle, grind the powdered spices and the garlic, adding just enough of the sour orange juice to make a thick paste. Spread the paste on the salmon so that it fully covers the side opposite the skin.

Put the banana leaf on a large piece of foil, and then place the salmon on it, skin-side down. Smoke the salmon in a water smoker or indirect-heat barbecue for 1½ to 1¾ hours, depending on its thickness. Remove the salmon and peel off the skin.

Serve the salmon with white Mexican Rice (p. 208), steamed zucchini, and the sauce. Serves 4.

❈ SWORDFISH WITH HOJA SANTA BUTTER SAUCE

■ This dish is very simple, and an excellent change of pace from more complicated foods. The *hoja santa* provides a taste that is both unexpected and seductive. ■

For the butter sauce simply combine all the ingredients. Prepare a charbroiler with hardwood or hardwood charcoal, and when it is ready broil the swordfish until it is just done, 3 to 4 minutes on each side. Place the cooked swordfish on each of 4 serving plates, garnish with ¼ of the butter sauce, and serve. This dish goes well with a salad, white rice (p. 242), and steamed squash or Puréed Spinach, Squash and Avocado (p. 113). Serves 4.

THE BUTTER SAUCE:

2 tablespoons butter

2 drops Worcestershire sauce

1½ tablespoons tightly packed, minced hoja santa

THE FISH:

4 swordfish steaks, 6–8 ounces each

BROILED RED SNAPPER & SHRIMP WITH AVOCADO & MANGO BUTTERS

THE AVOCADO BUTTER:

½ **teaspoon minced serrano chile**

2 **teaspoons lime juice**

1 **stick unsalted butter**

⅓ **cup avocado, chopped**

1 **tablespoon tightly packed fresh cilantro, minced**

⅛ **teaspoon salt or to taste**

THE MANGO BUTTER:

2½ **teaspoons lime juice**

½ **teaspoon minced lime peel**

½ **teaspoon minced orange peel**

½ **stick unsalted butter**

¼ **teaspoon ground nutmeg**

½ **teaspoon juice from a can of canned chipotle chiles**

⅓ **cup mango, peeled, seeded, and minced**

⅛ **teaspoon ground cinnamon**

⅛ **teaspoon salt**

■ This dish is rather mild and tropical in effect. Both the fish and shrimp can be broiled in either the oven or over hot coals. I prefer the latter. Also, the flavored butters can be made a day ahead if covered tightly with plastic wrap and kept refrigerated. ■

To make the avocado butter, place the *serrano* chile and lime juice in a small saucepan, bring to a boil, simmer for 30 seconds, and remove from the heat to cool. Put the cooled mixture with the remaining ingredients in a bowl, and, using a fork or an electric mixer, blend into a paste.

To make the mango butter, place the lime juice, lime peel, and orange peel in a small saucepan, bring to a boil, simmer for 30 seconds, and remove from the heat to cool. Place the cooled mixture with the remaining ingredients in a bowl, and, using a fork or an electric mixer, blend to a paste.

One-half hour before you are ready to cook the fish, place the shrimp in a bowl with the olive oil and lime juice to marinate. (If they are marinated any longer than ½ hour, the lime juice may begin to "cook" the shrimp as in *cebiche*.)

Preheat the broiler or light a fire. When the broiler or coals are ready, broil both the fish and shrimp until just cooked through. (If using a charbroiler, it is best to use a grill perforated with holes small enough to keep the shrimp from falling into the fire, or alternatively thread them on skewers.) When the fish and shrimp are cooked, place a fish filet on each of 4 serving plates, and spread the top of each with 2 tablespoons of the avocado butter. Mound the shrimp in equal portions on the top of the filets and top with 2 tablespoons of the mango butter. Serve accompanied by the lime halves. Serves 4.

THE FISH & SHRIMP:

1 pound medium-small shrimp

½ cup olive oil

3 tablespoons lime juice

½ teaspoon salt, plus additional for the fish

4 red snapper filets, 6- to 8-ounces each

4 limes, halved

✻ FISH FILET WITH PUMPKIN SEED PESTO

■ This pumpkin pesto, something between a compound butter and a sauce, adds texture and a more complicated, interesting taste to the usual *al mojo de ajo* (garlic sauce) treatment of fish in Mexico. It is good with any fish that can be cooked over charcoal—red snapper, freshwater bass, and yellowfin tuna are all good choices. ■

Place the garlic and olive oil in a small saucepan over medium heat, cook until the garlic is soft but not browned, and reserve. Place ½ teaspoon of the oil in which the garlic was cooked in a skillet over medium heat, add the pumpkin seeds, and heat, turning often, until most of the seeds have popped but have not turned brown. Place the seeds in a blender, add the garlic, oil, and remaining ingredients, except the fish, and blend until thoroughly chopped but not puréed. The pumpkin seeds should still have a coarse rather than smooth texture.

Prepare wood or hardwood charcoal coals and broil the fish. Top the fish with the pesto and serve with rice or roast potatoes. Serves 4.

4 large or 6 medium-sized whole garlic cloves, skins removed

½ cup olive oil

½ cup pumpkin seeds

1 tablespoon medium-packed minced parsley

2 tablespoons fresh cilantro, minced

1 tablespoon roasted poblano chile, peeled and minced

½ tablespoon pickled jalapeño chile, minced

2 tablespoons lime juice

½ teaspoon salt

4 fish filets, about 6 ounces each

✳ RED SNAPPER WITH TOMATILLO CREAM SAUCE

THE FISH:

4 red snapper filets, 6–8 ounces each

THE MARINADE:

5 cloves garlic, chopped

3 tablespoons olive oil

1½ tablespoons lime juice

THE SAUCE:

¾ pound tomatillos, peeled

2 medium-sized, canned chipotle chiles

1½ cups heavy cream

2 tablespoons roasted garlic

¾ cup chopped, fresh cilantro

3 tablespoons butter

1 teaspoon salt

1 teaspoon brown sugar

■ This dish is both earthy and elegant. It combines the smoky flavor of roasted garlic and *chipotle* chiles with the coolness of cream and cilantro. ■

To make the marinade, grind all the ingredients in a *molcajete*, or mortar and pestle. No more than 1 hour before you are ready to cook the fish, spread the marinade on the fish filets. If it is on longer, the lime juice will begin to "cook" the fish as with ceviche.

To make the sauce, place the *tomatillos* in a small pot, cover with water, bring to a boil, and simmer until they are quite soft, about 5 to 10 minutes. Drain the *tomatillos*, place them in a blender with the *chipotle* chiles, and blend for 1 minute. Strain the blended ingredients through the fine blade of a food mill and reserve.

Place the cream, garlic, and cilantro in a blender and blend for 30 seconds. Reserve.

The sauce can be prepared ahead to this point, at which time you should light a barbecue fire of hardwood or hardwood charcoal and allow it to burn down to coals.

About 10 minutes before the coals will be ready, finish the sauce. Heat a skillet over medium to medium-high heat. Add the butter, and when it has melted add the *tomatillo* mixture and cook for 2 to 3 minutes, or until it begins to thicken. Turn the heat to medium, add the cream mixture, salt, and sugar, and cook, stirring often, until it has thickened to the consistency of a medium-thick sauce. Keep it warm until you have broiled the fish.

Broil the fish about 4 to 5 inches from the coals until it is cooked through and slightly charred on both sides, about 3 to 4 minutes on each side. (Because of the nature of outdoor cooking, the suggested cooking time is only a guide.)

When the fish has been cooked, spoon the sauce onto each of 4 serving plates and top with the charbroiled fish. This dish goes well with white rice or Green Rice (p. 209) and steamed zucchini. Serves 4.

❋ FILET OF SOLE WITH APPLE-CREAM-CHIPOTLE SAUCE

■ A good farm-raised catfish filet can be substituted for the sole in this elegant dish adapted from a recipe in *Gourmet* magazine. It goes very well with Green Rice (p. 209). ■

Heat a medium-sized saucepan over medium-low heat, add the butter, and when it has melted add the onion and cook until soft but not brown, about 5 to 8 minutes. Add the flour and continue cooking 1 minute, stirring constantly. Then add the mushrooms and *chipotle* chiles, and cook, stirring frequently, until the mushrooms are soft and most of their juice has evaporated, about 15 minutes. Add the apple juice and brandy, increase the heat to medium high, and when the sauce comes to a boil reduce to a good simmer and cook until it has been reduced by between ⅓ and ½, about 15 minutes. Then add the cream, salt, and pepper and continue simmering until the sauce has thickened, about 10 to 15 minutes. Finally, add the parsley and turn the heat to very low to keep the sauce warm while you prepare the fish.

Dredge the fish filets in the flour and shake off the excess.

Heat a large skillet over medium to medium-high heat and melt the butter. When the butter has melted, add the filets and cook until well browned on the first side, about 2 to 3 minutes, turn, and continue cooking on the other side until just done.

Place the cooked filets on serving plates and spoon the sauce over them. Serve with Green Rice, slices of steamed zucchini, and lime wedges. Serves 4.

THE SAUCE:

3 tablespoons butter

3 tablespoons minced onion

1 tablespoon flour

2 cups diced mushrooms

2 medium-sized, canned chipotle chiles, seeded and minced

1½ cups apple juice

½ cup brandy

½ cup cream

¼ teaspoon salt

¼ teaspoon finely ground black pepper

2 tablespoons fresh parsley, minced

THE FISH:

4 sole, flounder, or catfish filets, about 5–8 ounces each

1 cup flour

4 tablespoons butter

Lime wedges

❋ Tamarind-Glazed Shrimp with ❋❋ Mango-Chipotle Cream Sauce

THE SHRIMP & BROTH:

2 pounds very large shrimp (preferably 6 per pound)

2 cups water

½ teaspoon dried thyme

I clove garlic, mashed

Olive oil

THE TAMARIND PASTE:

6 ounces piloncillo or brown sugar, cut into small pieces (use a serrated knife)

6 cloves garlic, minced and ground to a paste in a molcajete, or mortar and pestle

I canned chipotle chile, minced

I tablespoon liquid from the can of chipotles

I tablespoon tamarind paste (available at Oriental markets)

2 tablespoons rum

2 tablespoons water

¼ teaspoon salt

THE SAUCE:

½ cup mango, peeled and chopped

■ Tamarind came to Mexico by way of the Manila galleons, which sailed the route between Acapulco and Manila for over 200 years. In traditional Mexican cooking, it was used mostly to produce a soft drink. However, in *nueva cocina mexicana* it is being used in sauces that go particularly well with seafood and pork. Tamarind is extremely tart and needs to be paired with something quite sweet, in this case *piloncillo*, the dark brown, unrefined Mexican sugar that tastes like a combination of brown sugar and molasses. This dish is most successful with the largest shrimp you can buy. ■

Peel the shrimp, leaving the tails intact, and thread them onto 4 fairly short shish kebab skewers. (If you use wooden skewers, place them in water to cover for at least 1 hour to keep them from burning.) Place the shrimp shells in a saucepan, add the water, bring to a boil, and add the thyme and garlic. Simmer the mixture gently until it is reduced to 1 cup, about 15 to 20 minutes, then strain and reserve the liquid.

To make the paste, place the *piloncillo* in a small saucepan over low heat and cook, stirring often, until it is melted. (*Piloncillo* can be melted easily in a microwave, and without cutting it up first, but you must use medium power and no more than 30-second increments because it can easily overheat, creating an incredible mess and causing severe burns.) Add the remaining ingredients and cook over very low heat until the tamarind paste has melted, about 5 to 10 minutes. Reserve. This can be done well ahead of time, but if it hardens you will have to reheat it before using.

To make the sauce, place all the ingredients except the cream and butter in a blender and blend for 1 minute.

Meanwhile prepare a fire in a charbroiler with hardwood or hardwood charcoal. Just before the fire is ready for cooking, reblend the sauce mixture, place in a saucepan over medium-high heat, and bring to a boil. Add the cream and cook, whisking frequently, until the mixture begins to thicken slightly, about 6 minutes, and remove from the heat.

Brush the skewered shrimp with olive oil, place them over the fire, which should be quite hot, and cook for 1 minute. Turn the shrimp and brush the cooked side with the tamarind paste. Continue turning and basting until the shrimp are just cooked through. Remove them, and cover them with a loose tent of foil to keep them warm. Bring the sauce to a boil and continue cooking for about 4 to 5 minutes over medium-high heat, or until it reaches the consistency of a very thin sauce. Remove it from the heat, whisk in the butter, then spoon some onto each of 4 serving plates, and top with the glazed shrimp. Serve with white rice, packed into a decorative mold, if desired. Serves 4.

1 cup reserved shrimp broth

½–1 tablespoon liquid from the can of chipotle chiles

¼ cup loosely packed, chopped cilantro

¾ teaspoon salt

⅓ cup heavy cream

2½ tablespoons butter

CRAB IN GREEN CHILE-SAFFRON SAUCE

2 cups Chile and Cheese Chihuahua Style (p. 195), made with half the cheese

¼ teaspoon saffron

2 cups cooked crabmeat

½ cup grated Spanish manchego cheese

■ This is Mexico's answer to coquilles St. Jacques, and I think it is even better than the famous French dish. It is also extremely easy to make from freshly prepared or leftover Chile and Cheese Chihuahua Style. ■

Mix the saffron and crabmeat into the Chile and Cheese Chihuahua Style. If you are using leftover Chile and Cheese Chihuahua Style, place it in a double boiler with the saffron and crabmeat, cover, and cook until hot. Spoon the mixture into each of 4 shell-shaped ovenproof dishes or ramekins. Top with the grated cheese and place under the broiler for about 3 minutes or until the top is speckled with golden brown bits of cheese. Serves 4.

GREEN CEVICHE

■ Amando Farga asserts that *cebiche* was named by Captain Vasco Núñez de Balboa after his discovery of the Pacific Ocean in 1513 when he was given some by native fishermen; moreover, he states that the name itself comes from the verb *cebar*, which has several meanings, one of which means to penetrate or saturate.

Too many *cebiches* are just rehashed versions of the catsup-based shrimp cocktail, where the sauce overpowers the delicate fish. However, this recipe is as good as this dish gets; it is subtle yet assertive and supports rather than overwhelms the fish. Remember, though, that the fish must be perfectly fresh, both for the best taste and for health reasons. Any off-taste resulting from the formation of bacteria will come through the lime juice "cooking" process, and it is doubtful that lime juice kills bacteria as effectively as usual cooking methods.

The dish calls for partially ripe tomatoes, which means that they should be mostly green in color with just a tinge of red, and while they should not be soft they should also not be completely hard like green tomatoes. Since the amount of *cebiche* people prefer to serve varies, I have designed the sauce to be sufficient for ¼-pound portions, but the amount of sauce you add to the fish can be reduced for smaller portions. ■

Place the fish and onions in a nonreactive bowl. Combine the lime juice and salt and pour it over the fish, mixing well. Put the bowl in the refrigerator and allow the mixture to marinate for 2 to 3 hours or until it has turned opaque.

Put the roasted tomatoes in a blender and blend to a purée, about 30 seconds at high speed. Strain the mixture through the fine blade of a food mill. There should be about 1 cup of strained purée, so discard any excess. Rinse out and dry the blender bowl and return the purée to it. Then add the chile, cilantro, thyme, and marjoram, and purée about 30 seconds at high speed. In a bowl large enough to easily accommodate the sauce, whisk together the vinegar, lime juice, and corn oil. Little by little, whisk in the tomato/chile purée, then add the salt. Place the bowl in the refrigerator until the sauce is completely chilled.

When the fish is "cooked" and the sauce is cold, and about 15 minutes before you are ready to serve the dish, strain all the salted lime juice from the fish and place it in a bowl. Carefully stir in as much of the sauce as you wish to use and serve. Serves 4.

THE FISH:

1 pound boneless sea bass, cut into ¼- to ½-inch pieces

½ cup minced onions

1 cup lime juice

½ teaspoon salt

THE SAUCE:

2 medium to large, partially ripe tomatoes (about 1 pound), broiled until blackened and soft

1 large poblano chile, roasted, peeled, and chopped

2 tablespoons very tightly packed, fresh cilantro leaves

½ teaspoon dried thyme

½ teaspoon dried marjoram

1 tablespoon rice vinegar

2 tablespoons lime juice

3 tablespoons corn oil

1 teaspoon salt or to taste

Scallops with Tomatillo-Mango Sauce

THE SAUCE:

1 pound tomatillos

1 serrano chile

2 tablespoons medium-packed cilantro

2 tablespoons butter

2 cups finely chopped shiitake or Portobello mushrooms

1 cup chicken broth

¼ cup Kern's mango nectar

3 tablespoons whipping cream

½ teaspoon salt

THE CORN PUDDING:

2 cups milk

2 serrano chiles, stemmed, seeded, and minced

½ teaspoon salt

½ cup yellow cornmeal

4 ears corn, husked and grated with the coarse blade of a hand grater

2 tablespoons heavy cream

THE SCALLOPS:

1 pound sea scallops

Salt and pepper to taste

2 tablespoons butter

■ I adapted this recipe from one by Robert Del Grande published in Julia Child's *Cooking with Master Chefs.* Of all the American chefs specializing in southwestern cuisine whose cooking I have experienced, Del Grande's cooking best captures the essence of *nueva cocina mexicana.* I wanted to use this recipe both because it is delicious and because the corn pudding is a terrific innovation that can be used in many situations. In this version the addition of mango nectar to the sauce gives the dish a delightful hint of tropical sweetness. ■

To make the sauce, put the tomatillos and chile in a small saucepan, cover them with water, bring to a boil, and simmer them, covered, until they are very soft, about 5 to 10 minutes. Discard the water and put the tomatillos, chile, and cilantro in a blender and blend until puréed. Strain the mixture through the fine blade of a food mill and reserve.

Melt the butter in a small saucepan over medium-high heat, add the mushrooms and sauté until they are browned. Add 1 cup of the strained tomatillo sauce and the remaining ingredients, cook until the sauce thickens, and reserve.

To make the pudding, bring the milk, chiles, and salt to a boil. Slowly stir in the cornmeal. Add the grated corn and continue stirring until thick. Then add the cream, cover, reserve, and keep warm.

Salt and pepper one side of the scallops. Melt the butter in a skillet over medium to medium-high heat, and sauté the scallops until they are brown on both sides and just cooked through.

When the scallops are done, put a scoop of the corn pudding on each of 4 serving plates. Top each scoop with some scallops, then spoon on some of the tomatillo-mango sauce, and serve, possibly with the addition of some steamed squash. Serves 4.

Tortellini with Smoked Chicken & Tomato Cream Sauce

■ According to tradition, pasta came to Spain with the Moors, and the Spanish brought it with them to Mexico. Traditionally, it has taken the form of something between spaghetti and angel hair called *fideo*, and was used in *sopas secas* (literally "dry soups"), a category that also includes rice dishes where the starch is boiled in liquid until almost entirely absorbed. Prior to the widespread introduction of *nueva cocina mexicana*, upscale Italian food was popular in Mexico, particularly in areas such as Acapulco, where many Mexicans go on vacations, and was served to expand the Mexican repertoire of pasta dishes. This dish, which is delicious and easy to prepare, combines tortellini with a Mexican-style sauce seasoned with *serrano* chiles and cream. ■

Place the tomatoes and chiles on a baking sheet under a preheated broiler and broil until the skins are charred and the tomatoes soft. Blend the tomatoes and chiles and strain. You will need ⅔ cup of this sauce.

Melt the butter in a saucepan over medium heat, add the mushrooms, and sauté them for 1 minute. Add the garlic and cook an additional ½ minute. Add the ⅔ cup tomato-chile sauce, the cream, parsley, basil, salt, and pepper and continue cooking until the sauce has thickened.

Meanwhile, bring a large pot of water to a boil, add some salt, then boil the tortellini until they are al dente. Just before they are done add the smoked chicken to the sauce and heat it. Toss the tortellini with the sauce and serve with the Parmesan cheese. Serves 4.

1¼ pounds Italian-style tomatoes

2–3 serrano chiles

3 tablespoons butter

½ cup fresh shiitake mushrooms, coarsely chopped

2 cloves garlic, minced

⅔ cup cream

2 tablespoons minced fresh parsley

1 tablespoon minced fresh basil

½ teaspoon salt or to taste

½ teaspoon black pepper

18 ounces fresh tortellini

1 cup smoked chicken, coarsely chopped

Parmesan cheese, grated

✳ MULE DRIVER'S PASTA

3 tablespoons olive oil

2 tablespoons butter

6 cloves garlic, minced

4 serrano chiles, seeded and
minced

2 green onions, white and green
parts minced separately

½ teaspoon dried oregano

½ teaspoon dried thyme

½ teaspoon dried marjoram

1 small ancho chile, seeded and
minced

Heaping ¼ teaspoon salt

½ teaspoon black pepper

½ cup sun-dried tomatoes,
minced then soaked in warm
water for 20 minutes and
drained

½ cup panela cheese, grated

½ cup añejo cheese, grated

½ cup Spanish (not Mexican)
manchego cheese, grated

½ cup Oaxaca cheese, grated

1 pound spaghetti or medium
pasta shells

2 tablespoons fresh minced
parsley

2 tablespoons fresh minced
cilantro

■ This dish is usually much simpler, consisting just of spaghetti tossed with garlic, olive oil, butter, chiles and grated cheese. This version with the addition of sun-dried tomatoes and several herbs is superb. ■

In a saucepan, heat the olive oil and butter over low heat until the butter is melted. Add the garlic, *serrano* chiles, white part of the green onions (reserving the green part), oregano, thyme, and marjoram, and sauté until the garlic is soft but not browned. Remove the saucepan, and add the minced *ancho* chile, salt, pepper, and rehydrated and drained sun-dried tomatoes.

Place the cheeses in a bowl and mix together.

In a large pot, bring water to a boil and cook the spaghetti or shells until tender. Then strain it and place it in a bowl. Reheat the sauce and add it, ½ the cheese mixture, the reserved green part of the green onions, the parsley, and cilantro to the spaghetti or shells and toss.

Place the spaghetti or shells on each of 4 serving plates, top with a little more of the cheese, and serve with the remaining cheese in a bowl on the side. Serves 4.

PRIME RIB TACOS

■ This modern version of the taco is one of the all-time greats and quite easy to prepare. A fine party dish, it involves cooking a boneless prime rib in the oven or, preferably, in a water smoker or covered barbecue over indirect heat until *very* rare. The meat is then sliced and covered with a spicy "rub." Each slice is then sautéed and chopped into bite-sized pieces to make the taco filling. ■

Preheat the oven to 350 degrees or prepare a fire in a water smoker or in a covered barbecue, following the manufacturer's directions for indirect cooking, or use an electric water smoker.

To make the rub, combine all the ingredients. Cover the outside of the meat liberally with the rub, preserving enough to cover the meat after it is sliced, and roast or smoke it until a meat thermometer registers between 95 and 100 degrees. Allow the meat to cool for at least 45 minutes. Slice the meat into pieces ½ inch thick and cover both sides liberally with the rub. The meat can be prepared to this stage a day in advance and refrigerated.

When you are ready to make the tacos, heat a large, heavy skillet or griddle over medium to medium-high heat, put a film of oil on the surface, and fry the meat to the degree of doneness desired. (I prefer medium rare.) When the meat has cooked, remove it to a chopping block and slice it into ½-inch pieces. Serve the meat in a bowl accompanied by the tortillas, which should first be heated, the guacamole, and your favorite salsa. Serves 4 to 6.

THE RUB:

3 tablespoons chile powder made with ancho chiles

2 tablespoons chile powder made with pasilla chiles

2 teaspoons garlic powder

1 teaspoon onion powder

1 teaspoon salt

1 teaspoon ground black pepper

THE MEAT:

2 pounds boneless prime rib from the small end

THE ACCOMPANIMENTS:

12 or more flour tortillas

Guacamole made with minced onion and tomato

Salsa

✳ SQUASH BLOSSOM & CACTUS OMELETTE

8–12 eggs

1 large hoja santa leaf, minced

½ cup onion, minced

¼ cup raw pumpkin seeds

1 teaspoon cooking oil

4 medium nopal cactus paddles

2 ounces Oaxaca-style cheese, grated

2 ounces Spanish (not Mexican) manchego cheese, grated

2 ounces panela cheese, grated

2 ounces añejo cheese, grated

4 tablespoons butter

8 squash blossoms (or other edible flowers), stemmed

■ I have varied the number of eggs in this recipe to include either 2 or 3 per omelette. ■

Preheat the oven to warm.

Place either 2 or 3 eggs in each of 4 small bowls, add the minced *hoja santa* and onion, and beat. (If you cannot obtain the *hoja santa*, omit it.)

Toss the pumpkin seeds with the oil, place in a small skillet over medium heat, and cook, turning frequently, until the seeds pop and become slightly brown. Allow the seeds to cool, then coarsely grind them in a food processor or chop them finely by hand.

Remove all the spines and edges from the cactus paddles and chop them into ⅛-inch pieces. Simmer the cactus in water to cover for 5 minutes, then drain and rinse well in cold water.

Mix the chopped pumpkin seeds and cactus paddles with the cheeses and reserve.

Heat a skillet with a 7- to 8-inch base over moderate heat and add 1 tablespoon of butter. When the butter has melted and the foam subsided, pour in the egg mixture from 1 of the bowls and swirl it to coat the bottom of the pan. Continue cooking until the eggs have set, then add about ½ cup of the cheese mixture along one side and top with 2 squash blossoms. Continue cooking for about 30 seconds or until the eggs reach the desired firmness. Then slide the omelette onto a serving plate, folding the side that does not contain the filling over the side with the filling. Place the completed omelette in the warm oven and make the remaining omelettes in the same manner. Serves 4.

CHILES STUFFED WITH "TAMAL DE CAZUELA" & MOLE SAUCE

■ This dish uses a tamale-like filling adapted from a recipe by Robert Del Grande. It mimics the tamales that are made in a *cazuela* (a large clay cooking pot) instead of being individually wrapped and steamed. Because of the small amount of lard called for, it is also much lighter than more traditional tamales. The only disadvantage of this excellent dish is that the filling has to be stirred 30 to 40 minutes over medium heat. ■

With the coarse blade of a hand grater, grate shucked ears of corn into a bowl and reserve. Place the milk, lard, cinnamon, raisins, almonds, and salt in a medium-sized heavy pot and bring to a boil over medium-high heat. Slowly stir in the cornmeal with a whisk to avoid lumps. Then turn the heat down to medium and stir the mixture with a wooden spoon until it thickens, 3 to 5 minutes. Add the grated corn and continue stirring until the mixture is very thick and it becomes almost impossible to keep it from sticking to the bottom of the pot, about 30 to 40 minutes. Remove the pot from the stove, stir in the cream and cheese, and reserve.

After peeling the chiles, cut a slit down one side and remove the seeds. Stuff the filling into the chiles and place them, slit side up, on a large plate or baking dish. Heat the Puebla-Style Mole sauce, and when it just begins to boil, turn down the heat to warm and either microwave the chiles until heated through or place them in a 350-degree oven until they are hot. Then pour about ½ cup of the sauce onto each of 4 serving plates, place the stuffed chiles on the sauce, spoon the cream over the chiles and filling, and sprinkle on the pine nuts. Serves 4.

THE FILLING:

1 cup grated corn kernels (about 4–5 ears)

2 cups milk

1 tablespoon lard

⅛ teaspoon ground cinnamon

⅓ cup raisins

½ cup blanched, slivered almonds

½ teaspoon salt

½ cup white cornmeal

2 tablespoons cream

3 tablespoons grated Oaxaca or asadero cheese, or use ½ Monterey Jack cheese and ½ mozzarella cheese

THE CHILES:

4 poblano chiles, roasted, peeled, and seeded, but otherwise left intact

THE RESERVED FILLING:

2 cups Jim Peyton's Traditional Puebla-Style Mole sauce (p. 232)

⅓ cup crème fraîche, or substitute 2 tablespoons sour cream mixed with 3½ tablespoons whipping cream

⅓ cup toasted pine nuts

✳ ENCHILADAS PUEBLA STYLE

THE SAUCE:

2 ancho chiles, stemmed, seeded, deveined, and torn into small pieces

2 cups milk

4 tomatillos

2 tablespoons butter

½ cup cream

½ teaspoon dried thyme

1 teaspoon salt

1 teaspoon white vinegar

½ teaspoon sugar

THE ENCHILADAS:

¼ pound chorizo, skin removed

1 cup carrots, peeled and cut into ¼-inch pieces

1½ cups potatoes, peeled and cut into ¼-inch pieces

Cooking oil

8 corn tortillas

3 eggs, beaten

4 ounces asadero cheese, grated

4 ounces Spanish manchego cheese, or substitute aged Swiss cheese, grated

¼ cup minced onion

■ This dish combines the tortilla of traditional Indian cooking with the rich flavors of traditional French haute cuisine. Named for the city of Puebla, which epitomizes the baroque era of Mexico's history, it makes an excellent complement to many entrées. ■

Place the chiles in a blender. Heat 1 cup of the milk until nearly boiling, add it to the blender, and allow the chiles to rehydrate for 15 minutes. Meanwhile, simmer the *tomatillos* in water to cover until they are very soft. Drain the *tomatillos*, add them to the blender, and grind for a few seconds at low speed, then allow the mixture to sit for 5 minutes. Purée the chile mixture at high speed in the blender for 1 minute, add the remaining 1 cup milk, pulse briefly to mix, then strain it through the fine blade of a food mill. Melt the butter in a saucepan over medium heat, pour in the contents of the blender, and add the remaining sauce ingredients. Bring the sauce to a boil, simmer for 3 to 5 minutes or until it begins to thicken, then remove it from the heat.

Preheat the oven to 350 degrees. To make the enchiladas, first fry the chorizo over medium-low heat until it is well cooked but not crispy, about 7 minutes, and remove from the heat. Boil the carrots in water to cover until just soft, then place them in a strainer and cool them under running cold water. Cook the potatoes in the same way, add them to the strainer, and again cool under cold water. Heat about ½ inch of oil over medium heat until a drop of water sputters immediately. Using a basting brush, brush 1 tortilla with the sauce, dip in the beaten egg, drain, and place in the oil. Allow the tortilla to cook for 5 to 10 seconds, then, using kitchen tongs, turn and cook it a few seconds more. (The tortilla should be fried just long enough to make it pliable and to set the eggs but not brown them.) Remove the tortilla to drain on paper towels and repeat the process with the remaining tortillas. To wrap the enchiladas, combine the cheeses and place a small portion just off center on each softened tortilla, using about ¾ of the cheese in all. Spread 1 teaspoon of the chorizo on top of the cheese, sprinkle on some onion, and roll the tortillas loosely. Place 2 enchiladas on each of 4 ovenproof plates, spoon the sauce over them, top with the remaining cheese, sprinkle on the carrots and potatoes, and then place them in the oven for about 8 minutes or until the cheese is melted and the sauce is beginning to bubble. Serve the enchiladas alone or with an entrée like Stuffed Chicken Breasts in *Tomatillo*-Tequila Sauce (p. 146) and accompany with white rice. Serves 4.

✸ GREEN PIPIÁN CHILAQUILES

5 corn tortillas

Oil for deep-frying

1 boned, skinned chicken
    breast (or 2 half breasts)

1 pound tomatillos

2 serrano chiles

¼ cup cooking oil

⅓ cup pumpkin seeds

¼ cup blanched, slivered
    almonds

1 cup chopped onion

1 clove garlic, minced

¼ cup lightly packed, fresh
    cilantro

1 poblano chile, roasted,
    peeled, stemmed, seeded,
    and chopped

Chicken broth

¾ teaspoon salt or to taste

1 cup grated Oaxaca or
    asadero cheese, or substitute
    half Monterey Jack and half
    mozzarella

■ This dish presents one of the oldest traditional Mexican stews in the form of a traditional *antojito: chilaquiles*, where a sauce or stew is served over fried tortilla chips, usually at breakfast. The recipe for *Pipián verde* is from one I contributed to *Texas: The Beautiful Cookbook*. This dish is always a hit at either breakfast or brunch. ■

Cut 4 of the tortillas into strips about ½ inch wide by 1½ to 2 inches long. Cut the remaining tortilla in the same manner and keep it separate. Heat the oil in a deep fryer or heavy pot to 350 degrees. Fry 4 of the sliced tortillas until golden brown and crisp, drain them on paper towels, and reserve. Fry the remaining tortilla for only a few seconds, until it is just medium crisp, drain on paper towels, and reserve.

Place the chicken in a saucepan, cover with water, bring to a boil, and simmer until the chicken is just cooked through. Remove the chicken, allow it to cool slightly, then shred it, either by hand or in a food processor fitted with a plastic blade. Reserve the shredded chicken.

Place the *tomatillos* and *serrano* chiles in a saucepan, cover with water, bring to a boil, and simmer until the *tomatillos* are soft, about 5 to 10 minutes. Discard the water and place the *tomatillos* and chiles in the bowl of a blender and blend until puréed. Strain the mixture through the fine blade of a food mill and return to the blender.

Heat ½ tablespoon cooking oil in a small skillet over medium heat, stir in the pumpkin seeds, and cook, stirring frequently, until they expand like popcorn. Then place them in the blender. Add another ½ tablespoon oil to the skillet, then the almonds and cook, stirring frequently, until they are golden brown, but do not allow them to burn. Put them in the blender. Add 1 tablespoon oil to the skillet and cook the onions, stirring frequently, until they are soft but not browned. Add the garlic and continue cooking for 1 minute, then add the onions and garlic to the blender. Add the partially fried, reserved tortilla, cilantro, and *poblano* chile to the blender, and blend all the ingredients for about 30 seconds at high speed. Add chicken broth to the blender until the mixture totals 4 cups, then blend again briefly until well combined.

Heat the remaining 2 tablespoons cooking oil in a skillet over medium to medium-high heat, add the contents of the blender, and cook, stirring frequently, until the sauce is of medium consistency, about 10 to 15 minutes. Stir in the reserved, fried tortilla strips and the shredded chicken, and salt to taste and cook until just heated through. Place equal portions onto each of 4 serving plates, top with the grated cheese, and serve immediately. Serves 4.

✳ LITTLE CAZUELAS FROM CHILAPA

THE SHELLS:

1 cup Masa Harina or Maseca

Cooking oil

A deep fryer

THE FILLING & ASSEMBLY:

1 cup carrots, peeled and cut into ¼-inch pieces

1⅓ cups red potatoes, peeled and cut into ¼-inch pieces

1 tablespoon cooking oil

½ pound Oaxaca chorizo (p. 211)

2 tablespoons cooking oil

4 green onions, finely chopped

¼ teaspoon dried thyme

Salt to taste

½ cup grated añejo or cotija cheese

2 small to medium avocados, peeled, seeded, and chopped into ¼-inch pieces

Salsa salpicón (p. 203)

■ This recipe combines a unique corn shell from Guerrero with chorizo from Oaxaca and a sauce from the Yucatán, so it is a perfect example of *nueva cocina mexicana*. The corn shells are not difficult to make once you get used to the technique. In the village of Chilapa, they are made with small gelatin molds, but I have found the best tool for the purpose to be an 8-ounce nonstick soup ladle, about 3 to 3½ inches in diameter. *Cazuelas* are usually eaten with the hands, like a cupcake. ■

Mix water into the corn flour according to the directions on the package to make a dough that is not too wet or dry; then allow it to sit in a bowl, covered with plastic wrap, for 1 hour.

Heat oil in a deep fryer to 340 to 350 degrees.

Pinch off 8 pieces of *masa* weighing 1 to 1¼ ounces, and roll into balls about 1½ inches in diameter. Place a piece of plastic wrap or plastic garbage bag on both sides of an open tortilla press. Then, using very light pressure, press one of the balls into a circle about 4 to 4½ inches in diameter. Place an 8-ounce, Teflon-coated soup ladle (about 3 to 3½ inches in diameter) so that the bottom is in the middle of the circle of dough. Using the plastic, press the dough into the ladle so that it conforms to its shape and goes about halfway up the sides, to produce a shallow cup of dough. Peel off the plastic, leaving the dough attached to the bottom of the ladle, then press it into the ladle, if necessary. Holding the handle of the ladle, put it into the hot oil until it almost touches the bottom. The portion of the ladle that contains the dough should be completely submerged. After about 30 seconds, the dough that has now formed a shallow cup should slip off the ladle. Allow the cup to fry, scooping some oil into it until it becomes firm, about 30 seconds. Using kitchen tongs, carefully turn the cup so that the bottom faces up, then push the cup down into the oil for another 30 seconds. Continue frying the cup until it is a crisp golden brown and the oil nearly stops sizzling, turning the cup as necessary. Place the completed corn cup on paper towels to drain, and prepare the remaining cups in the same manner.

Simmer the carrots in water to cover until they are soft. Then remove them and cool them under cold running water in a strainer. Simmer the potatoes until they are soft, add them to the carrots, and cool them in the same manner, then pat the vegetables dry and reserve. Heat the 1 tablespoon oil in a skillet over medium heat, add the chorizo, and fry it, breaking it into small pieces, until it is a crisp, golden brown. Remove the chorizo to drain on paper towels. Turn the heat to high, add the 2 tablespoons oil and fry the potatoes, carrots, green onions, and thyme until the vegetables begin to brown. Return the chorizo to the skillet and continue frying until it is heated through, then add salt to taste. Place the cooked corn shells on a serving plate or plates and spoon the filling into them. Top the filling with some of the cheese, place the chopped avocado on top, and sprinkle on some more cheese. Serve the *cazuelas* with the Salsa *salpicón*. Serves 8.

"Turkish" Tacos

Cooking oil

12 corn tortillas

1 recipe Chiles rellenos filling
   (p. 251)

12 slices jalapeño Monterey
   Jack cheese, about 3½ inches
   by 1¼ inches by ⅛ inch thick

■ In Mexico, the word *turco* is often used to refer to almost anything from the Middle East, and the filling for these tacos, which is the same as the filling for the traditional *Chiles rellenos*, obviously has strong Moorish roots. These delicious morsels will surprise anyone whose concept of tacos has been formed by the Tex-Mex variety. ■

Preheat the oven to 350 degrees. Heat ½ inch oil in a small skillet over medium heat until a drop of water vaporizes immediately on contact. Using kitchen tongs, place a tortilla in the oil, fry a few seconds, then turn it over. It should begin to puff almost immediately; if not, increase the heat. Using the tongs, fold the tortilla in half and fry on both sides until it just begins to crisp but is still very pliable. You will have a taco shell that is just slightly crisp. Remove the tortilla to drain on paper towels. Prepare the remaining tortillas in the same manner. Then scoop some of the filling into each taco shell and add a slice of the cheese. Put the filled tacos in a baking pan, place them in the oven, and heat just until the cheese has melted. Serve immediately. Serves 4.

NORTHERN STYLE SQUASH BLOSSOM QUESADILLAS

■ These quesadillas have a delicious combination of flavors and textures, and are easy to prepare. ■

Put the oil in a skillet over medium heat and roast the pumpkin seeds until most of them have popped, but do not allow them to become too brown. Then place them in a *molcajete* and grind them for a few seconds or until they are well broken up. Reserve.

Melt the butter in a skillet over medium heat, add the squash blossoms, and sauté until they begin to soften, 1 to 2 minutes. Add the cream and stir to coat the blossoms, then add salt to taste and remove the skillet from the heat. Reserve.

Place as many flour tortillas as will fit on a griddle, *comal*, or skillet over medium heat. Brush some butter on top of each tortilla, and cook them until the bottoms are hot, about 30 seconds. Turn the tortillas over so that the buttered sides are down, and sprinkle on some of the cheese to cover half of each one to within about ½ inch of the edge. Sprinkle some of the roasted pumpkin seeds onto the cheese, add a strip or 2 of the *poblano* chiles, and 2 squash blossoms. Using kitchen tongs, fold the uncovered sides of the tortillas over the filling and continue to cook until the cheese is melted and the tortillas are golden brown on the outside. Serve immediately. Serves 4.

½ **tablespoon cooking oil**

½ **cup pumpkin seeds**

2 **tablespoons butter**

16 **squash blossoms**

¼ **cup very heavy cream**

Salt to taste

8 **flour tortillas**

2 **tablespoons melted butter**

¾ **pound Oaxaca cheese, grated**

2 **poblano chiles, roasted, stemmed, peeled, seeded, and cut into 1-inch strips**

PECAN PIE

1 unbaked pie crust,
   homemade or bought

1 egg yolk, beaten with a
   pinch of salt until it is thick
   and creamy

1 cup milk

4 tablespoons sugar

2 tablespoons light brown
   sugar

2 cups chopped pecans

1 pound pitted dates, finely
   chopped

¼ teaspoon salt

2 tablespoons honey

4 tablespoons butter, cut into
   4 pieces

1 teaspoon vanilla

32 pecan halves

■ In my first book, *El Norte: The Cuisine of Northern Mexico*, I included a confection called *Dulce de dátiles*, which was dates and pecans cooked with milk, sugar, and honey and then cooled and sliced into individual portions. In the description I wrote: "Good by itself, it also makes a potentially award-winning filling for pecan pie." Later, I decided to take my own advice, and in the spirit of *nueva cocina mexicana* created the following recipe. Although I have not entered it in any contests, I believe I was correct in this recipe's potential. ■

Line a pie pan with the crust and press a piece of aluminum foil on top of it to conform to its shape and cover the edges of the dough. Pour 1 pound rice or an appropriate amount of pie weights into the foil and mound along the edges to keep the sides of the crust from losing their shape. Then place the dough in the oven and bake for 20 minutes. Take the dough out of the oven and remove the foil and its contents. Prick the bottom of the crust all over with a fork, brush the top and halfway down the sides with the beaten egg yolk, and return the pan to the oven until it is a golden brown all over, about 5 to 7 minutes.

To make the filling, place the milk and sugars in a large saucepan, bring to a boil, and simmer until the mixture thickens and produces large bubbles, about 15 minutes. Then stir in the pecans, dates, salt, and honey and cook until the mixture is thick, just a few minutes. Stir in the butter, then when it has melted add the vanilla. Spoon the mixture into the pie crust and place the pecan halves in 8 lines going from the center to the sides of the pie, so that each piece will have a line of nuts down the center. Allow the pie to cool, then refrigerate it overnight. Before serving it bring the pie to room temperature. This pie is delicious served with a scoop of Moorish Ice Cream (p. 267). Serves 8.

RICE WITH COCONUT

■ This is an interesting and delicious version of the traditional *arroz con leche* that is easy to prepare and is always a hit. ■

Place the coconut milk, condensed milk, evaporated milk, ½ teaspoon cinnamon, and vanilla in a blender and blend at low speed until well combined. Bring 8 cups water to boil in a large pot, add the rice, parboil for 2 minutes, then pour the rice into a strainer, discarding the water. Place the milk and 2 cups of the blender mixture into a 3-quart pot and bring to a simmer. Cover the pot, turn the heat to very low, and cook the rice for about 13 minutes or until it is cooked but still has a fair amount of texture. You must be careful during the early stages of the cooking to keep the milk from boiling over. If the top on the pot starts to rise, remove. it, then remove the pot from the burner for a few seconds to allow it to cool enough to reduce the level of the liquids. Then replace the pot on the burner and continue cooking. You may have to do this several times. When the rice has cooked, add about 1 cup of it and the remaining liquid to the beaten egg yolk and stir for about 10 seconds, then pour the contents of the bowl into the pot with the majority of the rice. Continue cooking the rice over very low heat, stirring constantly, until the mixture thickens, adding a little more of the remaining liquid in the blender, if necessary. Allow the rice to cool to room temperature. Meanwhile put the coconut flakes on a cookie sheet or piece of foil, place it in the oven, and bake until it is golden brown, stirring it every few minutes so that it browns evenly. This will take about 10 minutes.

To serve, scoop portions of the rice onto serving plates, pour a little of the remaining milk mixture from the blender over them, then sprinkle on some cinnamon and a liberal amount of the toasted coconut, and top with a cherry. Serves 4.

I cup canned coconut milk

I cup sweetened condensed milk

I cup evaporated milk

½ teaspoon powdered cinnamon

I teaspoon vanilla

8 cups water

I cup rice

½ cup milk

I egg yolk, beaten in a medium-sized bowl

½ cup sweetened coconut flakes

Cinnamon

Maraschino cherries

✳ GELATINA DE CAJETA

1 14-ounce can sweetened condensed milk

1 10.9-ounce (310-gram) jar cajeta

3 cups water

3 egg yolks, beaten

3½ packages unflavored gelatin

1 cup cold water

1 cup half-and-half

THE GARNISH:

Almonds, toasted and finely chopped (optional)

Ground cinnamon (optional)

Mexican-style Eggnog (p. 270) or Irish cream liquor (optional)

■ The original recipe for this dish calls for condensed half-and-half, but since this product is difficult to obtain in the United States this recipe substitutes regular half-and-half with excellent results. Also, to prevent illness that might be carried by the egg yolks and to help them thicken, use a candy or quick-read thermometer to achieve the temperatures called for in the recipe. ■

Combine the condensed milk, *cajeta*, and water in a pot. (Because the *cajeta* is quite thick and sticky, it helps to warm it briefly in a microwave, but be sure and remove the metal cap first and be careful not to heat at a high temperature or overheat, or you will have a real mess.) Heat the mixture over medium to medium-high heat to between 160 and 165 degrees. To ensure that the egg yolks do not curdle, place them in a small bowl and add about ½ cup of the hot liquid to them, stirring constantly, then repeat with another ½ cup. Pour the yolk mixture into the pot and maintain the temperature at 160 degrees for 3 to 5 minutes, stirring constantly, then remove the pot from the heat.

In a small bowl, mix the 3½ packets unflavored gelatin, or enough to set 7 cups of liquid according to the directions on the package, with the 1 cup cold water, and allow to set for 3 minutes. Stir the gelatin mixture into the pot, and add the half-and-half, mixing well. Strain the mixture and pour it into 1 large or several small molds and place in the refrigerator until thickened, about 4 to 5 hours. This dessert is good garnished with toasted, finely chopped almonds, ground cinnamon, and either Mexican-style Eggnog or Irish Cream liquor. Serves 8.

❋ PUFF PASTRY DESSERT SALTILLO

■ I adapted this recipe from one served at Saltillo's fine La Canasta restaurant. It can be made with store-bought frozen sheets of puff pastry. Although the recipe calls for *ate de membrillo*, a thick paste of quince that has a rubbery texture, you can substitute any other thick fruit purée—apricot would be a good choice. Since this dessert deteriorates if reheated it should be eaten soon after it comes out of the oven. ■

Preheat the oven to 400 degrees. Thaw the puff pastry, cut it into 4 circles that will line the bottoms and sides of the ramekins, and 4 smaller circles that can be placed on top of the filling and pinched into the bottom pieces to seal the ingredients inside. Brush the ramekins with a little butter, then press the larger circles of puff paste into them so that the bottoms and sides are lined. Slice or spoon equal portions of the *ate de membrillo* or other fruit paste into the bottoms of each lined ramekin and top with equal portions of the grated cheeses. Place the smaller circles of puff pastry on the top and pinch them together with the bottom linings to seal.

Beat the egg until it is thick and creamy and brush some of it on the top of each prepared ramekin. Place the ramekins in the oven and bake until the pastry has cooked and the tops are golden brown, about 20 to 30 minutes. When the desserts are done, remove them from the oven and allow them to cool for 1 or 2 minutes. Using a heatproof glove, hold the ramekins while you run a thin knife around the edges, then unmold them onto serving plates. Top each pastry with a scoop of ice cream. Serves 4.

1 package frozen puff pastry

4 5-ounce dessert ramekins

2 tablespoons melted butter

8 ounces ate de membrillo, or substitute another thick fruit paste

4 ounces Gruyère cheese, shredded

4 ounces Spanish manchego cheese, shredded

1 egg

4 scoops ice cream (vanilla or strawberry are good choices)

❈ PUMPKIN CHEESE PIE

THE CRUST:

16 graham crackers

3 tablespoons sugar

1 teaspoon ground ginger

2 tablespoons butter, melted

THE FILLING:

2 3-ounce packages cream
  cheese

¾ cup pure, unseasoned
  canned pumpkin

2 large eggs

½ cup sugar

1 teaspoon vanilla

½ teaspoon ground nutmeg

¼ teaspoon ground allspice

1 teaspoon ground cinnamon

1 teaspoon ground ginger

THE TOPPING:

½ pint sour cream

1 tablespoon vanilla

3 tablespoons sugar

3 ounces minced pecans

■ This is an exceptional dessert. It combines the best cheese pie I have ever tasted with silky smooth puréed pumpkin. Because it must be prepared a day ahead, it is perfect for entertaining. ■

Place the graham crackers in a food processor fitted with a steel blade, and process them until they are completely pulverized. Alternatively, they can be pulverized in a blender or wrapped in a towel and pounded with the side of a hammer or other heavy object. Add the sugar and ginger, and pulse once or twice. Then with the machine running, slowly pour in the melted butter. Press the ingredients into the bottom and sides of an 8- or 9-inch pie pan and reserve.

Place all the filling ingredients in a blender and blend until the mixture is smooth. Pour the contents of the blender into the prepared pie pan, place a crust shield or a 1-inch piece of foil around the edges of the crust to prevent it from burning, and bake in a 400-degree oven for 20 minutes. Remove the pie, scrape off any burned portions of the crust around the edges, and allow it to cool for 5 minutes.

Place all the topping ingredients, except the pecans, in a blender and blend until smooth. Pour the topping over the pie after it has cooled slightly. Place the pie in the oven at 400 degrees for an additional 5 minutes and remove. Sprinkle on the pecans, and allow the pie to cool for about 30 minutes, then refrigerate it overnight. Serves 6 to 8.

 EGGNOG GELATIN

■ This dessert is similar in texture to *Gelatina de cajeta* (although a bit firmer) but has a different taste that comes from *rompope*, Mexican-style Eggnog. It is rich and creamy, especially considering that it is relatively low in fat. ■

Heat the condensed milk and water until it reaches a temperature of 160 degrees and is well combined and smooth. Place the gelatin in the cold water and allow to set for 3 minutes. Stir the gelatin into the milk-water mixture, add the Mexican-style Eggnog, and chill in individual or 1 large mold overnight. This dessert is good garnished with toasted, finely chopped almonds, powdered cinnamon, and either Mexican-style Eggnog or Irish cream liquor. Serves 8.

1 14-ounce can sweetened condensed milk

1 cup water

½ cup ice-cold water

2 tablespoons unflavored gelatin

1 cup Mexican-style Eggnog (p. 270)

Almonds, toasted and finely chopped (optional)

Ground cinnamon (optional)

# MANGO SORBET

THE SIMPLE SUGAR:

8 ounces (about 1 cup plus 2 tablespoons) granulated sugar

½ cup water

Juice from ½ lime

THE SORBET:

18 ounces (about 2½ cups) mango, peeled, chopped, and seed removed

⅔ cup simple sugar

⅔ cup water

■ In order to recreate the fruit sorbets I tried in some of Mexico's finest restaurants, I tried several recipes. The best and most similar to those made by professional chefs I found (not surprisingly) in Jacques Torres' *Dessert Circus*. Therefore, I adapted the recipes for this one and for Pineapple Sorbet, (making some minor alterations that make them a little simpler for the home cook). One item that is used by the professional chef, however, should not be changed, and that is the food scale. It really is the only way to successfully replicate recipes when using difficult-to-measure items such as chopped fruit.

To make sorbets, you must first make a simple sugar—a mixture of sugar and water and a little lime or lemon juice that is boiled to dissolve the sugar. ■

To make the simple sugar, place all the ingredients in a small saucepan, bring to a boil, stirring often, then remove from the heat and allow to cool. Refrigerate down to at least 60 degrees.

To make the sorbet, place all the ingredients in a blender and blend to a fine purée. Strain the mixture to remove the fibers. Chill the mixture down to at least 60 degrees, then freeze according to the directions on your ice cream maker. Serves 4 to 6.

PINEAPPLE SORBET

■ This is prepared in a manner similar to that of the Mango Sorbet and is also used in the chocolate *molcajete* dessert. ■

Place all the ingredients in a blender and blend to a fine purée, then chill the mixture down to at least 60 degrees. Pour the mixture into an ice cream maker and freeze according to the manufacturer's directions.

18 ounces chopped fresh or canned pineapple (If you use canned pineapple make sure to drain off all the liquid from the can. Do not use crushed pineapple.)

⅔ cup simple syrup

⅓ cup water

❊ MELON LIQUOR MARGARITA

Crushed ice

1 shot Midori melon liquor

1 shot lime juice

1 shot tequila

2 mint leaves

■ I am not particularly taken with the virtually endless parade of Margarita theme drinks, but this one is well worth trying. ■

Fill a cocktail shaker ¾ full of crushed ice, add the remaining ingredients, shake, and pour into serving glasses. Makes 1 drink.

❊ SILK STOCKINGS

1½ ounces silver tequila

2 ounces evaporated milk

1 ounce white crème de cacao

1 ounce grenadine

½ cup crushed ice

Cinnamon

1 cherry

■ This recipe, which I collected on a visit to the Sauza tequila distillery many years ago, remains one of the best after-dinner drinks I have ever had. Rich and creamy, it is a beautiful light pink color. ■

Put all the ingredients except the cinnamon and cherries into a blender and blend for at least 1 minute. Pour the liquid into a cocktail glass, sprinkle with cinnamon, and garnish with a cherry. Makes 1 drink.

MACAW COCKTAIL

Place all the ingredients in a blender, blend, and serve in 12-ounce pilsner glasses. Makes 2 drinks.

I shot light rum
I shot Midori melon liquor
¾ shot Kahlúa
I 6-ounce can pineapple juice
About I½ cups ice cubes

MAXIMILIAN'S COCKTAIL

■ This drink is a delicious combination of champagne and tequila. Since it combines the champagne of France with the tequila of Mexico, its name is fitting. ■

Fill a cocktail shaker with ice, add the tequila, lime juice, and sugar and shake about 30 times. Then pour the mixture into a wine or champagne glass and top with ice-cold champagne. Makes 2 drinks.

I½ ounces tequila
I½ ounces lime juice
2 teaspoons sugar
Champagne

CHAPTER 5
TRADITIONAL CUISINE

T raditional Mexican cuisine developed over centuries primarily through a combination of indigenous Indian cooking of Mexico with that of the European conquerors. The techniques and ingredients brought by the Spanish added important new dimensions to pre-Hispanic Indian cuisine. Sugar and milk added sweetness and richness to the *atoles* and chocolate drinks. Cheese, with its affinity for corn, made possible the quesadilla, and lard gave tamales a texture and flavor that transformed them from ordinary to divine food; the technique of frying tortillas in lard gave tacos an entirely new range of textures—from soft to crispy. In the north where corn was more difficult to grow, wheat resulted in flour tortillas. And distillation turned *pulque* into mescal and tequila.

Although Mexican cooking developed on two parallel paths—one for the upper class and another for the masses—this was nothing new in either Mexico or the world. Throughout the history of numerous cuisines, there have generally been two different cooking styles, aptly described by Jean-François Revel in *Culture and Cuisine:*

Cuisine stems from two sources: a popular one and an erudite one, this latter necessarily being the appanage of the well-off classes of every era. In the course of history there has been a peasant (or seafarer's) cuisine and a court cuisine; a plebeian cuisine and a family cuisine prepared by the mother (or the humble family cook); and a cuisine of the professionals that only chefs fanatically devoted to their art have the time and the knowledge to practice....

The first type of cuisine has the advantage of being linked to the soil, of being able to exploit the products of various regions and different seasons, in close accord with nature, of being based on age-old skills, transmitted unconsciously by way of imitation and habit, of applying methods of cooking patiently tested and associated with certain cooking utensils and recipients prescribed by a long tradition. It is this cuisine that can be said to be unexportable. The second cuisine, the erudite one, is based by contrast on invention, renewal, experimentation. (Revel 1982, 19)

Both these styles of cooking existed in Spain and in pre-Hispanic Mexico, and later in Mexico itself. While it was "court" cooking, largely of Spanish and French origin, that received the most attention in historical accounts, it is "peasant" cooking that has been "consecrated by tradition" and has endured in popularity as María Stoopen notes in *El universo de la cocina mexicana*. Consequently, it can be stated that traditional Mexican cooking derived from both "court" and "peasant" cooking, but not in equal measure.

Traditional Mexican cuisine can be divided into three basic categories. First, the most distinctive element of the cuisine is the category of dishes called *antojitos mexicanos*. This part of the cuisine evolved almost entirely through the incorporation of New World ingredients into existing pre-Hispanic dishes of both the "court" and "peasant" varieties. Included in this category are corn- and tortilla-based dishes such as tacos, quesadillas, tamales, enchiladas, *gorditas*, and *chalupas*. In addition, the *torta compuesta*,

Mexico's multifaceted version of the sandwich, is also often included in this category.

The following list of *antojitos mexicanos* provided by Alicia and Jorge De'Angeli in *Epazote y molcajete, productos y técnicas de la cocina mexicana* emphasizes the extensive variety of dishes in this category (for more detailed information on these dishes, see the Glossary): *chalupas, chilaquiles, enchiladas, enfrijoladas, entomatadas, envueltos, flautas, negritos, panuchos, papadzules, quesadillas, salbutes, tacos, tostadas, totopos, cazuelitas, garnachas, gorditas, molotes, pellizcadas, peneques, pintos, sopes, tlacoyos, burritos, chimichangas, empanadas, mochomos, pambazos, pastes,* and *tortas compuestas.* Under *tacos* the De'Angelis discuss the following types (differentiated, for the most part, by cooking process, *not* by ingredient, which would increase the number considerably): *Tacos al pastor, tacos al carbón, tacos al vapor, tacos de barbacoa, tacos de cazuela, tacos de comal o a la plancha, tacos dorados, tacos de canasta,* and *tacos de nada.* (De'Angeli 1993, 48–62)

Similarly, in *Esplendor y grandeza de la cocina mexicana*, Sebastián Verti catalogs over a hundred common regional tamales, many made with distinctive variations of corn *masa*, some with wheat and rice flour, and others with amaranth *masa*. They are filled with every imaginable vegetable and meat, and their dimensions range from the size of a small finger to some over two meters in length that contain whole turkeys and suckling pigs. A few of the more surprising fillings include: peanuts, coconut, olives, hard-boiled eggs, frog meat, and alligator meat, as well as various insects common in pre-Hispanic cooking.

The second category of traditional cooking includes the entrée dishes of roasted or sautéed meat, poultry, and seafood which came from Europe and were incorporated into the traditional cuisine, usually without the butter, cream, fruit, and vinegar sauces so popular in the Old World and with the Mexican elite. Instead, these foods are served with chile sauces and salsas.

And rather than being accompanied with potatoes, bread, European rice dishes, and vegetables, they are served with Mexican-style rice, beans, squash, and other indigenous vegetables. Steak or pork *ranchero* and red snapper Veracruz are examples of this category.

The third category of traditional Mexican cuisine includes what might be termed haute Mexican cooking, in which Old World ingredients were blended with the indigenous chile-based *moles* and *pipianes*. Many of these dishes, including the *moles*, evolved from pre-Hispanic "court" recipes such as those served to Montezuma to which Old World ingredients such as lard, chicken, pork, cinnamon, cloves, sesame seeds, and coriander were added.

Although evidence indicates that traditional Mexican cooking developed largely from the "peasant" branch of the cuisine, there is a notable exception: sweets and desserts, which came almost entirely from "court" cooking. In pre-Hispanic times, sweeteners were derived largely from stingless bees, cactus tunas, mesquite sap, honey ants, and *aguamiel*. These substances were used to flavor tamales, *pinole*, the famous *alegría*, popcorn, and *atoles*. Later, the Spanish brought chicken, eggs, sugar, almonds, cinnamon, and milk to Mexico, as well as nuns familiar with rich and elaborate Spanish confections of European and Arab origin made from these ingredients. Considering the numerous religious festivals, the general propensity for indulgence in society, and the fact that eating sweets was one of the few extravagances allowed in the convents, it is no wonder that the nuns produced remarkable recipes when they integrated New World fruits into their traditional confections.

In traditional Mexican cooking, all the methods familiar to Americans—frying, sautéeing, grilling, broiling, baking, braising, boiling, and steaming—are used, as well as several others. However, because modern ovens that allow baking and broiling were not available when the cuisine was first developed, these techniques are the least common.

Because of the heritage of cooking on *comales* placed on hearths of rocks, and later on wood stoves, frying and pan-broiling are probably the most popular cooking methods throughout Mexico. This is true even in the north, where cooking *al carbón* (over coals) is prevalent, especially in places like Chihuahua, where mesquite wood of an appropriate size for grilling is scarce. In fact, there are many restaurants which prepare the majority of their dishes, including tortillas, steaks, taco fillings, and even chimichangas, on an iron or stainless steel griddle. Traditionally, Mexicans even char tomato skins and roast onions and garlic on dry skillets or iron *comales*.

Braising, boiling, and steaming are other common cooking methods performed on stove tops. Mexico's plethora of stews—*cocidos, ollas podridas, pipiánes, estofados, guisados, cazuelas*, and *moles*—are either braised or boiled, depending on the recipe. Traditionally, tamales have been steamed; other foods that are steamed include vegetables and *tacos al vapor*.

Mexicans also use some cooking methods not normally practiced in the United States, the oldest of which is probably pit cooking. This method does not entail using a typical barbecue pit found in the American South and Southwest but an underground pit from which our slow-smoking devices probably derived. However, because of the amount of labor and wood required, this method is typically only used at large fiestas and some specialty restaurants. The exception is in the preparation of *barbacoa*, which usually consists of goat or mutton (or a cow or goat's head in the north) cooked in pits on Saturday nights to be consumed at Sunday feasts.

Another particularly Mexican cooking technique is called *al pastor*, which is practiced in small and large *taquerías* throughout the country. In this method, of Middle Eastern origin, thinly sliced pieces of meat, usually pork, are marinated, packed tightly onto vertical spits, often topped with a whole onion and pineapple, and then cooked in front of a heat source of wood, charcoal, gas, or electricity. As the meat cooks, it is sliced off and used to fill steaming tortillas. In northern Mexico, this dish is often called *tacos de trompo*, because as some of the meat is sliced off, the meat remaining on the spit becomes shaped like a top. Also in the north, especially in the state of Nuevo León, a variation of this cooking method is used for *cabrito al pastor*. To make this dish, a whole kid is placed on a spit over coals and slowly roasted until it is crusty on the outside and tender inside.

The goal of this book is not to provide an in-depth chronicle of existing recipes, an impossible task for one book, but to describe the cuisine, emphasizing its immense variety and depth. The following recipes were selected for their excellence and to reflect the cuisine's characteristics and cooking techniques.

TRADITIONAL CUISINE

❊ Drunken Sauce

■ This is the sauce that is traditionally served with *Barbacoa*. It is made with *pulque*, which I have not found in this country, so I have substituted beer with very good results. ■

Simmer the *tomatillos* in water to cover until they are very soft, 5 to 10 minutes, and place them in a blender. Simmer the chiles in water to cover for 15 minutes, drain, and put them in the blender. Add the garlic, beer, oil, vinegar, bay leaf, and oregano, and pulse for 10 to 15 seconds, or until the ingredients are well chopped but not puréed. Stir the cheese into the sauce and serve. Makes 1 small bowl.

5 ounces (5–6) tomatillos, husked

2–3 pasilla chiles, stemmed, seeded, and broken into small pieces

1 clove garlic, minced

¼ cup flat beer

1 tablespoon cooking oil

½ tablespoon rice wine vinegar

1 bay leaf, broken into pieces

½ teaspoon dried oregano

1 ounce cotija or añejo cheese, grated

❊ Chile & Cheese Chihuahua Style

Heat a saucepan over medium heat, melt the butter, add the onion and chiles, and cook until the onion just begins to soften, about 3 minutes. Add the tomato and cook for 2 more minutes. Add the remaining ingredients except the cheese, bring to a boil, and simmer, stirring often, until the mixture is thickened to the consistency of a thick cream soup, 5 to 10 minutes. Add the cheese, remove from the burner, and stir until the cheese is melted. Serve immediately with hot flour tortillas. Serves 4.

1½ tablespoons butter

½ cup onion, chopped

½ cup Anaheim or New Mexico chiles, roasted, peeled, seeded, and chopped

1 tomato, peeled, seeded, and chopped

¼ teaspoon dried oregano

½ cup cream

⅓ cup evaporated milk

¼ cup half-and-half

½ teaspoon salt

½ pound Oaxaca cheese, coarsely grated

# SHRIMP COCKTAIL

I pound medium shrimp, shells and tails removed and deveined

THE SAUCE:

I cup Heinz catsup

¼ cup onion, minced

I green onion, minced

¾ cup tomato, chopped

I tablespoon fresh parsley, minced

I tablespoon fresh cilantro, minced

I pickled jalapeño, stemmed, seeded, and minced

I tablespoon juice from the pickled jalapeño can or jar

I serrano chile, stemmed, seeded, and minced

I teaspoon Worcestershire sauce

I tablespoon extra-virgin olive oil

½ teaspoon whole oregano

½ cup tomato juice

Sliced limes

Saltines

■ Remember that shrimp cocktail you thought was the best you had ever eaten, the one you had under the thatched *palapa* just above the high tide line in La Paz—or Puerto Vallarta or Acapulco? Well, this is it. Similar concoctions, including the famous *campechana* and hangover restorative *vuelve a la vida* (return to life), can also be prepared by substituting some crabmeat, oysters, and/or squid for a portion of the shrimp. ■

Bring 1½ to 2 quarts water to a boil. Add the shrimp and cook until they are just done, then immediately immerse them in ice water to stop them from overcooking, which makes them tough. When the shrimp have been chilled, drain and dry them and place them in the refrigerator.

To make the sauce, combine all the sauce ingredients in a large bowl and chill the mixture in the refrigerator.

To make the cocktails, mix the chilled shrimp and sauce and spoon into 12-ounce pilsner or milk shake glasses and serve with the limes and saltines. Makes 4 small or 2 large cocktails.

✳ CEBICHE ESTILO COLIMA

■ This ceviche is of interest not so much because of the ingredients, which are fairly standard, but because of its texture—the fish is minced in a food processor before being "cooked" in the lime juice. It is traditionally served mounded on very small tortillas (about 2 to 2½ inches in diameter), topped with a slice of avocado, but you can substitute fried tortilla chips. It can be prepared with any firm, white fish with a low fat content—sea bass works well. ■

Cut the fish into very small pieces and place it in a food processor fitted with a steel blade. Process the fish in short pulses until it is just minced, but do not purée it or allow it to become pasty. (Do not worry if it seems to be just a little mushy as it will firm up during the "cooking" process.) Put the fish in a nonreactive bowl, add the lime juice, salt, chiles, and onions, and allow the fish to "cook" for at least 3 hours in the refrigerator. Meanwhile, fry the small or quartered tortillas, and drain them on paper towels. When the fish is fully "cooked," drain off as much of the lime juice as possible, mix in the cilantro, mound about 1 to 1½ tablespoons on each of the crisp tortillas, top with a slice of avocado, and serve. Makes about 24.

½ pound sea bass filets

1 cup lime juice

½ teaspoon salt

2 tablespoons minced serrano chiles

2 green onions, minced

About 24 small round tortillas, or tortilla chips made by deep-frying regular-sized, quartered tortillas

¼ cup finely chopped fresh cilantro

1 avocado, cut into 24 small slices about ⅛ inch thick

❋ CHILES RELLENOS SERVED AT ROOM TEMPERATURE

THE FILLING:

1½ cups peeled and finely
    chopped (¼-inch pieces)
    carrots

2 cups peeled, finely chopped
    (¼-inch pieces) red potatoes

1½ tablespoons olive oil

2 tablespoons chorizo

2 tablespoons loosely packed,
    finely chopped fresh parsley

½ teaspoon dried thyme

½ teaspoon salt

¼ teaspoon ground black
    pepper

¼ cup olive oil

2 tablespoons rice wine vinegar

¼ teaspoon salt

THE CHILES:

2 tablespoons olive oil

1 cup thinly sliced onions

2 cloves garlic, minced

2 cups light brown sugar

1 cup water

8 ancho chiles, slit along 1 side
    and seeds removed

■ This recipe, inspired by one called *chiles palominos* in the series of books on Mexican cooking published by México Desconocido, makes an excellent first course or light luncheon dish. The original recipe features both *chiles poblanos* and *chiles anchos* (the dried *poblano*) stuffed with carrots and potatoes. While the *poblanos* were good, the *anchos*, with important modifications, were sublime, and this version possibly qualifies as a *nueva cocina mexicana* recipe. They can be prepared well ahead of serving. Moreover, a very low-fat vegetarian version can be made by omitting the chorizo and not frying the vegetables. This dish is most successful when prepared with high-quality *ancho* chiles, that is chiles that are still quite pliable. Overdried brittle ones will work but are much more difficult to use. ■

Bring 6 cups water to a boil in a pot, add the carrots, and simmer until they are just tender. Put the carrots in a strainer under cold running water to cool. Cook the potatoes in the same way. When the vegetables are cool, drain and dry them (a salad spinner works well).

Place the 1½ tablespoons olive oil in a skillet over medium heat, add the chorizo, and sauté until it is cooked to a crispy brown. Turn the heat to medium high, add the dried carrots and potatoes, the parsley, thyme, salt, and pepper, and cook, stirring constantly, until the vegetables just begin to get crusty. Remove the vegetables to a bowl to cool. Meanwhile, mix the ¼ cup olive oil, vinegar, and salt to make a vinaigrette. When the carrots and potatoes have cooled to nearly room temperature, mix in 2 tablespoons of the oil and vinegar dressing and reserve while you prepare the chiles.

Pour the 2 tablespoons olive oil into a skillet over medium heat and fry the onions until they just begin to brown. Add the garlic, cook for 1 minute, then remove the skillet from the heat.

Place the sugar and water in a large saucepan and bring to a boil over medium to medium-high heat. Add the fried onions and garlic, then add the chiles and cook at a bare simmer for 10 minutes, turning the chiles several times without tearing them. When done, they should be very soft. Carefully remove the chiles to a strainer to drain, cool to room temperature, and reserve the syrup.

When the chiles have cooled, stuff them with the potato-carrot mixture. (This can be done a day ahead and the chiles refrigerated. Simply warm them in a microwave when you are ready to use them.) Just before serving, place them on 4 serving plates, spoon some of the onions from the sugar mixture over the chiles, then drizzle some of the remaining vinaigrette over them. Serves 4.

 PICKLED ONION RINGS

Mix all the ingredients except the onions together in a saucepan and bring to a boil. Simmer for 5 minutes and pour into a nonreactive bowl over the onions. Cover and allow to steep for 1 hour. Serves 4.

1 cup vinegar

⅓ cup water

6 tablespoons orange juice

1 teaspoon dried oregano

2 cloves garlic, crushed

2 serrano or jalapeño chiles, minced

½ teaspoon salt or to taste

2 onions, thinly sliced and separated into rings

THE BROTH:

7 cups water

2 split chicken breasts (4 pieces), skins and as much fat as possible removed

5 cloves garlic, toasted in their skins on an ungreased comal or skillet over medium heat until soft

I cup onion, chopped and toasted on an ungreased comal or skillet over medium heat until just beginning to brown

¼ teaspoon dried oregano

2 tablespoons fresh cilantro, loosely packed

2 serrano chiles, stemmed, seeded, and minced

THE SOUP:

I tablespoon cooking oil

¾ cup onion, finely chopped

2 green onions, with the white and green parts separated and minced

I cup green pepper, minced

I tomato, peeled, seeded, and minced

2 key limes or ½ Persian lime, sliced into ⅛-inch rounds

½ teaspoon salt or to taste

4 corn tortillas, cut into strips ⅛- to ¼-inch wide and 1½-inches long

2 tablespoons fresh cilantro, minced

Lime wedges

LIME SOUP

■ This soup, the most famous in the Yucatán, is mild with a unique flavor and is especially refreshing as a luncheon dish on a hot humid day. It is best made with Mexican or key limes, which resemble the more bitter ones used in the Yucatán. Although it can also be made with the large Persian limes, the flavor will not be the same. ■

To make the broth, place all the ingredients in a pot, bring to a boil, turn down the heat, and simmer until the chicken is just cooked through, about 12 to 15 minutes. (It is important that the chicken remain tender and moist.) Remove the chicken, allow it to cool, then remove the meat from the bones, shred, and reserve it. Strain the broth and reserve it.

To prepare the soup, heat a pot over medium heat, add the oil, and cook the onion, white parts of the green onions, and green pepper until they are soft but not brown. Add the tomato and continue cooking for 3 minutes, stirring often. Add the strained broth and half the lime slices and barely simmer for 5 minutes. Meanwhile, heat oil in a deep fryer to 340 to 350 degrees. Remove the lime pieces, turn the heat to high, and bring the soup to a rolling boil. Add the shredded chicken, green parts of the green onions, remaining limes, and salt. Allow the soup to heat on high for 30 seconds, then ladle it into 4 serving bowls. Just before serving deep-fry the tortilla strips, shake the frying basket to remove as much oil as possible, place equal amounts of the chips in each soup bowl, garnish with the cilantro, and serve immediately with lime wedges. Serves 4.

❋ SOUP TLAPAN STYLE

■ This is one of the most famous soups in central and southern Mexico and as with other popular dishes there are many versions. Essentially it is chicken and vegetable soup and is closely related to *caldo Xoxitil*, which, however, also has rice as an ingredient. The key to the success of this soup is the quality of the broth, so it is advantageous to begin with the richest chicken broth you can make or buy. In addition, the *epazote* imparts a special flavor without which the soup will still be good but more ordinary. ■

Place the broth and chicken breasts in a pot, bring to a boil, and simmer until the breasts are barely done. Remove the breasts (reserving the broth), and when they are cool enough to handle either shred or coarsely chop them and reserve the meat. Heat the olive oil and sauté the onions until they are soft and beginning to brown. Then add the garlic, and continue cooking for another 30 seconds. Add the reserved broth and the remaining ingredients except the avocado and lime wedges, and simmer for 15 minutes. Then add the reserved chicken meat and cook just long enough to heat the soup thoroughly. Ladle the soup into bowls and top with the chopped avocado. Serve with lime wedges. Serves 4.

8 cups chicken broth

¾ pound skinned, boned chicken breasts

1 tablespoon olive oil

1 cup finely chopped onions

2 cloves garlic, minced

¾ cup finely chopped carrots

2 large tomatoes, broiled until soft and the skins are blackened then strained through the fine blade of a food mill

1½ cups garbanzo beans

1 cup finely chopped zucchini

½ cup green peas

4 epazote leaves

1 teaspoon lime juice

1 canned chipotle chile and ½ tablespoon sauce from the can, or to taste

2 medium-sized avocados, peeled, seeded, and coarsely chopped

Lime wedges

TARASCAN SOUP

5 small ancho chiles, stemmed
and seeded

1 tablespoon olive oil

⅔ cup onions, chopped

2 cloves garlic, minced

2 14½-ounce cans whole
unsalted tomatoes

5 cups chicken broth

2 bay leaves

¼ teaspoon dried thyme

¼ teaspoon dried marjoram

¼ teaspoon dried oregano

4 tortillas, cut into 1½- by
⅛-inch strips

Oil to deep-fry the tortilla
strips

Salt

4 ounces queso fresco, coarsely
grated or chopped

¼ cup crème fraîche, or
substitute Monterey Jack

■ This is one of the world's truly great soups, and whenever I am in Pátzcuaro in the state of Michoacán I have it with nearly every meal. After I tried it the first time, I found several recipes for it in different books, all of them calling for beans. I was surprised because none of the restaurant cooks I had discussed the ingredients with had mentioned beans, and I was fairly certain there were none in any of the soups I had tried. So I developed a recipe from the list of ingredients given to me that was very close to those I had sampled. When the *Guía Gastronomía* on Michoacán came out, I found the solution to the mystery. A description of *sopa purépecha* (the original name of the Tarascan Indians) that contained beans noted that many people called this soup *sopa tarasca* but that the true *sopa tarasca* did not contain beans and was nearly identical to the soup I had developed. ■

Simmer the chiles in water to cover for 15 minutes, then place 1 of them in a blender and reserve the remaining 4. If the chiles are large, cut them in half and use 2½ instead of 5. You may also want to reduce the amount of chile if they are particularly hot or if you want a less piquant result. Sauté the onions in the olive oil over medium heat until they are soft but not browned. Add the garlic, and cook 1 minute more, then place the mixture in a blender. Put the tomatoes and their juice in the blender and blend for 1 minute. Strain the mixture and put it in a pot. Add the broth, bay leaves, thyme, marjoram, and oregano, bring the liquid to a boil, then cook at a very low simmer for 15 minutes. Meanwhile, deep-fry the tortilla strips until they are a crisp golden brown, and drain them on paper towels.

When you are ready to serve the soup, add salt to taste, and place equal portions of the reserved chiles, fried tortillas, and cheese in each of 4 soup bowls. Ladle the soup into the bowls, top with a tablespoon of the cream, and serve. Serves 4.

Salsa Salpicón

■ This typical sauce from the Yucatán is particularly interesting because of the radishes it contains. Even if you are not particularly fond of radishes, try this sauce since their usual assertive taste virtually disappears. As with other sauces containing both *habanero* chiles and sour orange juice, you should allow the chiles to "cook" in the acidy juice for at least 3 hours before serving. ■

Mix all the ingredients together and place in the refrigerator for 3 hours or overnight before using. Makes 1 small bowl.

½ cup radishes, finely chopped

½ cup purple onion, finely chopped

1–2 habanero chiles, minced

2 tablespoons fresh cilantro, minced

⅓ cup sour orange juice, or substitute ¼ cup orange juice and 1½ tablespoons lime juice

¼ teaspoon salt

Garlic & Chile de Árbol Sauce

■ I have found this sauce in a *taquería* in Saltillo and in a specialty food store in Mexico City. It is as interesting as any sauce I have ever tried but is quite hot and should be used sparingly on broiled meats and poultry. ■

Cut the tomatoes into small pieces and mince them in a spice or coffee grinder, then remove them. You do not want to pulverize them, just cut them into pieces about ⅛ inch. Break the chiles into small pieces, put them and their seeds into a grinder, and process them in the same manner as the tomatoes. Then put all the ingredients, except the dried cilantro, in a small saucepan and bring to a simmer over medium to medium-low heat. Turn the heat down as low as possible while still maintaining just a bare simmer, and cook, stirring occasionally, until the garlic and onion have caramelized but are not quite hard, about 45 minutes to 1 hour. During the last 15 minutes of cooking, add the cilantro. Allow the sauce to cool before serving. Makes 1 small bowl.

4 sun-dried tomatoes (not cured in oil)

3–4 de árbol chiles

¼ cup minced garlic

¼ cup minced onion

½ teaspoon salt

½ cup corn oil

1½ tablespoons dried, minced cilantro

✳ CHIPOTLE CONDIMENT

1 ounce (a little over ⅓ cup) dried chipotle chiles, stemmed and rinsed

¾ cup hot water

1½ tablespoons rice vinegar

1½ tablespoons piloncillo (15 grams), or substitute 1 tablespoon plus 1 teaspoon brown sugar and ½ teaspoon molasses

¼ inch cinnamon stick

2 whole cloves

Pinch dried oregano

Pinch dried thyme

Pinch dried marjoram

¼ teaspoon salt

1 clove garlic, coarsely chopped

¼ cup finely chopped onion

1 tablespoon corn oil

■ This concoction, somewhere between a condiment and a sauce, is quite different from our North American concept of a Mexican salsa. Extremely hot, it is not a dipping sauce to be eaten with tortilla chips but should be used in very small quantities on charbroiled meats. ■

Put the chiles in a small bowl, cover them with the water, and place them in a refrigerator overnight. They will swell up and become somewhat soft.

Place the chiles and their soaking water in a small saucepan, add the remaining ingredients, except the onion and oil, bring to a boil, and simmer, covered, for 20 minutes. Add the onions and oil and simmer, uncovered, for 2 to 3 minutes longer. Allow the mixture to cool. Then pour it into a *molcajete*, and grind it just until the chiles are broken up. The mixture should be quite rough in texture, more like a thin chutney than a sauce. Serve with broiled meats. Makes about 1 cup.

❊ Yucatán Tomato/Habanero Sauce

■ This sauce is the same one used for *papadzules* and with other Yucatán dishes. In spite of the use of Mexico's hottest chile, it is quite mild because the chile is cooked with the sauce, then removed, which imparts just the right amount of heat and flavor. ■

Place the tomatoes in a saucepan, cover them with water, bring to a boil, and simmer for 5 minutes. Remove the tomatoes to a bowl. When the tomatoes have cooled, cut each of them into 4 pieces and scrape out as many of the seeds as you can, but otherwise leave them intact in the bowl. Place the ½ tablespoon olive oil and onions in a skillet over medium heat and cook until the onions are just beginning to turn golden. You want just enough caramelization to add a little flavor but not so much that it becomes overpowering. Place the onions in a food mill fitted with a coarse, grating blade, add the tomatoes and any juice that has accumulated in the bowl, and strain the mixture.

Place 1 tablespoon olive oil in a saucepan over medium heat, add the strained tomato-onion mixture, the reserved chiles, and the salt. Simmer the sauce until it thickens, about 10 to 25 minutes, depending on the water content of the tomatoes, then discard the chiles. Makes 1 small bowl.

1 pound tomatoes
½ tablespoon olive oil
½ cup onion, sliced
1 tablespoon olive oil
2 habanero chiles
¼ teaspoon salt

# BLACK BEANS

Heaping 1 cup of black beans

½ tablespoon lard or olive oil

1 piece bacon, minced

½ cup finely chopped onion

2 cloves garlic, minced

½ cup chopped tomato

½ teaspoon oregano

Heaping ¼ teaspoon salt

1 ancho chile, stemmed and
    seeded (optional)

■ This is a delicious version of the classic "pot beans" that has a few more ingredients than usual, giving it some of the qualities of the famous northern dish *frijoles a la charra*, which is made with pinto beans. It is also the first step in making the best version of *frijoles refritos*, or refried beans, that I have ever tasted: *frijoles negros maneados*. Please note that the *ancho* chile is listed as optional. It provides a nice touch of heat to this dish and is a necessary ingredient if you plan to make *frijoles negros maneados*. ■

Wash and carefully pick over the beans and reserve. Add the oil to a pot over medium heat, then add and cook the bacon until it begins to render its fat. Add the onion and cook until it begins to soften, then add the garlic and cook for 1 minute. Add the tomato and continue cooking until it begins to soften and give off its juice, then add the beans, oregano, and chile, if you are using it, and enough water to cover the beans by at least 2½ to 3 inches. Bring the liquid to a boil, partially cover the beans with a lid, leaving just a crack for steam to escape, then cook the beans at a brisk simmer until they are very tender, about 1 hour, depending on the altitude and condition of the beans. When the beans are done, remove the chile and add the salt if serving the beans in this form or leave it in the pot if you are planning to prepare *frijoles negros maneados*. Serve the beans with broiled meat or poultry or reserve them to make *frijoles negros maneados*. Serves 4.

ORPHAN'S RICE

■ In the second edition of *El Norte: The Cuisine of Northern Mexico*, I included a recipe for this dish from northern Mexico. For this book, I am including the following version from Mexico City, which, since it contains saffron instead of curry powder, is much closer to its Moorish roots. ■

Heat the broth until very hot but not boiling, add the saffron and salt, allow it to sit for 10 minutes, and reserve it.

Heat a heavy pot or Dutch oven over moderate heat until it is hot, add the oil, and sauté the rice, stirring frequently, for 3 minutes or until a few grains just begin to brown. Add the onion and garlic and cook 1 minute more, stirring constantly. Then add the broth mixture, bring to a boil over high heat, cover the pot, turn the heat down to low, and simmer for 15 minutes.

Meanwhile, fry the bacon medium crisp, drain on paper towels, chop finely, and mix with the ham. Heat the butter in a medium-sized skillet over moderate heat, add the pecans, almonds, and pine nuts, and sauté, stirring frequently, until the almonds turn a light golden brown. Do not allow the nuts to overcook or they will be bitter. When the rice is done stir the bacon, ham, nuts, and parsley into it, replace the cover, and remove the pot from the heat. Allow the rice to continue steaming for 15 minutes. Serves 6 to 8.

21 ounces chicken broth

Pinch saffron (about ⅛ teaspoon)

¾ teaspoon salt

3 tablespoons cooking oil

1½ cups long grain rice

1 tablespoon onion, minced

1 clove garlic, minced

1½ ounces bacon (about 1 thick slice or 2 thin slices)

1½ ounces ham, finely chopped (about ¼ cup)

1 tablespoon butter

¾ cup pecan halves

½ cup blanched, slivered almonds

⅓ cup pine nuts

1 tablespoon minced parsley

MEXICAN RICE

2 small or 1 large tomato, totaling 10 ounces

4 peeled garlic cloves

⅓ cup chopped onion

1½ cups olive oil or 3–4 tablespoons

1¼-inch slice of onion

1½ cups long grain rice

¾ teaspoon salt

2⅓ cups chicken, turkey, or pork broth, or substitute water

⅓ cup carrots, peeled and cut into julienne strips about 1 inch long

⅓ cup frozen baby peas, thawed

■ This is the most important rice dish in Mexican cooking. The following recipe is a revised version of one I included in my book *La cocina de la frontera*. The revisions make it even better. This rice is best fried in a large amount of oil and then drained. Although very little of the fat will be incorporated into the dish, if you do not want to use this much oil, fry the rice in 3 to 4 tablespoons of it and skip the draining. ■

Place the tomatoes on a baking sheet as close under a broiler as possible, and broil them until the skins are charred, 15 to 20 minutes. Then put the tomatoes in a blender. Mince 2 of the garlic cloves, add them and the chopped onion to the blender, and purée at high speed for about 30 seconds. Reserve the mixture.

Place the oil, 2 whole cloves garlic, and onion slice in a heavy pot or Dutch oven over medium heat. Continue heating until the garlic begins to brown, then remove it and the onion. Discard the onion and reserve the cooked garlic. Add the rice and continue simmering, stirring frequently, until the rice begins to turn golden. If you are using the larger amount of oil, pour the contents of the pot into a strainer over a bowl to drain off the excess oil. If you are using the lesser amount of oil, continue with the next step. Turn the heat to between medium and medium high, replace the rice if you have drained it, add the contents of the blender, and cook, stirring frequently, until the moisture is nearly gone and the rice no longer sticks together. This is very important because if too much moisture remains, the result will be gloppy. It is better to overcook rather than undercook at this stage.

While the rice is cooking, place the salt, broth or water, and reserved fried garlic cloves in a blender and blend at high speed for 1 minute. When you have finished cooking the rice and tomato mixture, pour the contents of the blender into the pot, add the carrots, and stir well. Bring the contents to a boil, cover the pot, turn the heat to very low, and allow the rice to cook for 15 minutes. Stir in the peas, replace the top, and allow the rice to steam for 15 minutes. Serves 6.

GREEN RICE

■ This recipe is the favorite among those to whom I have given demonstrations and cooking classes. People are amazed that it is so delicious, elegant, and easy to prepare. Since it was first published in the second edition of *El Norte: The Cuisine of Northern Mexico*, I have not been able to improve it. I am including it in this book because it is such a perfect accompaniment to many *nueva cocina mexicana* dishes. Green Rice goes very well with *poblano* chiles stuffed with meat, fruit, and nuts, and/or cheese. It is also a fine accompaniment to meat, fish, and poultry recipes, especially those with a cream sauce. ■

½ cup very tightly packed fresh cilantro

1 cup very tightly packed fresh spinach

1¼ cups chicken broth

1¼ cups milk

1 teaspoon salt

1 tablespoon olive oil

3 tablespoons butter

1½ cups long grain rice

¼ cup minced onion

1 clove garlic, minced

Place the cilantro, spinach, and broth in a blender and blend until the vegetables are puréed. Add the milk and salt to the blender and blend until they are well combined.

Heat a heavy pot over medium heat, add the olive oil and butter, and when the butter is melted add the rice and fry, stirring about every 30 seconds, until it *just* begins to brown, about 5 minutes. Then add the onion and garlic and cook 1 more minute, stirring constantly. Add the contents of the blender, stir well, turn the heat to high, and bring to a boil. Cover the pot, turn the heat to very low, and cook for 20 minutes. Remove the cover, stir the rice carefully, and cook 5 minutes more. Remove the pot from the heat, replace the lid, and allow the rice to steam for 10 minutes. Serves 6 to 8.

✳ POTATOES & CARROTS

2 cups red potatoes, peeled and cut into ½-inch pieces

1½ cups carrots, peeled and cut into ½-inch pieces

1½ tablespoons olive oil

2 tablespoons chorizo

½ teaspoon dried thyme

¾ teaspoon salt

¼ teaspoon ground black pepper

⅓ cup cotija or añejo cheese, grated (optional)

■ This is one of the most popular Mexican dishes, particularly in central and south Mexico, and an excellent low-fat dish. It is served with all kinds of entrées and as a topping for dishes such as *tacos potosinos* and *pollo estilo guerrero*.

After being cut and boiled, the potatoes and carrots are often served as is or with the addition of salt and pepper or a little thyme, oregano, or marjoram. On other occasions the boiled vegetables are mixed with cooking oil or lard and fried, frequently with herbs and a little chorizo, which produces an especially savory yet not too fatty result. I have provided the more elaborate version of the recipe, but it can be simplified, if desired. ■

Boil the potatoes in water to cover until they are just tender, then strain them under cold water to stop the cooking. Boil the carrots in the same way. Then heat the olive oil in a skillet over medium heat, add the chorizo, and cook it until it is well browned. Turn the heat to medium high, add the remaining ingredients, except the cheese, and fry, stirring constantly, until the vegetables just begin to brown. Serve topped with the cheese, if desired. Serves 4.

Oaxaca Chorizo

■ The town of Toluca, located about 40 miles west of Mexico City, is justly famous for its chorizo, and it is from there that most chorizo recipes come. However, fine chorizo is made all over Mexico, and I am particularly partial to the variety made in Oaxaca, of which the following recipe is typical. ■

Put the cut-up meat in the freezer until it just begins to freeze, about 15 minutes. Simmer the chiles in water to cover until they are very soft, 20 to 30 minutes. Cool the chiles under cold water, drain, then remove the stems and most of the seeds. Put 1 or 2 chiles at a time meat side down in a food mill fitted with a medium or fine blade, and crank the machine until the chile pulp is separated from the skins. Process the remaining chiles in the same manner and reserve the pulp. In a spice or coffee grinder, grind the cloves, cinnamon, oregano, marjoram, thyme, bay leaf, and salt to a powder. Mix the partially frozen pork with ¼ cup of the chile purée, rubbing it in by hand. (Reserve any remaining purée for another use.) Add the spices and garlic, and mix well. Put the meat in a food processor fitted with a steel blade, add the vinegars, and process in pulses until the meat is coarsely ground. Alternatively, you may put the meat through the coarse (not chile grind) blade of a meat grinder, then mix in the chile paste, spices, and vinegar. Allow the chorizo to absorb the flavors overnight before cooking, then freeze the remainder in useable portions. Makes about 1¼ pounds.

1 pound fatty, boneless pork shoulder, cut into ½-inch cubes

5 ancho chiles

1 pasilla chile

2 whole cloves

¾-inch piece of cinnamon stick

Heaping ¼ teaspoon dried oregano

Heaping ¼ teaspoon dried marjoram

Heaping ¼ teaspoon dried thyme

1 bay leaf, broken into small pieces

¾ teaspoon salt

2 cloves garlic, minced

2 tablespoons red wine vinegar

2 tablespoons cider vinegar

❋ PORK & FRUIT MOLE

2 pounds lean pork loin, cut into bite-sized pieces

2 small ancho chiles, stemmed and seeded

I pasilla chile, stemmed and seeded

I chipotle chile, stemmed and seeded, or substitute I canned chipotle in adobo sauce

I tablespoon sesame seeds

I small tomato

2 ¼-inch slices white onion

2 large cloves garlic

½ medium plantain, halved lengthwise

2 tablespoons blanched, slivered almonds

2 tablespoons dark rum

2 tablespoons raisins

⅓ cup chicken broth

⅓ cup pineapple juice

2 tablespoons lard or cooking oil

Chicken broth

Heaping ¼ teaspoon ground cinnamon

Scant ¼ teaspoon ground allspice

■ This is one of the best-known traditional stews from Mexico's interior, particularly around Mexico City and Oaxaca, where it is included as one of the famous 7 *moles*. The Spanish name *manchamanteles* literally means "tablecloth stainer," and even though it contains chiles and other New World ingredients it seems to be the closest of these dishes to medieval Spanish cooking. It is an excellent dish suitable for nearly any occasion. ■

Cover the pork with water, bring to a boil, and simmer for about 45 minutes or until tender. Allow the pork to cool in the broth and reserve.

Toast the chiles on an ungreased skillet over medium heat until they are fragrant but not scorched. Place them in a blender, cover with hot water, and set aside for about 30 minutes.

Meanwhile, toast the sesame seeds in an ungreased skillet until golden brown; toast the tomato, onion, and garlic on the ungreased skillet until the tomato is charred and becoming soft, and the onion and garlic are soft and beginning to brown. Fry the plantain in a little oil in a small skillet over medium heat, until it is golden brown and soft; next fry the almonds in the same oil just until they turn golden. Then place the rum and raisins in a small dish and allow to soak for 10 minutes.

Pour off all the water from the chiles in the blender and add the above ingredients, then add the chicken broth and pineapple juice, and process at high speed for at least 1 minute. Strain the resulting purée through the fine blade of a food mill and reserve.

Place the lard or oil in a large heavy pot over medium-high heat, add the blended purée, and fry, stirring constantly, until it becomes quite thick but does not burn. Add additional broth until the sauce reaches the desired consistency. Next add the cinnamon, allspice, salt, and vinegar, then add the cooked pork, and simmer for 15 minutes.

Sauté the garnish in a little butter and deglaze with a fruit brandy or liquor. Spoon over each serving, if desired. Serves 4.

¼ teaspoon salt

I teaspoon cider vinegar

THE GARNISH:

Sesame seeds

Almonds

Cilantro

Small amount of onion, finely chopped

Pineapple, chopped

Mango, chopped

Serrano chile, chopped

Butter

Quince liquor or a fruit brandy such as peach

2 pounds lean, pork loin, cut
   into 1- to 2-inch pieces

1 medium onion, skinned and
   halved

2 cloves garlic, skinned

2 bay leaves

½ teaspoon oregano

½ teaspoon thyme

½ teaspooon marjoram

3 tablespoons lard or olive oil

2 cups thinly sliced onion

2 cups peeled red potato, cut
   into ¼-inch pieces

2 cloves garlic, minced

¼ pound chorizo, minced

4 medium tomatoes, broiled

4 canned chipotle chiles

1 tablespoon lard or olive oil

½ teaspoon thyme

½ teaspoon marjoram

½ teaspoon oregano

1½ teaspoons sugar

1 tablespoon rice vinegar

½ teaspoon salt

Lettuce leaves to serve as a
   bed for the stew

2 small avocados, or 1 large,
   peeled and sliced

Hot corn tortillas

THE DRESSING:

2 teaspoons rice vinegar

¾ teaspoon sugar

½ tablespoon olive oil

PUEBLA STEW

■ This classic pork stew from Puebla is called *Tinga Poblana*. Flavored with chorizo and *chipotle* chiles it is delicious either served with white rice, or more traditionally, on a bed of lettuce with steaming corn tortillas. ■

Place the pork in a large pot and cover with water by about 2 inches. Bring the liquid to a boil and skim off the scum that rises to the surface. Add the onion, garlic, bay leaves, oregano, thyme, and marjoram, cover the pot, and simmer until the pork is very tender, 45 minutes to 1 hour. Allow the pork to cool in the broth, then remove the pork, reserving the broth for another use (such as making rice). Shred the pork, either by hand or in a food processor fitted with a plastic blade, and reserve.

Heat the 2 tablespoons lard or oil in a skillet over medium heat, add the onion and potato, and cook until they are soft, about 4 to 5 minutes. Then add the garlic and chorizo, turn the heat to medium high, and continue to cook until the onion and potato begin to brown and the chorizo becomes brown and crisp, about 5 minutes. Remove the mixture to a bowl and reserve. Meanwhile, blend together the broiled tomatoes and 2 of the *chipotle* chiles, and strain the mixture through the fine blade of a food mill. With the heat under the skillet at medium high, add the remaining 1 tablespoon lard or olive oil, then add the meat. Let it fry for about 30 seconds without stirring, turn it, and allow it to cook for another 30 seconds. Then, stir-fry it until the meat *just* begins to become crisp. Turn the heat down to medium and add the reserved potato/ chorizo mixture and the strained tomato/chile mixture, and stir to mix well. Add the thyme, marjoram, oregano, sugar, vinegar, and salt, and simmer for 5 minutes. Serve the stew on a bed of lettuce leaves, topped with sliced avocado, with hot corn tortillas. Just before serving mix together the dressing ingredients and spoon over the avocado. Serves 4.

❋ YUCATÁN-STYLE BARBECUED PORK

■ Throughout most of Mexico, lamb and goat are the prime ingredients that go into the *Barbacoa* pit, but not in the Yucatán. Here the rocky land provided little grazing, and the Spanish settlers relied more on pork than in other areas. So it was only natural that the Indians used this succulent meat to replace the venison and turkey in their pits, although they retained the traditional *recado*, or seasoning paste. Like most *Barbacoa* these days, this dish is usually cooked in a steamer or wrapped in foil and baked, and thus does not have the traditional smoky flavor. For this recipe, I adapted a technique presented in *Cook's Illustrated* as a simplified method of preparing southern-style "pulled pork" barbecue. It does an excellent job of imitating the *Barbacoa* pit. ■

Grind the annato seeds and cumin to a powder in a spice or coffee grinder. Add the oregano, allspice, cinnamon, salt, coriander, and ground chile and grind until the spices are thoroughly mixed. Place the powder in a small bowl, then mix in the garlic, orange juice, and lime juice. You want a smooth paste that spreads easily. If the *recado* is a little dry, add some more orange juice and lime juice.

Rub the *recado* into the butt roast, and put it in the refrigerator overnight. Roll the banana leaves up, fold them in half, and steam them for 20 to 30 minutes to make them pliable. When the leaves have cooled, place them shiny side up on a work surface. Put the meat on the leaves, wrap into a tight bundle, and tie with the string.

Pour 3 quarts boiling water into the pan of a water smoker and smoke the pork for 4 hours at between 225 and 250 degrees. Check the smoker after 2 hours and add additional boiling water to the pan, if necessary. When done, the internal temperature of the pork should be 160 to 170 degrees. Place the pork in a foil loaf pan, seal it with heavy-duty aluminum foil, place it in an oven preheated to 325 degrees, and bake for 1 hour 45 minutes. Remove the package

THE RECADO:

1 tablespoon annato seeds

½ teaspoon whole cumin

1 teaspoon dried oregano

¼ teaspoon ground allspice

¾ teaspoon ground cinnamon

1 teaspoon salt

1 teaspoon ground coriander

1½ teaspoons ground ancho chile

4 cloves garlic, minced and mashed

2 tablespoons orange juice

½ tablespoon lime juice

THE PORK:

1 2½- to 3-pound half Boston butt roast

Banana leaves to wrap the pork

String to tie the bundle

from the oven, and place it in a large paper grocery bag, fold the bag tightly to seal it, and leave for 45 minutes. Remove the pork from the roasting pan and unwrap the banana leaves. It should be so tender it will literally fall off the bone. Cut the pork into 2-inch pieces, removing as much fat as possible, and place it in a food processor fitted with a plastic blade. Process until the pork is shredded or shred it by hand. Serve the pork with guacamole, sour orange juice, Yucatán *Habanero* Sauce, corn tortillas, and marinated red onions. Serves 4.

BIRRIA

THE SAUCE:

2 pounds tomatoes

½ teaspoon salt or to taste

THE MEAT:

2 medium-sized ancho chiles, stemmed, seeded, and deveined

3 guajillo chiles, stemmed, seeded, and deveined

3 cascabel chiles, stemmed, seeded, and deveined

2 cloves garlic

½ cup rice vinegar

■ To say this dish is assertive is like saying that Elizabeth Taylor is pretty or that Luciano Pavarotti has a good voice. A specialty of the state of Jalisco, whose commercial center is Guadalajara, it is indeed powerful in only the way that Mexican cooking can be. In Spanish the word *birria* literally means "horror," "piece of junk," "trash," or "rubbish," and too often it is prepared in a manner that justifies its name. The meat for this dish, a fatty cut of either goat or lamb, was originally prepared in a *barbacoa* pit, which has the effect of both steaming and smoking it at the same time. The reason so much *Birria* is second rate today is that it is usually steamed in a large pot, sometimes with maguey leaves to mimic the traditional method. If great care is not taken, steaming fatty meat and serving it with its juices can result in a greasy mess. But when *Birria* is properly prepared, there is no more "Mexican" dish, just as there is no more "Mexican" place than Guadalajara, in terms of embodying the mixing of Indian and Spanish cultures. In the following recipe, the meat is first smoked in a water smoker, which burns off some of the fat and imparts a deep smoky flavor; next it is steamed until the meat literally falls off the bones; then it is glazed in the oven with a sweetish chile sauce, shredded, and served in bowls with a broth redolent of flavors from the cooking process. Since lamb is more available in this country, that is what is specified, but it can be just as easily made with goat or kid.

While this dish is quite time-consuming, its steps, such as the tomato sauce, the meat, and the final sauce, can be done on different days. In fact, the entire dish can be completed ahead of time and refrigerated for several days, because as with most stews it improves as the meat absorbs the flavors. ■

To prepare the sauce, place the tomatoes on a baking sheet and put them in the oven as close to the heating element as possible. Broil the tomatoes until they are charred and soft, about 20 minutes. Put the broiled tomatoes in a blender and blend at high speed for 30 seconds, then strain the tomatoes, stir in the salt, and reserve. The tomato sauce will later be mixed with the cooking broth and some chile sauce.

To prepare the meat, toast the chiles for a few seconds on each side in an ungreased skillet over medium heat, pressing down on them with a spatula in the process. Place the chiles in a blender, add about 2 cups of very hot water, and allow them to rehydrate for 20 minutes. Drain the chiles, replace them in the blender, add the remaining ingredients, except the lamb and beer, and blend at high speed for 1 to 2 minutes. Place the lamb in a nonreactive bowl, pour in ⅓ cup of the chile sauce, rub it into the meat, and place it in the refrigerator for 1 to 3 hours. Reserve the remaining sauce.

To smoke the meat, I prefer to use an electric water smoker rather than one fired by charcoal because you have more control over the temperature. Soak some mesquite or other hardwood smoking chips in water to cover for ½ hour. Drain and place the chips on the "gravel" near the burners. If you are using a wood or charcoal-fired smoker,

½ cup warm, flat beer

1 teaspoon ground cumin

1 tablespoon dried marjoram

¼ teaspoon black pepper

¼ teaspoon ground cloves

¼ teaspoon ground cinnamon

3 tablespoons sugar

¾ teaspoon salt

3 pounds lamb shoulder, cut into chunks about ¾ inch thick and a few inches across

1 12-ounce bottle of beer

THE GARNISH:

½ cup minced onion

½ cup loosely packed, fresh minced cilantro

light the coals, allow them to turn grey, then add the chips. Heat 2 quarts of water with the beer, and pour it into the water dish of the smoker. Place the marinated lamb in a colander, put it on the grill, cover the smoker, and smoke for 2 hours. The temperature should remain between 225 and 250 degrees.

Remove the colander with the meat and transfer it to a large steamer set on your stove. Add as much liquid from the smoker's water dish as you can to the steamer, while still keeping it below the level of the meat (there should be at least 6 cups, so you will need to use a large, deep pot and place something like a gelatin mold inside on which to set the colander with the meat). Cover the pot, using a thin towel to seal the top, and steam over low heat for 1¾ hours. While you are steaming the meat, place a metal or pottery bowl in the freezer into which the broth will be poured and chilled to facilitate removing fat. Also preheat the oven to 325 degrees.

When the meat has steamed, remove it to a baking sheet or pizza pan, and allow it to cool for 10 minutes. Pour the broth into the chilled bowl and place it in the freezer. There should be at least 3½ cups; if not, add some water. Brush some of the reserved chile sauce on the meat, then place it in the oven until the sauce turns into a glaze, about 20 minutes. Remove the meat and allow it to cool for 10 minutes. Then remove the meat from the bones, discard any large remaining pieces of fat, and shred it, either by hand or in a food processor fitted with a plastic blade. Next place the shredded meat into each of 4 soup bowls. There should be about ¾ cup of meat in each one. Take the bowl of cooking broth from the freezer and remove any solidified fat with a strainer. Then place 3 cups of the broth in a saucepan with the puréed tomato mixture, add 2 tablespoons of the remaining chile sauce, and bring to a boil. Cook the sauce until it begins to thicken, about 5 minutes, then ladle about 1 cup of it into each serving bowl on top of the shredded lamb. Sprinkle on some onion and cilantro and serve with hot corn tortillas. Serves 4.

BARBACOA

In the north of Mexico, *Barbacoa* is usually made with goat, but in the rest of the country with lamb. Traditionally, the meat is wrapped in roasted maguey leaves and placed in a large pit, about 2½ feet deep, in which wood has been burned to coals. The meat is placed on a grill set over a cauldron containing water, herbs, and vegetables. The pit is then sealed, and the meat is cooked for at least 6 hours or overnight. The process combines indirect heat from the coals and steam from the pot and maguey leaves. The result is succulently moist with a nice smoky flavor. With typical Mexican gallows humor, cooks often place a cross on the mound of earth covering the pit, with a sign saying, "Rest in peace." And sometimes a bottle of tequila or mescal will be buried in the mound and attached to the cross with a rope. The "disinterring" and imbibing often becomes a ceremony in itself. The cooked meat is shredded and served accompanied by bowls of soup, Drunken Sauce (p. 195), guacamole, and corn tortillas.

Unfortunately, because the meat is now so often cooked in a steamer on top of a stove, the same as with other styles of *Barbacoa*, including *cochinita pibil* and *Birria*, the meat lacks the traditional smoky flavor. The method I have developed for the following recipe, which uses both a water smoker and a steamer, produces a truly authentic flavor, with relatively little effort, especially compared to the pit process. The only thing it lacks is the flavor imparted by the maguey leaves, which I did not include because I doubted many cooks would have access to them.

Place the olive oil, garlic, and salt in a blender and blend for 1 minute. Pour over the lamb pieces and marinate in the refrigerator overnight.

Before cooking, place the lamb pieces in a metal colander. Bring the water and beer to a boil, and place in the pan of a water smoker with the remaining ingredients except the carrots and garbanzo

⅓ cup olive oil

3 cloves garlic, chopped

½ teaspoon salt

1 4-pound leg of lamb, boned and the meat cut into large pieces (about 4 inches by 2 inches thick)

2 quarts plus 1½ cups water

1 12-ounce bottle beer

1 onion, quartered

4 carrots, cut in half

1 teaspoon dried thyme

1 teaspoon dried oregano

2 bay leaves

¾ cup carrots, peeled and cut into ½-inch pieces

1 16-ounce can garbanzo beans, drained and rinsed in cold water

beans. Put the colander with the lamb on the grill and smoke at between 225 and 250 degrees for 2 hours. Remove the colander with the lamb from the smoker and place it in a steamer with at least 6 cups of water below it. Then bring the water to a boil, put a thin towel over the pot, place the lid over it, and, if necessary, something heavy over it to keep the seal as tight as possible. Turn the heat down to a simmer and steam the meat for 2 hours. Meanwhile, pour the liquid from the pan in the smoker into a bowl and place it in a freezer until the fat solidifies. Remove the fat and strain the liquid into a pot, add the garbanzo beans and carrots. Simmer covered for 20 minutes, adding water as necessary to produce enough "soup" for 4.

When the lamb has finished steaming, remove it from the pot, and, using tongs to keep from burning your hands, remove any remaining fat and cut the meat into small pieces. Place the lamb in a food processor fitted with a plastic blade and process until the meat is finely shredded. (You will probably need to do this in 2 batches.) The meat can also be shredded by hand. Place the soup in small bowls (it is quite strong and a little goes a long way) and serve the lamb in a large dish so that people can help themselves, accompanied by Drunken Sauce, guacamole, and hot corn tortillas. Serves 6 to 8.

# PACHOLAS

■ This traditional dish, which is found in several regions of the interior, including Jalisco and Guanajuato, is one that I have never seen in this country nor found in a restaurant in Mexico. It is nevertheless a delicious recipe; although simple, it is for that very reason an excellent foil to more complicated dishes. *Pachola* is essentially a hamburger steak that is traditionally formed on a *metate*, the stone implement usually used to grind corn for tortillas and tamales. What makes this different from the usual hamburger steak is both its shape and the ingredients other than meat. ■

6 ancho chiles, stemmed and mostly seeded

2 slices white bread, crusts removed and chopped

½ cup milk

1½ pounds hamburger (preferably 85 percent lean)

1 tablespoon minced onion

2 cloves garlic, minced

½ teaspoon ground cinnamon

¼ teaspoon ground cloves

½ teaspoon salt

2 tablespoons olive oil

Place the chiles in a saucepan, cover with water, bring to a boil, then simmer, covered, for 15 minutes. Drain the chiles in a strainer, and run cold water over them until they are cool enough to handle. Then put the chiles in a food mill fitted with the finest blade and grind, producing several tablespoons of chile purée, without any of the skins or remaining seeds. Reserve 2 tablespoons of the purée and save any left over for another purpose. Place the chopped bread in a small dish, cover with the milk, and allow to sit for 15 minutes. Then remove the bread and squeeze out as much of the moisture as possible.

Thoroughly mix the meat with the 2 tablespoons chile purée, the soaked and squeezed bread, and the remaining ingredients, except the olive oil. The meat can be mixed by hand in a bowl, in a food processor, or in the bowl of a stand mixer (unless, of course, you have a *metate* and wish to use it). I prefer to use a stand mixer because it mixes all the ingredients well and produces a light texture.

To form the patties, separate the meat into 4 pieces of equal size, then roll each of them into a cylinder about 7 to 8 inches in length. In Mexico, the cylinder is placed on the *metate* and pressed with the *mano* into the shape of an elongated football, about 9 to 10 inches long, about 5 inches wide at the center, and about ¼ to ⅓ inch thick. One edge of the *mano* is then pressed into the center of the meat, the long way, and down to the *metate*, thereby cutting the football-shaped patty in half lengthwise. Each half is then scraped off the *metate* onto a griddle. This works well if you have a *metate*, and nearly as well if you follow the directions using a chopping block and a rolling pin, except that you use a knife to cut the patty in half and then remove it from the block with a long-bladed spatula. The result will be 8 patties that are between 9 and 10 inches in length, 2½ inches in width at the center, tapering to less than 1 inch at each end, and about ¼ to ⅓ inch thick.

When all the patties have been made, fry them in a little of the oil on a griddle or very large heavy skillet over medium-high heat until they are browned on both sides and just cooked through. Serve 2 patties per person, one on each side of a mound of Potatoes and Carrots (p. 210), mashed potatoes or another vegetable; or for a very light meal serve 1 patty per person. Serves 4 to 8.

DISCADA

■ The name of this classic northern Mexican dish comes from the implement in which it is cooked: the disk of a plow measuring about 26 inches in diameter. It is usually prepared over campfires and served with refried pinto beans to cowboys hungry after a long day in the saddle. Fortunately, the traditional *disco* is very similar to a wok, which is used in this recipe. There are as many versions of this dish as there are cooks, but this one, which I adapted from a recipe in México Desconocido's *Guía Gastronomía, Comida chihuahuense*, is particularly interesting because of the flavoring ingredients: A1 sauce, Worcestershire sauce, and Maggi seasoning liquid. Although the ingredients may be foreign, the result is pure Mexican.

There is a great deal to the notion that the atmosphere in which food is prepared and consumed has a lot to do with its enjoyment. Just as pizza seems to taste best in a pizzeria in Naples or in a small café overlooking the Amalfi Coast, this dish is best cooked over a campfire after a late afternoon horseback ride.

While this dish is cooked in a wok, it is not supposed to be like a typical Chinese dish in which the vegetables are crispy and the juices are thickened into a sauce with cornstarch; instead, the juices are supposed to make a slightly watery sauce. Also, while the recipe is best served immediately after preparation, it is still delicious the next day. If you wish to make it a day in advance, purée 3 large tomatoes in a blender, then fry them in 1 tablespoon lard or cooking oil until they begin to thicken. Add the meat and continue cooking, stirring constantly, until everything is hot. ■

Mix the first 3 ingredients together and reserve. Heat a large wok over medium heat, add the bacon and chorizo and fry, breaking the

3 teaspoons Worcestershire sauce

2¼ teaspoons A1 sauce

1½ teaspoons Maggi seasoning liquid

4 ounces (about 4 slices) bacon, minced

8 ounces chorizo

Cooking oil

3 green onions, minced

1 cup white onion, minced

1 cup Anaheim chiles, stemmed, seeded, and minced

1 cup red or green bell pepper, stemmed, seeded, and minced

4 cloves garlic, minced

1½ pounds top sirloin, cut into ¼-inch pieces

½ cup loosely packed cilantro, minced

chorizo into small bits, until it has browned and rendered its fat. Spoon the contents of the wok into a strainer set over a bowl. When the fat has drained off, pour it into a measuring cup and add cooking oil until you have ¼ cup plus 2 tablespoons, or a total of 6 tablespoons. Leave the bacon and chorizo in the strainer. Turn the heat to high, and when the wok is very hot add 3 tablespoons of the fat, and when it begins to smoke add the green onions, onion, chiles, bell pepper, and garlic. (Be careful not to let the oil catch fire.) Stir-fry the vegetables until they are soft, then spoon them into the strainer with the chorizo and bacon. Reheat the wok until it is very hot, add the remaining 3 tablespoons fat, again being careful not to allow it to catch fire, and then add the top sirloin. Allow the meat to cook undisturbed until the bottom begins to become brown and crispy, 30 seconds to 1 minute, then turn it with a spatula or large spoon, and allow the other side of the mass to brown. Stir-fry the meat until it is barely cooked through, then add the bacon, chorizo, vegetables, and the reserved sauces and cilantro. Cook just until the ingredients are well mixed and hot, then serve on plates with refried beans, guacamole, and hot flour tortillas. Serves 4.

❈ STEAK TAMPIQUEÑA

■ Deciding whether to designate this recipe as traditional or *nueva* was difficult because this dish may well be the first notable example of *nueva cocina mexicana*. The dish was first served by José Inéz Loredo in the legendary Tampico Club of Mexico City. Loredo was born in San Luís Potosí and at age twelve began to work at a local hotel. Later, his family moved to Tampico, where he was employed at the Hotel Imperial, the best in town, and he subsequently became mayor of the city. In 1939, he moved to Mexico City, where he opened the Tampico Club in the historic center on Calle de Balderas. It was here that he served the typical steak of Tampico on a plate combined with *rajas* and various *antojitos*. The dish became a sensation, and spread around the country, where it is now served, in one form or another, in virtually every restaurant.

In attempting to present the "authentic" Steak *Tampiqueña*, I learned once again that nothing in Mexico is simple or straightforward. I found the "authentic" recipe in *Epazote y molcajete productos y técnicas de la cocina mexicana*, by Alicia and Jorge De'Angeli, two of Mexico's most renowned culinary authorities. They stated that the recipe in their book had been supplied by chefs at the Tampico Club when it was presented in 1946, and they carefully noted the few changes they had made to the original. I also found the "original" recipe in a magazine article about the Caballo Bayo, another Loredo restaurant, supplied by Señor Loredo's granddaughter, who now runs the business. The only problem was that the recipes were not quite the same.

I usually urge readers to view my recipes as a starting point from which they can add their own touches. However, in this case, I also encourage readers to prepare this recipe exactly as written at least once because it is a perfect vehicle for teaching Mexican cooking techniques, and such a good example of both the most popular Mexican steak and the way *antojitos* are served in Mexico. In this country, Mexican-American restaurants have accustomed us to

THE TOMATILLO SAUCE:

½ pound tomatillos, husked, stemmed, and seeded

1–2 serrano chiles

1 tablespoon minced fresh cilantro

¼ teaspoon salt

THE RAJAS:

½ tablespoon lard

2 ounces (about ¼) onion, thinly sliced into strips 2½–3 inches long

4 ounces (about 1 large or 2 small) poblano chiles, roasted, peeled, seeded, and cut into thin strips about 2½–3 inches long

THE MEAT:

1 tenderloin steak, about 2½ inches thick and weighing 9–10 ounces

Juice of 1 lime

Salt and pepper to taste

4 corn tortillas

I tablespoon melted lard

**The reserved tomatillo sauce
and rajas**

The steaks

**2 ounces Oaxaca cheese,
grated**

**4 strips Oaxaca cheese, 3½
inches long, 1½ inches wide,
and ⅓ inch thick**

I lime, halved

having *antojitos* served on a hot plate covered with a chile sauce and melted cheese. In these restaurants, the plate is prepared and put under the intense heat of a salamander, then carefully placed on the table. However, in Mexico *antojitos* are traditionally prepared on a griddle, then placed on the plate as they are completed, and served without the extra sauce and final heating, arriving at the table somewhere between hot and lukewarm.

To me these styles produce a different but equally good result. But if you have not traveled in Mexico and experienced the traditional style I suggest you try this recipe and decide for yourself. It is very important to use lard in order to experience the authentic flavor, and it has less saturated fat than butter. I have presented the recipe to serve 2, which will be a more manageable task. The *tomatillo* sauce and *rajas* can be prepared and the steak cut well ahead of time, but everything else must be assembled just before serving. ■

To make the *tomatillo* sauce, simmer the *tomatillos* and chiles in water to cover until they are very soft but not falling apart, 5 to 10 minutes. Then place the *tomatillos* in a blender, chop the chiles into small pieces, and add them and the remaining ingredients to the blender. Pulse the blender several times until the sauce is well mixed but not completely puréed; it should still have some texture.

Melt the lard in a small skillet over medium heat, add the onion strips, and sauté until they just begin to brown. Add the chiles and continue cooking for 3 to 5 minutes or until the chiles become soft but not limp.

The steak is cut in the Mexican fashion, that is in somewhat the same way a chef slices the peel from an orange in one piece. Place the steak on a chopping board on its side (see diagram p. 227). If you are right handed, place the knife on top of the steak about ¼ inch from the right edge and carefully slice downward until you are about ¼ inch from the bottom. Turn the steak a half turn to the left, which will again position the knife at the top of the steak, and again cut down to within ¼ inch from the bottom, making sure that the strip you are removing stays in 1 piece and is about ¼ inch thick. Continue slicing in the same manner to "unroll" the meat into a strip ¼ inch thick and about 2½ inches wide. The result will

be 1 long thin strip about 12 to 14 inches long. Cut the strip into 2 portions, and, using a meat pounder or edge of a cleaver, lightly pound to remove any irregularities resulting from the slicing. With just a little practice, you will be able to do this quickly and accurately. Sprinkle some lime juice over the steaks, salt and pepper to taste, and reserve.

Heat a griddle over medium-high heat, and put the *tomatillo* sauce and *rajas* on low heat to keep them warm.

When the griddle is hot, soften 2 tortillas in lard. Rather than melting lard in a skillet and passing the tortillas through it, I suggest you "paint" a little melted lard on each side of each tortilla with a pastry or basting brush, then place them in a plastic tortilla warmer or wrap them in a towel and microwave them for 30 to 45 seconds, or until they are hot and pliable. Submerge the tortillas in the sauce (or spoon some of the sauce onto each side to coat them), put a little of the grated cheese on each, reserving some for the final garnish, roll into enchiladas, and place one on the side of each serving plate.

Put the remaining 2 tortillas on the griddle—they should become hot and begin to puff almost immediately. Place a strip of cheese on one side of each tortilla and fold the tortilla in half to cover the cheese. Brush a little melted lard over the top side of the quesadilla, turn it, then brush a little more lard on the other side. Cook the quesadillas, turning them as needed, until they begin to brown and the cheese is melted. Then place them on the serving plates, across from the enchiladas. Spoon a little lard onto the griddle and place the remaining 2 strips of cheese on it. Fry the cheese until it begins to melt, then turn and fry on the other side until it is melted but still has its shape. Using a spatula, place the fried cheese on the serving plates, leaving room for the steak. Spoon a little more lard onto the griddle and cook the steaks as you like them, then place them in the middle of the serving plates. Put the *rajas* on the plates next to the steaks. Spoon a little of the *tomatillo* sauce over the enchilada, sprinkle on some of the reserved grated cheese, and serve with lime halves. Serves 2.

❋ "Pickled" Quail

■ This dish, the original of which is a specialty of Valladolid, is Spanish in origin and is my favorite of the *en escabeche* dishes. It makes a fine appetizer or a light lunch or supper, served with a salad and crunchy bread. The recipe also works with chicken or duck. ■

Heat the oil over medium heat until a drop of water evaporates almost immediately. Then cook the quail in batches and when they are just cooked through, remove and reserve them. At the end, add the onion, green and red bell peppers, and garlic and cook until the onions *just* begin to soften. Add the garlic and cook 2 minutes more. Add the reserved quail and the remaining ingredients, bring to a boil, then immediately remove the pot from the heat. Allow the mixture to cool, then refrigerate for 24 hours. To serve, drain the quail and put them on serving plates, and using kitchen tongs or a slotted spoon mound the vegetables on top of them. Serves 4.

1½ cups olive oil

8 quail, partially deboned, if possible

1 purple onion, thinly sliced

1 green bell pepper, thinly sliced

1 red bell pepper, thinly sliced

3 whole, peeled cloves garlic

1½ cups mushrooms, thinly sliced

1½ cups rice vinegar

3 tablespoons lime juice

½ cup dry white wine

1½ cups chicken broth

3 bay leaves

¾ teaspoon thyme

¾ teaspoon marjoram

¾ teaspoon oregano

Heaping ¼ teaspoon sage

4 whole cloves

3 tablespoons capers

12 whole peppercorns

12 pickled serrano chiles

1½ teaspoons sugar

¾ teaspoon salt or to taste

CHICKEN GUERRERO

2 medium to large potatoes,
   peeled and cut into ¾-inch
   pieces

2 medium carrots, peeled and
   cut into ½- to ¾-inch pieces

4 large, skinless, boneless half
   chicken breasts

Flour

⅓ cup cooking oil

10 green onions, cut into
   2-inch lengths

3 tablespoons dry white wine

2 large cloves garlic, minced

½ teaspoon dried thyme

8 dried pequín chiles

Salt and pepper to taste

■ I had this dish in a small restaurant in the famous silver city of Taxco after a long day of looking at incredible works of art I could not afford. Although it is Spanish in origin, the addition of the chiles nevertheless makes it entirely Mexican. It is deceptively simple and is a perfect antidote for the palette when it becomes sated with richer, spicier fare. ■

Boil the potatoes until they are just tender, then run them under cold water to cool. Dry them on paper towels and reserve. Boil and cool the carrots in the same manner, and reserve them.

Place 1 of the half breasts between 2 sheets of plastic wrap and, using a meat pounder, pound it until it is less than ¼ inch thick. It is best to begin pounding from the middle to keep from shredding the edges and to turn the meat about halfway through the process. Prepare the remaining breasts in the same manner. Dust 1 side of each half breast with flour, press it into the meat, then shake off the excess.

Heat a large skillet over medium-high heat, add about 1½ tablespoons of the oil, and when it begins to smoke sauté the chicken, floured side down, until it is a crispy golden brown. Turn the chicken and continue cooking until it is just done. Depending on the size of the chicken and your skillet, you will have to do this in several batches, adding a little oil for each one. When the chicken is done, remove it to warm serving plates.

If necessary, add a little more oil to the pan, then add the cooked potatoes, carrots, and green onions, and sauté until the potatoes begin to brown. Then add the wine, garlic, thyme, chiles, salt, and pepper. When heated, spoon the mixture over the chicken and serve. Serves 4.

SAFFRON CHICKEN

■ This appears to be a very old Spanish recipe because saffron and wine are not used nearly as much in everyday cooking as they once were, and because the ingredients are all Spanish except the small amount of chile. Besides being delicious, it provides an interesting insight into a style of Mexican cooking that is not well known outside of Mexico. ■

Dry the chicken pieces thoroughly. Heat the oil in a skillet over medium-high heat, brown the chicken on both sides, and remove to a plate. Reduce the heat to medium, add the onion and chile, and cook until the onion is soft but not browned. Then add the garlic and cook 1 minute longer. Add the flour and, stirring constantly, cook for 1 minute. Remove the skillet from the heat and stir in about ¼ cup of the chicken broth. When it has thickened, add another ¼ cup, then replace the skillet on the burner and continue slowly stirring in the broth and then the wine. Next add the saffron, thyme, marjoram, salt, pepper, and the reserved chicken pieces. Bring the liquid to a boil, then simmer until the sauce has thickened enough to coat the back of a spoon, about 30 minutes. Remove the chicken and strain the sauce through the fine blade of a food mill. Melt the butter in a saucepan over medium heat, stir in the strained sauce, and continue cooking until it is fairly thick. Meanwhile, remove the breast meat from the bones, being careful not to burn yourself, and divide it among 4 serving plates. Then pour the thickened sauce over the meat, garnish with the almonds and serve with white rice, sautéed mushrooms, and squash, if desired. Serves 4.

2 split bone-in chicken breasts, with most or all of the skin removed

¼ cup olive oil

1 cup chopped onion

1 serrano chile, stemmed, seeded, and minced

1 garlic clove, minced

3½ tablespoons flour

3 cups rich chicken broth

1 cup dry white wine

Heaping ¼ teaspoon saffron

¼ teaspoon dried thyme

¼ teaspoon dried marjoram

¼ teaspoon salt

⅛ teaspoon ground black pepper

½ tablespoon butter

2 ounces sliced almonds

✳ JIM PEYTON'S TRADITIONAL PUEBLA-STYLE MOLE

THE CHILES:

7 mulato chiles

4 ancho chiles

4 pasilla chiles

I canned chipotle chile

½ cup cooking oil or lard

THE VEGETABLES:

I tomato

½ cup chopped onion

3 cloves garlic

4 finely chopped tomatillos

½ tablespoon cooking oil or lard

THE SPICES & SEEDS:

3 whole cloves

½ stick cinnamon

½ teaspoon coriander seeds

½ tablespoon chile seeds

I ½ tablespoons sesame seeds

¼ teaspoon aniseed

¼ teaspoon black pepper

¼ cup toasted pumpkin seeds (optional)

THE FRUITS & NUTS:

I tablespoon cooking oil or lard

¼ cup raisins

■ Virtually all experts on Mexican cooking agree that Puebla-style Mole, or *Mole poblano* is the cuisine's most important dish. The reasons for this go far deeper than flavor and taste. The very creation of *Mole poblano* reflects the development of Mexican culture, and the dish, a complex and enchanting fusion of ingredients, celebrates the resplendence and uniqueness of that culture.

Mole poblano emerged from the convents of Puebla, for which it is named, during Mexico's baroque period. There, nuns collaborated with Indian women, blending Old World and New World ingredients and cooking techniques to create the most famous dishes of traditional haute Mexican cuisine, including *Mole poblano*, the most famous of all. It is no accident that this quintessential dish contains the most important ingredients in Mexican cooking: tortillas, tomatoes, chocolate, and chiles. Moreover, the chiles, which are the heart and soul of the dish, are arguably the most important ones in Mexican cooking: *anchos*, *mulatos*, *pasillas*, and *chipotles*.

In researching this subject, I first studied recipes considered "originals," from the various convents, principally Santa Clara, Santa Mónica, and Santa Teresa. These old recipes, which were reproduced in books, differed in some aspects considerably. The table at the end of the recipe reproduces these recipes with the ingredients averaged when there were differences between the various sources.

In reading these old recipes, you will notice that the old recipe from the convent of Santa Mónica *is* different from the others in the proportion of chiles. Also, in the original recipes there is a variety of ingredient measurements, including weight, volume, and number. I weighed several samples of all the chiles to arrive at an average number by weight. In reviewing the recipes, you will also notice that ingredients given by weight are sometimes out of proportion. For example, two recipes call for 50 grams of cinnamon, which is equivalent to about 8 to 12 sticks—certainly much more than we would use today.

The next step in my research was to analyze more modern recipes for *Mole poblano*, a time-consuming task given the many cookbooks that contain a recipe for this dish. However, it became readily apparent that the newer recipes differed from the originals in two respects. The newer recipes had similar ratios of chiles, and those ratios were consistently different from those in the Santa Clara and Santa Teresa recipes. The respective percentages of *mulatos*, *anchos*, and *pasillas* in the older recipes averaged 71 percent, 14 percent, and 15 percent, while in the newer recipes they averaged 49 percent, 25 percent, and 26 percent. The newer recipes also had fewer of the very hot *chipotles*, perhaps because they contained fewer *pasillas* in the old recipes, which are hotter than *anchos* and *mulatos*. The more recent recipes also called for much less chocolate, and some had additional ingredients, including peanuts, plantains, pumpkin seeds, and sometimes plums. In order to show the differences, I have included both in two recipes or as options in my basic recipe, whichever route is chosen. Both can be prepared according to the same instructions. In my newer recipe which is in the first column of the table on p. 237, I have changed the amount of chiles and chocolate while adding ingredients not found in the historic recipes, *which are shown for historical purposes only.*

Mole poblano, as most *moles*, is a complicated dish, both in terms of preparation and flavor with the former creating the latter. However, it is not so much difficult to prepare as time-consuming. For understanding and ease of preparation, it is best to break the dish down to basic elements, which include the poultry, chiles and vegetables, spices and seeds, fruits and nuts, thickeners, sauce, chocolate, and the garnish.

Mole poblano can be made with either turkey or chicken, with turkey being the most traditional. Turkey, browned and roasted or boiled, is the best choice when serving a crowd, but requires more

¼ cup almonds

2 tablespoons peanuts

½ sliced plantain (optional)

THE THICKENERS:

½ corn tortilla

½ slice bread

2 tablespoons cooking oil or lard

THE SAUCE:

3¾ cups broth

2 tablespoons lard

1½ ounces Mexican chocolate

1½ tablespoons sugar or to taste

1½ teaspoons salt or to taste

THE CHICKEN & ASSEMBLY:

1 tablespoon sesame seeds

6 boneless, skinless chicken breasts

12 very thin slices onion

preparation because of its size and produces less consistent portions—one reason why many restaurants now serve this dish with chicken breasts. If chicken breasts are preferred, they can either be browned and then boiled with other seasonings until tender, which produces the broth used in the sauce, or boneless, skinless breasts can be poached just prior to serving. The latter method is easiest and best because there is less chance that the breasts will be overcooked and dry. In any case, it is the sauce not the meat that is the star of this dish.

The chiles used are a combination of *anchos*, *mulatos*, and *pasillas*, and quite often *chipotles*. The *anchos* provide the sweetness of dried fruit, such as figs and dates; the *mulatos* add another level of sweetness plus definite overtones of chocolate; the *pasillas* contribute more heat than the *anchos* and *mulatos* with less sweetness, but with a depth of flavor that has overtones of chocolate and tobacco; the *chipotles*, which are used in moderation, give a burst of smoky heat. As a first step in creating your own favorite combination, you might consider rehydrating and puréeing a sample of each of these chiles. This has been done by Mexican cooks since the invention of the first *mole*, and is one reason there are so many versions. Some cooks simply toast the chiles before rehydrating them, but most fry them in lard or cooking oil to enhance their flavor.

In Mexico, chiles are traditionally ground in stone mills after being rehydrated, which creates a very smooth texture. Most home recipes call for chiles to be blended with some broth and then strained. This works well but adds more liquid to the paste than the stone-ground method. I have found that simply processing the rehydrated chiles through the fine blade of a good food mill produces a very smooth, pure paste with little effort and mess, so the following recipe uses that method.

In addition to the chiles, most *moles* include tomatoes, onion, garlic, and sometimes *tomatillos* as well. These items are usually fried, except for the tomatoes, which are best broiled (on a *comal* or under a broiler) until slightly charred and some of the juices have caramelized.

Spices and seeds used in the dish include cloves, cinnamon, coriander seeds, chile seeds, sesame seeds, aniseed, sugar, black pepper, salt, and occasionally pumpkin seeds. These items, except for the sugar, pepper, and salt, are usually toasted on a *comal* to bring out their flavors.

Fruits and nuts incorporated include raisins, almonds, and sometimes peanuts and plantain. They are usually toasted or fried before being added to the other ingredients.

Thickeners include corn tortillas, bread, and sometimes powdered cookies. The tortillas and bread are usually fried in oil until golden brown.

The chocolate, a Mexican chocolate often made with almonds and cinnamon, is frequently added toward the end of the cooking process.

The traditional garnish for *Mole poblano* is sesame seeds, toasted to a rich golden brown, and thinly sliced raw onion rings.

In the following recipe, I have tried to make the steps as easy and logical to follow as possible. Nevertheless, it is much better to prepare the sauce in advance, not only because you will be less tired when the meal is served, but because a superior result is achieved if the flavors are given time to develop. ■

THE CHILES:

Remove the stems and as many seeds as possible from the chiles, reserving 1 tablespoon of the seeds. Heat the oil or lard over medium heat, then fry the chiles in 2 batches, except for the *chipotle*, until they begin to puff up. Remove the chiles to a strainer to drain, then put them in a pot, cover them with water, bring to a bare simmer, and allow them to cook, covered, for 20 minutes. Drain the chiles and allow them to cool enough to handle. In 3 or 4 batches, put the chiles through the fine blade of a food mill, grinding until as much of the pulp as possible has passed through the blade. (It helps to clean the blade after each batch.) Reserve the chile pulp.

THE VEGETABLES:

Broil the tomato 2 to 3 inches from the heat until it is charred and soft, about 20 minutes, then place it in a blender. Fry the onions, garlic, and *tomatillos*, if using, in the oil or lard over moderately low heat until the onions are golden brown, then add to the blender.

THE SPICES & SEEDS:

Heat an ungreased small skillet over medium heat, add the cloves, cinnamon, coriander seeds, reserved chile seeds, sesame seeds, aniseed, black pepper, and pumpkin seeds, if using, until the sesame seeds begin to turn golden brown, removing the cinnamon if it begins to scorch. Place the toasted ingredients in a coffee or spice grinder, grind to a powder, and add to the blender.

THE FRUITS & NUTS:

Heat the oil or lard in a small skillet over medium heat, and fry the raisins, almonds, peanuts, and plantain, if using, until the almonds begin to turn golden brown. Drain the mixture and add to the blender.

THE THICKENERS:

Heat the oil or lard in a small skillet and fry the tortilla and bread until the tortilla begins to turn golden but not crisp and the bread is golden brown. Cool the tortilla and bread, tear them into small pieces, and add to the blender.

THE SAUCE:

Blend the vegetables, spices and seeds, fruits and nuts, and thickeners thoroughly, adding just enough broth to allow the blender to work properly. Put the mixture through the fine blade of a food mill and reserve.

Heat the lard in a medium-sized heavy pot over medium-high heat, add the reserved chile paste, turn the heat to medium, and cook, stirring almost constantly, until the paste is quite thick, about 5 minutes. Add the reserved blended and strained purée and continue cooking about 2 minutes. Gradually stir in the broth, chocolate, sugar, and salt, bring to a boil, then cook, uncovered, at a bare simmer, stirring often, until the sauce begins to release its oil, causing a glossy sheen to appear on top.

THE CHICKEN & ASSEMBLY:

Toast the sesame seeds in an ungreased skillet until they turn golden brown, and reserve. Poach the chicken breasts in water to cover until just cooked through. Place a breast in the center of each plate and cover liberally with the sauce. Sprinkle some toasted sesame seeds over each plate and garnish with the onion slices. *Moles* are traditionally served only with hot corn tortillas, but white rice makes a nice addition. Serves 4.

	JIM PEYTON'S NEWER RECIPE	SANTA CLARA	SANTA MONICA	SANTA TERESA
CHILES	10 Mulato 2 Ancho 3 Pasilla 1 canned Chipotle ½ cup cooking oil or lard	1 kilo, about 67 165 grams, about 11 125 grams, about 14 10 grams, about 5 —	125 grams, about 8 25 grams, about 2 — — —	1 kilo, about 67 125 grams, about 8 100 grams, about 11 14 grams, about 7
VEGETABLES	1 tomato ½ cup chopped onion 3 cloves garlic ½ tablespoon cooking oil or lard	— 1 head, roasted —	— 1 small 5 cloves, roasted	— 1 head, roasted
SPICES & SEEDS	3 whole cloves ½ stick cinnamon ½ teaspoon coriander seeds 1 tablespoon chile seeds ½ tablespoon sesame seeds ½ teaspoon anis seed ½ teaspoon black pepper	pinch of ground 50 grams 1 tablespoon ? cup 1 ? tablespoon 1 tablespoon sugar to taste	3 teaspoons ground 1 stick 1 tablespoon 2 tablespoons 2 teaspoons 1 tablespoon	25 grams 50 grams 1½ tablespoons ½ cup 1½ tablespoons 25 grams
FRUITS & NUTS	½ scant cup raisins ½ scant cup almonds 1 tablespoon cooking oil or lard	500 grams 500 grams —	55 grams — —	50 grams — —
THICKENERS	½ corn tortilla ½ slice bread 2 tablespoons cooking oil or lard	1 3 slices fried —	— 2 slices fried —	— 3½ tablespoons powdered cookies —
BROTH	3½ cups	3½ cups		
LARD	2 tablespoons	2 tablespoons		
FINAL FLAVORING & GARNISH	1½ ounces Mexican chocolate 1½ tablespoons sugar, or to taste 1½ teaspoons salt, or to taste 1 tablespoon sesame seeds 12 very thin slices onion	2 tablespoons		
CHICKEN	6 boneless, skinless breasts			

❊ Oaxacan Black Mole

Cooking oil

¼ pound whole almonds

2 French-style dinner rolls, cut into strips 1 inch wide

1 large plantain (about 1 foot long), peeled and sliced in 1-inch pieces

¼ pound sesame seeds

1 onion, chopped

12 cloves garlic, peeled

¼ pound raisins

2 tablespoons dried thyme

3–3½ tablespoons loosely packed broken cinnamon sticks

4½ pounds tomatoes, chopped

3 heaping tablespoons sugar

1½ teaspoons salt

½ pound pasilla chiles, stems, veins, and seeds removed but seeds reserved

3½ ounces chilhuacle chiles, stems, veins, and seeds removed but seeds reserved

2½- to 3-pound chicken, cut into serving pieces, or an equal amount of bone-in breast

■ When I wrote *La cocina de la frontera* I included a recipe for *mole negro* that I had learned on a trip to Oaxaca from Carmen Solís, one of the area's finest cooks. I also wanted to include a recipe for this dish in this book as it is my favorite. I tried several recipes, but did not find one I liked as much as Carmen's, so I decided to include it in this book as well.

Mole negro includes one of the most difficult to find chiles, even in Mexico, the chile *chilhuacle*. However, I have recently found this chile at a local market, so perhaps it will be more easily available in the future. If you cannot find the *chilhuacles* you can use additional *pasillas*. ■

Heat a skillet over medium heat, add a little oil, and fry the almonds until just browned. Remove the almonds to drain.

Add a little more oil and fry the bread pieces until they are well browned but not burned; then remove them to drain.

Fry the plantain until well browned, then remove to drain.

In a small saucepan, fry the sesame seeds in just enough oil to coat them until just browned and add the onion and garlic. Continue to cook until the onion is soft but not burned; then add the raisins, thyme, and cinnamon sticks and fry 1 or 2 more minutes.

Place the fried almonds, bread, and plantain in a bowl with the sesame seed mixture and reserve.

Place the tomatoes in a large pot over medium heat, bring to a boil, and simmer for 5 minutes. Add 3 heaping tablespoons sugar and the salt and continue to cook until the tomatoes begin to turn into a sauce but are still watery, 10 to 15 minutes. Blend and strain the mixture.

Toast the chiles. This is the most difficult part of the recipe since the chiles must be toasted much more than in most recipes but not completely burned. Heat a *comal* or iron griddle over medium heat and toast the chiles until they are blackened but not too burned. The blackening process is important to both the color and taste of the sauce. When I asked Carmen why her sauce was not quite as black as other sauces, she told me the commercial pastes overburn the chiles and make up for the bitter taste by adding too much sugar. I found her method results in a much more subtle taste.

I suggest you experiment with 1 chile at a time until you get the feel of it. The chiles are properly done when they become very dry and brittle and are easily crumbled. The problem is that if you wait for this stage to occur, they may be too burned. The reason for this is that after you remove the chiles from the *comal*, they continue to cook. So begin by toasting 1 chile until it is just blackened, then remove it from the heat. Wait 1 or 2 minutes and if it is not quite brittle and easy to crumble, cook the next one a while longer. You will soon get the timing down.

Toast the reserved chile seeds (there should be about 1 cup) on the *comal* or griddle until they are a blackish brown.

At this point most Oaxaca cooks take the sesame seed-spice mixture to one of the many mills in the central markets and have them ground with the chiles and finally with the tomato mixture, which is added during the process to "lubricate" the grinding machinery. Since you undoubtedly will not have access to this equipment, you must try to imitate the fine grind. Use a blender, adding just a little of the sesame mixture with just enough of the tomato mixture to allow the blades to operate. As the mixture is puréed, put it through a food mill using the finest blade that will work. The process is tedious and messy, but it is necessary to obtain a properly smooth sauce. Reserve any tomato sauce not blended into the mixture.

1 onion, quartered

12 cloves garlic, peeled

⅓ cup lard or cooking oil

Additional sugar

¼ pound Mexican chocolate, or substitute semisweet chocolate

Meanwhile, simmer the chicken with the onion and garlic for about 20 minutes. Remove the chicken and strain and reserve the broth, discarding the garlic and onion.

Cook the puréed spice and chile mixture in ⅓ cup lard or cooking oil. At this point you will need to add additional sugar to taste. Add the sugar, little by little, until the taste is no longer bitter but not too sweet. Continue cooking the paste until it releases its fat and stops sticking to the pan, about 15 minutes.

Add the reserved tomatoes with any tomato juice that has accumulated, and cook for 5 minutes. Then add the chocolate and stir until well mixed.

Taste the sauce again and add more sugar, if necessary; then add enough of the broth in which the chicken was cooked to make about 3 cups of sauce. It should be thick enough to stick to a spoon but not too thick.

Cook the sauce until the fat begins to render, about 5 minutes; then add the cooked chicken and heat through.

You can serve the chicken immediately with Oaxaca-style white rice at the end of the Chicken Stew recipe (p. 241). Better yet, leave the chicken in the sauce and refrigerate overnight, to absorb the flavors, then reheat and serve. Serves 4.

CHICKEN STEW

■ Chicken stew? Doesn't sound like much? It didn't to me either. But my interest was somewhat pricked when Carmen Solís, with whom I was studying cooking in Oaxaca, informed me that it is one of the seven famous *moles*. What a surprise as I watched the dish begin to unfold and could see something special was happening.

Estofado de pollo is one of those dishes that appeals to nearly everyone. The heat level, which is not intense in the first place, is easily adjusted. It is also very easy to prepare and can be made a day or two in advance; in fact, it's much better that way.

The whole, cut-up chicken is cooked with the stew. If you are careful, there will be lots of sauce left over. Simply refrigerate it, then use it to simmer boneless, skinless chicken breast for 5 minutes or so, or until it is done, and you will have several other meals in no more time than that. ■

Heat 2½ tablespoons lard or olive oil in a large pot over medium heat. Add the onions and garlic and cook until just soft but not browned. Then add the tomatoes.

Chop half the olives and raisins (reserving the remaining portions), add them to the pot, and continue to cook for 2 minutes. Add the sugar, thyme, cinnamon sticks, and salt and cook 5 minutes.

Meanwhile, boil the almonds for 5 to 10 minutes, allow them to cool, and then remove the skins.

Place the cooked sauce mixture and half the almonds in a blender and blend for 1 minute. You may have to do this in 2 batches.

Sprinkle the chicken pieces with garlic salt; then fry them in the remaining 2½ tablespoons lard or olive oil over medium to medium-high heat in a large pot or Dutch oven until well browned.

5 tablespoons lard or olive oil

2 small onions, chopped

10 small cloves garlic, peeled and chopped

3¼ pounds tomatoes, chopped

1 8- to 10-ounce jar pitted green olives

¼ pound raisins

2 tablespoons sugar

1½ tablespoons dried thyme

2–2½ tablespoons loosely packed, broken cinnamon sticks

Salt to taste

¼ pound whole almonds

2½–3 pounds chicken, cut into serving pieces, with ⅔ skins removed

Garlic salt

½ of 7-ounce can of pickled serrano chiles (105 grams net weight)

¼ cup parsley, minced

Strain the blended sauce into the pot with the chicken. Add the reserved whole olives and raisins, the almonds, the ½ can of chiles with its juice, and the parsley to the pot and simmer, covered, for 20 minutes.

Serve with white Oaxaca-style rice, which is made as follows: fry 1½ cups long grain rice in 2 tablespoons of oil for 3 minutes over medium heat. Add ¼ cup minced onion and 1 clove minced garlic and continue cooking 1 minute. Add 3 cups water and 1 teaspoon salt, bring the water to a boil, turn the heat to low, and steam the rice, covered, for 20 minutes. Serves 4 with lots of sauce left over, which can be used on poached chicken breasts.

 ## BATTERED SHRIMP

THE BATTER:

¾ cup flour

¼ teaspoon salt

½ teaspoon chile powder

¾ cup plus 1 tablespoon beer

THE SHRIMP:

**1 pound medium shrimp
(26–28 per pound)**

Oil for deep-frying

■ This is a traditional Mexican shrimp dish with strong Spanish roots. It is good served with your favorite hot sauce and relishes. ■

Mix the batter until smooth and refrigerate for at least 1 hour.

Meanwhile, shell the shrimp but leave the last section of the tail intact. Devein the shrimp and dry them thoroughly. Then heat the oil to 345 to 350 degrees. When you are ready to cook the shrimp, using kitchen tongs, dip 1 of the shrimp in the batter, then put it into the oil, holding it so it is not touching the bottom or sides of the fryer for a few seconds to keep it from sticking. Release the shrimp and prepare the rest of them in the same way. Serves 4.

❋ SHRIMP WITH GARLIC SAUCE

■ This dish is a favorite in traditional Mexican cooking, especially along seacoasts. One of the best renditions of this classic Mexican dish I have tried, this version is quite easy to prepare. ■

To make the sauce, place the oil and garlic in a small saucepan over very low heat. Cook the garlic, keeping the heat very low, until it just begins to brown, then remove the pan from the heat. When the oil has cooled, pour it and the garlic into a blender and blend, beginning at low speed and gradually increasing to high speed for about 30 seconds. Pour the oil and garlic back into the saucepan, add the remaining ingredients, and reserve. Just before serving, heat the contents of the pan over medium heat until the contents just begin to simmer, then remove from the heat.

Shell the shrimp, but leave the last section of the tail intact. Devein the shrimp, dry thoroughly, and put them into a plastic bag. Mix together the flour, salt, and pepper, add it to the shrimp in the bag, and shake to coat thoroughly. Remove the shrimp, shaking them to remove excess flour.

Heat a skillet over medium-high heat and add ½ the oil. Allow the oil to heat for a few seconds; it should be very hot but not quite smoking. Add ½ the shrimp to the oil and sauté them until they are crisp and golden brown on both sides, then remove them to drain on paper towels. Heat the remaining oil and cook the rest of the shrimp in the same fashion.

To serve, place some lettuce leaves on each of 4 serving plates, place the shrimp on top of them, then spoon the hot garlic sauce over them. Either *Ancho* Chile Rice (p. 109) or Roasted *Ancho* Potatoes (p. 112) go very well with this dish. Serves 4.

THE GARLIC SAUCE:

½ cup olive oil

10 cloves garlic, chopped

2 tablespoons butter

1 tablespoon minced parsley

½ teaspoon ground ancho chile

½ teaspoon dried thyme

½ teaspoon dried marjoram

1 tablespoon lime juice

Salt and pepper to taste

THE SHRIMP:

1¼ pounds very large shrimp (12 to the pound)

⅓ cup flour

¼ teaspoon salt

¼ teaspoon black pepper

⅔ cup olive oil

Several soft lettuce leaves

MARINATED FISH

THE FISH:

4 filets fish, 6–8 ounces each

Salt and pepper to taste

2 tablespoons olive oil

THE ESCABECHE:

4 jalapeño chiles, broiled whole

¾ cup olive oil

1 cup sliced onions

¾ cup carrots, julienned

2 jalapeño chiles, stemmed, seeded, and cut into thin slices

¾ cup very thinly sliced green beans

1 cup red or yellow bell pepper, cut into thin strips

4 cloves roasted garlic

½ teaspoon dried oregano

¼ teaspoon white cumin seed

½ teaspoon coarsely ground black pepper

1 large or 2 small sticks cinnamon

4 whole cloves

2 bay leaves

⅔ cup orange juice

¼ cup lime juice

¼ cup rice wine vinegar

■ *Escabeche* literally means "pickled," and the preparation of dishes *en escabeche* resembles that process to varying degrees. In the case of chiles and other vegetables *en escabeche*, the ingredients are actually pickled in the sense that they are at least partially preserved by the process. However, fish and poultry *en escabeche* are normally consumed the day of or day after preparation. They are usually sautéed, then allowed to cool in a mixture of oil, vinegar, herbs, and spices. The following version of *Pescado en escabeche* can be made with any firm filet of fish. When testing the recipe, I used catfish with fine results. Since freshness is of the utmost importance to this dish, catfish may be a good choice because of its availability and often superior freshness in inland areas due to being farmed and shipped under better conditions than other seafood. This dish is excellent only if the fish is perfectly fresh—with absolutely no odor. In fact, the rule I follow is if fish is not fresh enough to use for sushi, it is not fresh enough to use for anything. *Pescado en escabeche* serves well as a summer luncheon or supper dish, or as a first course, and can be prepared and refrigerated for 2 to 3 days before serving. ■

Salt and pepper the fish and sauté it in the olive oil in a skillet over medium heat until just cooked through, and reserve.

Meanwhile prepare the *escabeche*.

Broil the 4 *jalapeño* chiles a few inches from your broiler until they are charred and soft, about 15 minutes. Remove them and put them in a plastic bag to "sweat" for 15 minutes, then peel, slice, and reserve them.

Heat the olive oil over medium heat until a drop of water just sputters, add the onions, carrots, sliced *jalapeños*, green beans, bell pepper, and garlic, and simmer for 3 minutes. Then add the remaining ingredients, bring to a simmer, and cook for 10 minutes. When the *escabeche* is done, pour it over the cooked fish filets and allow them to cool to room temperature. To serve, drain the filets and place them on each of 4 serving plates. Drain and spoon the cooked vegetables over the fish. This dish is also excellent if refrigerated overnight, then brought to room temperature. Serves 4.

¾ **cup sliced mushrooms**

1½ **tablespoons minced fresh parsley**

1½ **tablespoons minced fresh cilantro**

¾ **teaspoon salt**

PAPADZULES

THE TOMATO SAUCE & BROTH:

1 pound tomatoes

2 habanero chiles

7–10 epazote leaves

¼ teaspoon salt

2¼ cups water

½ tablespoon olive oil

½ cup onions, sliced

1 tablespoon olive oil

¼ teaspoon salt

THE PUMPKIN SAUCE & FINAL ASSEMBLY:

7 ounces pumpkin seeds (the narrow green ones not the fat white ones), about 1½ cups plus 2 tablespoons, or 200 grams

1–1¼ cups reserved broth

Salt to taste

8 corn tortillas

4 hard-boiled eggs, peeled, finely chopped, and salted to taste

¼ cup pumpkin seed oil

■ *Papadzules* are a specialty of the Yucatán resembling either enchiladas or soft tacos but unique. They consist of corn tortillas wrapped around a filling of chopped hard-boiled eggs and topped with a sauce made from ground squash seeds, another sauce of tomato, and garnished with some of the fragrant, dark green oil that is squeezed from the sauce (or, much easier, purchased in a supermarket). I attempted several times to make this dish with little success until I tried Diana Kennedy's suggestion of grinding the pumpkin seeds in a spice grinder rather than in a blender or food processor. The result was sublime. For the recipe to be successful, timing is important, especially since it is prepared from hot ingredients and served immediately rather than baked in the oven, as are some similar dishes.

Note that some recipes call for broiling the tomatoes rather than boiling them. You can certainly use this method, but I think the tomatoes then overpower the other subtle tastes. Also, traditionally the pumpkin oil for the garnish is extracted from the ground seeds after they are sprinkled with a little of the broth by twisting the resulting paste in a porous piece of cloth. To me, this has always been the most difficult part of the recipe because, to a large extent, the amount of liquid added and temperature determine the success of the operation. As a result, the garnish of oil is often left off, which is a shame since it is very important to the overall success of the dish. Today, however, pumpkin seed oil is available in grocery and specialty food stores, which makes the dish quite easy to prepare. ■

Place the tomatoes, chiles, *epazote*, ¼ teaspoon salt, and water in a saucepan, bring to a boil, turn down the heat, and simmer for 5 minutes. Remove the tomatoes to a bowl, strain, and reserve the broth and the 2 chiles but discard the *epazote*. When the tomatoes have cooled, cut them into 4 pieces and scrape out the seeds, but otherwise leave them intact in the bowl. Put the ½ tablespoon olive oil and onions in a skillet over medium heat and cook until the onions are just beginning to turn golden. You want just enough caramelization to add a little flavor but not so much it becomes overpowering. Then place the onions in a food mill fitted with a coarse blade. Add the tomatoes and any juice that has accumulated in the bowl, and strain the mixture.

Put the 1 tablespoon olive oil in a saucepan over medium heat, add the strained tomato mixture, 2 reserved chiles that were cooked with the broth, and ¼ teaspoon salt. Simmer the sauce until it thickens, about 5 to 10 minutes. Then discard the chiles and turn the heat to very low while you make the pumpkin sauce.

Place the pumpkin seeds in a large skillet over medium-low heat. Cook the seeds until most of them have popped, shaking the pan from time to time. It is important that the seeds do not turn brown since this will affect the color of the sauce. Place the seeds in a spice or coffee grinder, and process them until they are ground into a powder. You will probably have to do this in several batches. Place the ground seeds in the top of a double boiler, small bowl, or saucepan set over but not quite in simmering water. Meanwhile, heat the reserved broth to about 180 degrees, but do not let it boil. Stir the broth into the pumpkin seeds until a medium-thick paste is formed, and add salt if you wish.

Usually the tortillas are dipped into this sauce, which heats and coats them, and then they are wrapped around the chopped egg. However, this is quite messy, and the tortillas have a tendency to fall apart, causing consternation just before you are ready to serve the meal. Instead, heat the tortillas, either by toasting them on an ungreased griddle or wrapping them in a towel and microwaving them for 30 to 45 seconds. Then spoon some of the pumpkin sauce onto either side of each tortilla, place some of the egg just off center, then roll as you would for enchiladas, making 2 per person.

Meanwhile, bring the reserved tomato sauce to a boil, and have the pumpkin seed oil handy. Once the *Papadzules* have been rolled, spoon some more of the pumpkin sauce over them so that they are well covered. Then spoon some of the tomato sauce over the center of the *Papadzules*, enough to cover the middle one-third to one-half. Dribble some of the pumpkin seed oil onto the portions that are not covered by tomato sauce and serve. Serves 4.

MEXICAN "TRILOBITE" BREADS

1 cup warm water (between 90 and 100 degrees)

2 teaspoons sugar

2¼ teaspoons dried yeast

3 cups all-purpose, unbleached flour

½ tablespoon salt

2½ tablespoons cooking oil

■ Mexican "Trilobite" Breads, or *teleras,* are the rolls most often used in Mexico to make *tortas* or Mexico's very special version of the sandwich. They are a cross between French bread and American sandwich bread in that they have more body and crust than the American variety but are still soft enough to use for sandwiches without being difficult to eat. They are particularly interesting because of their shape, which is like a rounded football with three ridges on the top, resembling a trilobite. ■

Mix together ½ cup warm water, the sugar, and yeast, and allow to proof for 5 minutes.

Place the flour and salt in a bowl and mix well. (These breads can easily be made in a food processor fitted with a plastic blade.) Stir the remaining ½ cup water and cooking oil into the yeast mixture, and gradually add it to the flour and salt. Form into a dough, knead for 5 minutes by hand or for 45 seconds in the food processor, place it in a lightly greased bowl, cover with plastic wrap or a towel, and allow it to rise for between 1¼ and 1½ hours, or until it stops rising vigorously.

Deflate the dough and cut it into pieces about 4½ ounces each. There should be about 5 pieces. Allow the divided dough to rest for 10 minutes. Then flatten each piece of dough into the shape of a rounded football about 5 inches long, 3⅓ inches wide, and about ½ inch thick. Take a heavy cylindrical object between ¼ and ½ inch in diameter (I use a knife honer), and place it lengthwise on the top of a roll about halfway between the edge and the center. Press it down as far as it will go without going through the dough. Place on the other side of the roll, again about halfway between the edge and center, and press down again. The result will be 3 ridges and 2 indentations along the length of the roll. Place the rolls on a lightly greased baking sheet, cover them with a light, damp towel, and allow them to rise for about 1 hour. Meanwhile, preheat your oven to 425 degrees.

When the rolls have risen, place them in the oven and immediately turn the heat down to 400 degrees. Bake the rolls until they are brown and reach an internal temperature of between 190 and 205 degrees, about 15 minutes. Makes 5 rolls.

CORN BREAD

THE BATTER:

4 eggs

4 cups fresh corn kernels (cut from about 4 ears)

1 stick melted butter

½ cup sugar

½ cup plus 2 tablespoons flour

1 teaspoon baking powder

½ teaspoon salt

PREPARATION:

1 stick butter, melted

4 cups corn oil

■ This specialty from the state of Nuevo León is more like a pancake than bread. In the village of Santiago, just south of Monterrey, the streets are lined with food stalls that serve this specialty. The cooks have specially made iron skillets set on gas burners in which they place butter and oil, then batter, and allow the mixture to cook, covered, for about 10 minutes. Then the bread is turned and cooked again until it is golden brown on both sides and served with a dollop of honey. This dish is not for people who wish to limit fat and calories in their diets but makes a wonderful occasional snack or breakfast food.

In Mexico, this dish is prepared with high-starch field corn, and as with tamales made of fresh corn it is much more prone to solidify than is the sweet corn available in our markets. As a result, I have added some flour to the recipe, which produces a satisfactory, although not identical, result.

You will need a heavy, deep skillet with a firmly fitting top, preferably iron or a well-made Teflon pan. Also, because it takes about 20 minutes to make one bread it is preferable to make as many at the same time as you can. ■

To prepare the batter, place all the ingredients in a blender and blend at high speed until completely puréed, about 45 seconds.

Mix the melted butter and corn oil. Heat a 5- to 6-inch heavy skillet over just under medium heat, and add about 1½ tablespoons of the butter-oil mixture. When the fat is hot and the foam has subsided, pour in about 1 cup of the batter. Cover the pot and cook until the bottom is a crisp golden brown, about 10 minutes. Invert the partially solidified bread onto a plate, heat another 1½ tablespoons of the butter-oil mixture, then, using a spatula, replace the bread with the unbrowned side down. Cook again, covered, until the bottom is golden brown, and the bread is fairly firm, about 10 minutes. Place the bread in a warm oven, and cook the remaining batter in the same way. Serve the breads with honey. Serves 4.

Chiles Rellenos

■ This dish is not battered and fried as are most chiles rellenos served in the United States. It was undoubtedly from one like this that the incomparable *Chiles en nogada* was developed. However, since it is not fried or served with a rich sauce of cream and cheese it is a very light version of what was to become the most famous dish in traditional Mexican cooking after *Mole poblano*. Because it can be successfully prepared a day or two in advance and assembled at the last minute using a microwave oven, it is perfect for entertaining. ■

To make the filling, heat a skillet over medium heat, add the oil and fry the onions until they are soft but not browned. Then add the garlic and cook 1 minute. Add the ground meat and fry it, stirring continuously, until it is browned and well broken up.

Chop the tomatoes finely and add them to the pan with ¼ cup of the juice from the can, then add the remaining ingredients. Cook, stirring frequently, until most of the juice has either evaporated or thickened, about 10 minutes. Stuff the chiles with the filling and reserve.

To make the sauce, sauté the onions in a large saucepan over medium heat until they are soft but not brown. Add the remaining ingredients, except the squash blossoms or zucchinis, and simmer the sauce until it has thickened, lowering the heat as necessary, about 30 minutes.

ASSEMBLY:

Place a stuffed chile on each plate. Heat the completed dish in a 350-degree oven for about 5 to 10 minutes, or microwave each plate for about 45 seconds. Meanwhile, steam the squash blossoms or zucchini until just tender, about 1½ minutes for the blossoms and 2 minutes for the zucchini. Spoon some of the sauce over and around the chiles. Then place some of the squash blossoms or squash around the chiles and serve. Serves 4.

THE FILLING:

2 tablespoons canola oil

½ cup chopped onion

2 cloves garlic, minced

¾ pound lean (85 percent lean) ground beef

1 14½-ounce can unsalted whole tomatoes

½ cup coarsely chopped pecan bits (not the finely minced ones)

⅓ cup minced, dried apricot

⅓ cup minced, dried pears

⅓ cup minced, dried apples

¼ cup raisins

1 teaspoon dried thyme

½ teaspoon dried marjoram

½ teaspoon dried sage

1 teaspoon salt

4 large poblano chiles, roasted, skinned, and seeded but otherwise left whole

THE SAUCE & GARNISH:

3 tablespoons olive oil

½ cup minced onions

8 medium-sized tomatoes, peeled, seeded, and finely chopped

1½ tablespoons juice from a can or jar of pickled jalapeños

¾ teaspoon dried thyme

Salt and pepper to taste

18 whole squash blossoms, or 3 zucchinis, thinly sliced

❈ EGGS MOTUL STYLE

THE TOMATO SAUCE & BROTH:

1 pound tomatoes

¼ teaspoon salt

2¼ cups water

½ tablespoon olive oil

½ cup onions, finely chopped

1 tablespoon olive oil

2 habanero chiles, left whole

¼ teaspoon salt

THE BEANS:

2 cups black beans, cooked

**½ cup broth in which the beans
    were cooked**

3 tablespoons lard or olive oil

2 cloves garlic, minced

¾ teaspoon ground cumin

½ teaspoon salt

THE TORTILLAS:

Cooking oil

8 corn tortillas

THE EGGS & ASSEMBLY:

The fried tortillas

The refried beans

**About 6 tablespoons lard or
    butter**

■ This is the Yucatán's answer to the more common *huevos rancheros* served in other parts of Mexico. ■

Bring enough water to a boil to cover the tomatoes, put them in the water, turn down the heat, and simmer for 5 minutes, or until they are fairly soft. Place the cooked tomatoes in a bowl, and discard the water. When the tomatoes have cooled, cut them into 4 pieces and scrape out as many of the seeds as you can, but otherwise leave them intact in the bowl. Place the olive oil and onions in a skillet over medium heat and cook until the onions are *just* beginning to turn golden. You want just enough caramelization to add a little flavor but not so much that it becomes overpowering. Place the onions in a food mill fitted with a coarse, grating blade. Add the tomatoes and any juice that has accumulated in the bowl and strain the mixture.

Place the 1 tablespoon olive oil in a saucepan over medium heat, add the strained tomato mixture, the chiles, and ¼ teaspoon salt. Simmer the sauce until it thickens, about 10 to 25 minutes, depending on the water content of the tomatoes, then discard the chiles and reserve the sauce.

Place the beans and their cooking broth in a blender. Purée the beans, then strain them through the medium blade of a food mill. Heat the lard or oil in a skillet over medium heat, add the garlic, then the cumin and salt. Next add the beans, stirring constantly, until they thicken to the point where they are no longer runny but can still be easily spread. Cover the beans to keep them warm and reserve.

Put about ½ inch oil in a small skillet and heat over medium to medium-high heat until a drop of water immediately evaporates. Fry the tortillas on both sides until they are just beginning to stiffen; they should not be crisp. Drain the tortillas on paper towels and reserve.

Place 1 tortilla on each of 4 serving plates, and spread on a layer of beans.

Heat a skillet over medium heat, melt a little lard or butter, fry the plantain pieces until they are golden brown, and reserve. Add a little more lard or butter and fry the ham until it is warmed through but not brown, and reserve. Add a little more lard or butter and fry the eggs, 2 at a time, either sunny side up or over easy. When they are done, place each pair on the bean-covered tortillas. Spoon a little of the sauce over the eggs and sprinkle on some of the cheese. Top the eggs with the remaining tortillas. Spoon some more of the tomato sauce over the tortillas, then sprinkle on the reserved ham, the peas, and additional cheese. Serve immediately, garnished with the fried plantain. Serves 4.

1 or 2 plantains, sliced cross-wise on the diagonal into 8 pieces about ¼ inch wide

½ cup finely chopped ham

8 eggs

Tomato sauce

4 ounces grated queso fresco

⅓ cup frozen baby peas, simmered in water to cover until tender

✳ Chorizo, Avocado & Chipotle Sandwiches

1½ tablespoons cooking oil

4 teleras (p. 248), halved
    lengthwise, or substitute
    small French bread rolls

2 cups shredded iceberg lettuce

½ cup very thinly sliced onions

1½ tablespoons cooking oil

2 teaspoons white vinegar

¾ teaspoon sugar

½ tablespoon cooking oil

10 ounces chorizo

1½ tablespoons cooking oil

2 cups red potatoes, peeled and
    cut into ¼-inch pieces

Salt and pepper to taste

1 avocado, pitted, peeled, and
    cut into ⅛-inch slices

4 canned chipotle chiles, halved

■ These sandwiches, also called *Pambacitos*, are very similar to those prepared at the famous Café de Tacuba in Mexico City. When I am in the mood for a sandwich, these are usually my first choice. ■

Place the 1½ tablespoons oil in a skillet over medium to low heat, put in the halved rolls, cut side down, and cook them until the bottoms are brown and crusty (like croutons), then put them on serving plates, fried sides up.

Mix the lettuce and onions in a bowl and reserve. Whisk the 1½ tablespoons oil, vinegar, and sugar into a dressing and reserve. Place the ½ tablespoon oil in a skillet over medium heat, add the chorizo, and fry until it is just cooked through. Turn the heat to medium high, add the remaining 1½ tablespoons oil and the potatoes, and fry until they are brown and crusty. Add salt and pepper to taste.

Pour the oil and vinegar dressing into the lettuce and onions, toss well, then put some of it onto the bottom of each roll. Spoon equal portions of the fried potatoes and chorizo on top of the lettuce, top with sliced avocado and *chipotle* halves, and cover with the tops of the rolls. Cut the *Pambacitos* in half, if desired, and serve. Serves 4.

�֍ SHEPHERD'S OR "TOP" TACOS

■ These are tacos made from large, thin strips of marinated pork roasted on vertical spits in front of gas, electric, or charcoal fires. Usually a pineapple and onion are also placed on the skewer atop the meat. As the meat cooks, it is sliced off and rolled into small, hot corn tortillas and served with some onion and pineapple. As the meat is sliced, the remaining portion of the spit assumes the shape of a top, thus its second name. Because the meat can be up to a foot in diameter and several feet in height, and can take a number of days to cook and be used, this method may present a serious health hazard (since so much meat remains uncooked at a temperature ideal for bacteria growth). However, the method described below avoids this hazard and produces the best *Tacos al pastor* I have ever tried. ■

To make the marinade, combine all the marinade ingredients in a blender, and blend until the chiles are roughly chopped. Allow the chiles to absorb the liquid for 20 minutes, then blend again for 1 minute. Place the meat in a nonreactive bowl, cover with the marinade, and put in the refrigerator to marinate for 2 to 3 hours. After marinating, remove the meat and reserve ¼ cup of the marinade. Mix this with 1 tablespoon cooking oil, and use this mixture to baste the meat as it cooks.

To prepare the meat, start a fire of hardwood or hardwood charcoal, preferably in a barbecue with a cover or rotisserie attachment. When the fire has burned to grey coals, roast the meat 8 to 12 inches from the coals for about 50 minutes to 1 hour, or until it reaches an internal temperature of 145 to 150 degrees, basting at least every 10 minutes.

To serve, chop the meat into small pieces, place in a heated serving dish, and serve with hot corn tortillas, guacamole, and your favorite hot sauce. Serves 4 to 6.

THE MARINADE:

2 ancho chiles, stemmed, seeded, and torn into small pieces

2 cloves garlic

1 teaspoon dried oregano

⅓ cup orange juice

2½ tablespoons lime juice

½ teaspoon salt

¼ teaspoon ground black pepper

THE MEAT:

1¾ pound boneless pork loin roast in 1 piece (not 2 pieces tied together)

✳ CHILES IN WALNUT SAUCE

THE CHILES:

6 medium large to large poblano chiles

4 cups water

2 tablespoons salt

THE FILLING:

¾-pound lean, boneless pork loin, cut into ¾-inch pieces

3 ounces ham, chopped

2 tablespoons cooking oil

½ cup onion, finely chopped

2 cloves garlic, minced

14 ounces tomatoes, about 1 very large or 2 medium, broiled

½ cup peeled and finely chopped pear

⅓ cup peeled and finely chopped apple

¼ cup peeled and finely chopped plantain, or substitute banana

¼ cup raisins

⅓ cup blanched, slivered almonds

⅓ cup dry sherry

Scant ⅛ teaspoon powdered cloves

Scant ¼ teaspoon powdered cinnamon

■ Chiles in Walnut Sauce, or *Chiles en nogada*, is second in importance in Mexican cooking only to *Mole poblano*. This significant dish can also be served as an entrée. As was noted in the historical section this dish was invented in Puebla to honor Iturbide for his command of the Mexican army, which gained independence from Spain. It was designed to reflect the colors of the newly designed Mexican flag: green, white, and red. The green is represented by the chile, the white by the *nogada*, or walnut sauce, and the red by the garnish of pomegranate seeds.

Not only is this a unique and delicious dish, but except for peeling the nuts, which takes about 20 minutes, it is relatively easy to prepare. The preparation of the chiles and filling can be done several days in advance. The sauce is best prepared no more than 1 or 2 hours before serving. However, nuts should be peeled and left to soak the afternoon before. Because of this and the fact that *Chiles en nogada* is served at room temperature, when your guests arrive all you need to do is pour the sauce over the already stuffed chiles, add the garnish, and serve. One caveat is that this assumes that the dish is served without being *capeado*, or fried in an egg batter. The latter method is considered more traditional, but the fried batter *and* the cream and cheese sauce can be very rich together. However, this dish came from Puebla, where the baroque is celebrated, so I have also included directions for the fried version. ■

Roast and peel the chiles, leaving them as intact as possible. Make a slit along one side of each chile and carefully remove the seeds and as many of the veins as possible. Because it is possible for *poblano* chiles to be much hotter than is desireable for this dish, mix the salt and water together, pour it over the chiles, and allow them to soak for at least 4 hours or overnight, if necessary. Some cooks add a tablespoon or so of vinegar, which seems to help as well, but too much will create an acid taste. Drain and dry the chiles and reserve them. They can be prepared 1 to 2 days in advance.

To make the filling, place the pork in a pot, cover with water, bring to a boil, and simmer, uncovered, until the meat is tender, about 45 minutes, adding additional water as necessary. Allow the pork to cool slightly, then chop it finely with the ham. I use a food processor fitted with a steel blade, which makes this task quite easy. This meat must be very finely chopped for the filling to have a smooth texture.

Heat the oil in a skillet over medium heat, add the onion, and cook until the onion is soft but not browned. Add the garlic and cook about 1 minute more. Add the finely chopped pork and ham, and cook, stirring frequently, until it is heated through, about 5 minutes, but do not allow it to brown. Meanwhile, blend the broiled tomato, then strain it through the fine blade of a food mill. There should be about 1 cup of strained tomato. Add the strained tomato to the skillet and, stirring frequently, cook the mixture until it thickens, about 10 minutes. Add and stir in the remaining ingredients and cook, stirring often, for about another 10 minutes or until it thickens. The filling may be prepared 1 or 2 days in advance.

To make the nut sauce, place the walnuts in a bowl, cover them with boiling water, and allow them to soak for 5 minutes. Strain off the water, and when the nuts are cool enough to handle, peel them. This is very important because if the nuts are not peeled the sauce will not have either the proper color or consistency. Cover the peeled nuts with the milk, reserving about 1 cup, and allow them to soak, refrigerated, for 12 hours.

About ½ hour before preparing the sauce, cut the bread into small pieces, cover them with milk and allow them to soak. Drain the nuts and place them in the jar of a blender. Drain, squeeze, and add the bread, cream, sherry, sugar, and cinnamon, and blend until puréed. Add the cheese, salt, and between ¼ cup and ½ cup of the reserved milk, or enough so that the blender will operate properly, and purée the sauce. While it should not be too thick, it must be

¾ teaspoon salt or to taste

½ teaspoon sugar or to taste

THE NUT SAUCE (NOGADA):

1 cup, packaged, peeled large, intact walnut pieces

1 quart milk

1 slice white bread, crust removed

1 cup thick Mexican cream, crème fraîche, or ⅓ cup sour cream and ⅔ cup whipping cream

2 tablespoons dry sherry

1 tablespoon sugar

¼ teaspoon cinnamon

8 ounces queso fresco, about 1½ cups, or ½ cream cheese, ½ Monterey Jack cheese

¼ teaspoon salt or to taste

THE ASSEMBLY & GARNISH:

Pomegranate seeds

THE BATTER:

4 eggs

¼ teaspoon salt

1 tablespoon flour for the batter

Flour for coating the chiles

Cooking oil

thick enough so that when it is poured over the stuffed chiles it will not run off, about the consistency of a medium-thick milk shake. You should have about 3 cups of sauce.

Bring the chiles, filling, and sauce to room temperature. Stuff each chile with about ⅓ cup of the filling and place one in the center of 6 serving plates, with the slit side down. If you are serving the chiles without first frying them, spoon about ½ cup of the sauce over each stuffed chile, sprinkle some pomegranate seeds over each plate, and serve.

OPTIONAL INGREDIENTS FOR SERVING THE CHILES BATTER FRIED:

If you are serving the chiles *capeado,* separate the eggs, then beat the whites to between soft and hard moist peaks. Add the salt, beat the yolks and fold them into the whites. Sift the 1 tablespoon flour over the batter and fold it in. To fry the chiles, heat about ¾ inch oil in a skillet over medium to medium-high heat until a drop of water sputters and vaporizes almost immediately. In the meantime, dredge the stuffed chiles in flour and dust off the excess. When the oil is hot, dip 1 of the chiles into the egg batter, coating it thoroughly, then carefully lay it into the hot oil. Allow it to cook until it is golden brown on the bottom, then turn and brown again on the other side. Drain the cooked chile on paper towels. Prepare the remaining chiles in the same manner, allow them to cool to room temperature, add the sauce and garnish, and serve. (I have found that an excellent tool to use for handling these and other *chiles rellenos* is one of the small, thin stainless steel spatulas used for turning fish.) Serves 4 as an entrée, more as a snack.

# CORN TORTILLAS

■ I am convinced that the main thing standing between the average cook and truly authentic Mexican cooking is the corn tortilla, and unfortunately this is perhaps the most important element of the cuisine. The reason for this is that most of the corn tortillas sold in the United States are of very poor quality, and preparing corn tortillas from scratch—to have the dough the right consistency, the heat just right, and the necessary elasticity—is looked upon as an insurmountable chore. For the best quality, tortillas need to be consumed shortly after being made, so until the demand for them makes it feasible for *tortillerías* to become neighborhood fixtures we are left with the option of making them at home. Fortunately, technology has come to the rescue in the form of the Tortilla Chef, a waffle iron-like machine produced by Vitantonio. With this device and a little practice, making first-class corn tortillas is no longer a frustrating process.

Corn tortillas are best made with *masa* ground from *nixtamal*. Unfortunately, this dough has an even shorter shelf life than prepared tortillas, and the shortage of *tortillerías* makes its use unfeasible for most people. Fortunately, decent *masa* can be prepared using dried, ground corn sold as Masa Harina and Maseca. In fact, more *tortillerías* are using this method, although the dough does not have as much elasticity as dough made directly from *nixtamal*. However, this disadvantage can be circumvented by adding a little all-purpose flour to the dough, a common practice in Mexico. This not only produces a very good result but makes the dough more pliable and thus easier to shape and cook.

Although the Tortilla Chef is an admirable tool, the directions provided leave something to be desired. If your dough is dry enough that it is immediately released from the hot press when it is opened, it will undoubtedly suffer from "lacing," which means that it will be covered with a spider web of wrinkles and have a poor texture. However, the directions below provide a simple solution to this problem. ■

2 cups Masa Harina or Maseca

2 tablespoons all-purpose flour, sifted

1½ cups cold water

Place the corn flour in a bowl and stir in the sifted flour. Stir in the water, a little at a time, to make a moist dough, adding a little more water, if necessary. Work the dough just until smooth, then place it in a bowl, cover with plastic wrap, and allow it to rest for 1 hour. Break off a piece of the dough to test in the Tortilla Chef, then after you are sure it has the proper water content make the rest of the dough balls. For regular-sized 6-inch tortillas, break off and roll the dough into 12 balls. For small 3½- to 4-inch tortillas, break off and roll into 26 balls.

Open and preheat the Tortilla Chef for 7 to 10 minutes. Place a ball of dough slightly off center (toward the hinges of the press), and quickly press the dough ball into a tortilla with a firm motion, then immediately open the machine. If the dough is the right consistency, it will stick to the *top* of the press. If the dough releases immediately and remains on the bottom of the press, add a little more water to the dough and try again. Slide a thin plastic spatula between the dough and the press, beginning at the bottom. If the dough seems determined to stick, simply close the press for about 1 second, reopen it, and try again—you may have to repeat this process for the first couple of tortillas, but after this it should go more quickly. Ease the dough onto the bottom of the press, and allow it to bake for about 30 seconds. Then turn it and cook on the other side, at which point the tortilla should begin to puff. The tortilla is done when the dough is just cooked through. Place the completed tortilla in a tortilla warmer or wrap in a towel and prepare the remaining tortillas in the same way. Because the Tortilla Chef can accommodate only 1 tortilla at a time, the process can seem slow. But it can be speeded up considerably if you heat a large skillet or *comal* over medium heat and use it as an extra cooking surface. Makes 12 to 26 tortillas.

TROPICAL DREAM

■ This delicious recipe from the state of Quintana Roo, which is between Belize and the Yucatán, has a real tropical feel and is fairly easy to prepare. It was inspired by one in *Dulces mexicanos* by Rita Molinar. ■

Preheat the oven to 400 degrees. Slice the bananas lengthwise as for banana splits, and place the halves, rounded sides up, on a lightly greased baking sheet with the pineapple rings. Sprinkle the bananas and pineapple with lime juice, brush them with melted butter, then sprinkle on a coating of coconut. Place the sheet in the oven and bake until the coconut begins to turn golden brown, about 5 minutes.

Meanwhile, place the marmalade and rum in a small saucepan, bring to a boil, and simmer for about 2 minutes. When the coconut has browned, remove the baking sheet and place the fruit on serving plates as follows: put a pineapple ring in the middle of each plate, and place a split banana (2 pieces) around it. Brush the banana and pineapple with the marmalade sauce, put a scoop of the ice cream on each pineapple slice, and serve. Serves 4.

4 bananas

4 pineapple rings

Juice of 2 limes

2 tablespoons melted butter

¾ cup sweetened coconut, grated

1 cup marmalade, made from either oranges or a tropical fruit

¼ cup dark rum

4 scoops coconut ice cream

FLAN

½ cup sugar

4 eggs

2 396-gram cans sweetened condensed milk

10 ounces evaporated milk (this usually comes in 12-ounce cans so pour it into either a liquid measure or into an empty condensed milk can that is the right size)

Please note that when reading the amount of the contents on sweetened condensed milk it is given by weight, whereas the contents of evaporated milk is given by volume, which can create confusion. So, the can of sweetened condensed milk labeled as 396 grams, equivalent to 14 ounces, is actually 10 ounces by volume. The can of evaporated milk is 12 ounces by volume which is 2 ounces more than the amount specified in the recipe. I find it easiest to add the sweetened condensed milk first, then use the empty (10 ounce by volume) can to measure the evaporated milk.

■ In the introduction to *Your Mexican Kitchen*, by Natalie Scott, William Spratling, the American expatriate architect who began the artistic silver-working trade in Taxco, said in reference to Mexican cooking, "The elements are so simple and the results so vastly varied." Had he added the words *elegant* and *delicious*, he would have perfectly described the following recipe from Blanca de Loera of Guadalajara, which turns four humble ingredients into a thing of beauty.

In Mexico, flan is traditionally made in a mold with a top that locks in place. Because this piece of equipment may be difficult to find, I have provided instructions for making the recipe in an ordinary pie pan. With this method, the flan will not be quite as firm or the traditional shape, but the results will still be spectacular. It should be prepared at least a day before serving so it has ample opportunity to chill. ■

Preheat the oven to 375 degrees. The caramel topping for the flan can be made in either the flan mold or a small skillet. I use a skillet to prolong the life of the mold. Place the sugar in either the flan mold or a small skillet over medium heat until it has melted and turned a rich golden brown. Pour the melted sugar into either a flan mold or pie pan. Allow the sugar to cool for a few minutes.

Place the remaining ingredients in a blender, blend for 2 minutes, then pour the contents into the flan mold or pie pan. Cut a piece of aluminum foil to fit the top of the mold or pie pan, and place it directly on top of the liquid. Close the mold or wrap another sheet of foil over the pie pan to seal it. Next put the mold or pie pan in a large casserole dish and add warm water until it reaches about halfway up the mold or pan. Then place the flan in the oven and bake it for 1 hour if you are using a mold or 45 minutes if using a pan. Remove the flan and allow it to cool for about 1 to 1½ hours before refrigerating it. This waiting period is important as the flan will continue to cook. If it is refrigerated too soon, the process will be stopped and the flan's texture will not be as firm as it should be.

To unmold the flan, put the bottom of the mold or pan in warm water for about 10 seconds, run a sharp thin knife around the edge of the flan to loosen it, then invert it onto a plate. Serves 6 to 8.

 ## THREE "MILKS" CAKE

■ This is one of the richest and best desserts in any cuisine, but it is seldom found in cookbooks. It is the favorite cake of ladies at tea time, as well as a dessert for lunch or dinner. The following recipe came from Saltillo, but did not include the directions for the frostings. I experimented with the two other recipes I had and found that the one from *Mexico: The Beautiful Cookbook* by Susanna Palazuelos, with some modification, was closest to those I have tried in Mexico. ■

Preheat the oven to 325 degrees, and grease and flour the bottom but *not* the sides of a 9-inch springform pan.

All ingredients should be at room temperature.

Combine the flour, baking powder, and salt, then sift them. Beat together until thick ½ cup of the sugar and the egg yolks, about 2 minutes at medium speed. Then beat in the milk and vanilla and

THE CAKE:

2 cups cake flour

1 teaspoon baking powder

¼ teaspoon salt

¾ cup sugar

7 eggs, separated

½ cup milk

1 teaspoon vanilla

Heaping ¼ teaspoon cream of tartar

1 can evaporated milk

1 can condensed milk

1 can condensed cream, or substitute heavy cream

THE FROSTING:

3 egg whites

⅛ teaspoon cream of tartar

3 ounces water

¾ cup sugar

1 tablespoon lime juice

**Candied cherries or
    strawberries**

pour into a large bowl. Sift the flour mixture over the egg yolk mixture, but do not stir it in. Then beat the egg whites with the cream of tartar until soft peaks are formed. Continue beating and add the remaining ¼ cup sugar little by little until stiff peaks are formed. Then carefully fold the egg white mixture into the ingredients in the bowl. Combine the ingredients well without deflating the whites. Pour the batter into the greased, floured springform pan, and place it in the oven for 35 to 45 minutes, or until a cake tester or skewer comes out clear.

While the cake is baking, blend the two milks and the cream. When the cake is done, take it out of the oven, allow it to cool a few minutes, remove it from the pan, and slice it into 2 layers. Place the bottom layer into a large, flat-bottomed pan and slowly pour half the milk-cream mixture over it. With a fork or sharp knife, perforate the slightly browned top, place it in another flat-bottomed pan, and pour the remaining mixture over it. Allow the cake to soak up the liquid for at least 30 minutes, basting it from time to time.

To make the frosting, mix the egg whites with the cream of tartar and beat to soft peaks. Place the water, sugar, and lime juice in a small saucepan, bring to a boil over medium to medium-high heat, cover, and continue boiling for 1 minute. Gradually pour the sugar mixture into the beaten egg whites, beating constantly. Place the bowl over a pot of simmering water and continue beating until the frosting is thick and glossy. Allow it to cool.

When the cake has absorbed as much of the milk-cream mixture as possible, place the top layer on to the bottom layer, frost the cake, garnish with the fruit, and refrigerate. Makes 1 cake.

ROYAL EGGS

■ This historical dessert is a fine example of the rich, baroque confectionary so typical of the convents during Mexico's early days. It is also very easy to prepare and illustrates the Mexicans' genius for creating something rich and delicious from just a few ingredients. Although by today's standards it is frighteningly rich in egg yolks, when served in small portions it makes a beautiful, satisfying, and not too fattening finish to any meal. ■

Preheat oven to 325 degrees. Brush a 7-inch square baking pan liberally with the butter. Beat the yolks and baking powder together until the yolks are thick and creamy, about 2 minutes with an electric mixer or about 4 by hand. Pour the beaten yolks into the buttered baking dish and seal it with foil. Place the dish in a larger dish, add about 1 inch of water around the baking dish, place in the oven, and bake for 20 minutes. Remove the baking dish, and allow it to cool, still covered, for 10 minutes.

While the eggs are cooking, make the syrup. Place all the ingredients except the sherry in a small saucepan, bring to a boil, and simmer for 5 minutes. Add the sherry and remove the pan from the heat.

ASSEMBLY & SERVING:

Remove the foil from the baking dish and cut the yolk mixture into rectangles about 2 inches by 1½ inches. Pour ¾ of the syrup over the eggs and allow the eggs to soak it up for about 10 minutes. Arrange 2 or 3 of the rectangles on each serving plate and top with some more syrup, making sure you include some of the raisins and almonds. Serves 4.

THE EGGS:

I tablespoon melted butter

6 egg yolks

I teaspoon baking powder

THE SYRUP:

I cup water

¾ cup sugar

2 3-inch cinnamon sticks

2 whole cloves

¼ cup raisins

¼ cup blanched, slivered almonds

2 tablespoons dry sherry

# COCONUT ICE CREAM

1 14-ounce (396-gram) can
sweetened condensed milk

¾ cup evaporated milk

2 cups half-and-half

1 cup canned, unsweetened
coconut milk

⅓ cup dried, sweetened, flaked
coconut

Powdered chocolate

Powdered, dried coffee

■ Coconut ice cream has always been a personal favorite. However, too often it is nothing more than vanilla ice cream with coconut flavoring added—but not this version, which is the best I have ever had. It uses both coconut milk and dried coconut flakes to produce a truly authentic flavor and smooth texture. Be warned that there are many brands of canned coconut milk on the market, and not all of them are good. You want one that is smooth in texture and neither lumpy nor greasy.

Because different ice cream makers have different capacities, I suggest you mix the ingredients as specified in the recipe, then add only the amount to your machine it will hold. Also, since many popular models of ice cream makers have limited ability to freeze the contents, it is helpful to chill the ingredients for several hours in the refrigerator before using the ice cream maker. ■

Mix together the condensed milk, evaporated milk, half-and-half, coconut milk, and flaked coconut and place them in the refrigerator to chill several hours before you make the ice cream. To make the ice cream, put the chilled mixture in your machine and follow directions. Serve the ice cream sprinkled with the chocolate and coffee. Makes about 1½ quarts.

Moorish Ice Cream

■ I tried this terrific ice cream in Campeche and was fortunate enough to find a recipe for it in *Guía Gastronomía* the series of books on Mexican cooking published by México Desconocido, which I used as a basis for the following one. ■

1 cup plus 2 tablespoons sugar
2½ teaspoons cornstarch
Pinch salt
1¾ cups milk
⅓ cup sweet or medium sherry
2 egg yolks
½ cup evaporated milk
¾ cup cream
¾ teaspoon vanilla
½ cup prunes, soaked in water for 1 hour, drained, and finely chopped
⅓ cup coarsely chopped walnuts

Have ready a steel bowl sitting in another bowl containing a mixture of ice and water.

Place the sugar and cornstarch and pinch of salt in a pot, gradually stir in the milk, bring to a boil, and turn down to a bare simmer. Add the sherry and simmer for 1 minute, then remove from the heat. Beat the egg yolks in a large bowl until they are smooth and creamy. Beat in ½ cup of the hot liquid, beat in another ½ cup of the liquid, then slowly whisk in the remaining liquid, then return the mixture to the pot. Put it back on the burner over medium to medium-high heat. Heat the mixture until it begins to thicken and reaches 182 degrees on a thermometer. Add the evaporated milk, cream, and vanilla. Then pour the mixture into the bowl in the ice bath. Whisk the mixture until it begins cooling to stop the eggs from cooking further. Strain the mixture, stir in the prunes, and place the mixture in the refrigerator to cool for at least 3 hours. Then make it into ice cream according to the directions for your machine, adding the nuts at the beginning of the process. Makes about 1½ quarts.

✳ Pollas el Conquistador

1 cup evaporated milk

1 ounce powdered chocolate

1 cup ice cubes

½ teaspoon vanilla

1 teaspoon vodka

1 ounce "beet liquor" (made the night before serving by placing 1 sliced, canned beet in a container with 1 ounce cane liquor, or light rum)

½ ounce brandy

½ ounce sweet sherry

■ I do not know whether this drink is traditional or not, but it was featured in the series of books on Mexican cooking published by México Desconocido as the specialty of Señor Orlando Pérez of Campeche and is one of the most interesting cocktails I have ever tried. It is very much an adult milk shake that is good as an afternoon refresher or after-dinner drink. One of the ingredients, "beet liquor," must be made in advance. ■

Blend the ingredients for 1 minute and serve. Makes 4 8-ounce drinks.

Coco Loco

■ This drink is a delicious example of an ideal cocktail for a tropical climate.

In tropical Mexico, drinks are often served in coconuts. This is easily accomplished because coconuts from the tree have a thick but relatively soft husk. To make a drink container, Mexicans simply carve a level base on the husk with a machete, chop off the top, and pour off the coconut water. However, because most coconuts in our grocery stores come with the husk removed and only the hard, round nut remaining, to serve drinks in them requires placing them in a container that will sit flat on a bar or table. To open a coconut, strike it with the blunt side of a cleaver about a third of the way down from the "eyes" until it cracks and you can pry off the top. If this fails, drill two of the eyes with a large-diameter drill bit, drain off the coconut water, and saw off the top. (A jigsaw works well, but be careful because the coconut can easily slip and cause a serious accident.) ■

Put all the ingredients except the orange and cherry in a cocktail shaker. Shake, pour into the coconut, and serve with the garnish. Makes 1 drink.

Water from 1 coconut (reserve the coconut in which to serve the drink)

½ shot light rum

½ shot tequila

½ shot gin

½ shot vodka

½ shot grenadine

Crushed ice to fill the cocktail shaker

Orange slice

Maraschino cherry

✳ MEXICAN-STYLE EGGNOG

1 quart milk

1¼ cups sugar

1 stick cinnamon

3 whole cloves

½ teaspoon nutmeg

¼ teaspoon baking soda,
   dissolved in 1 tablespoon of
   the milk

Heaping ⅓ cup almonds,
   ground to a powder in a
   spice or coffee grinder

10 egg yolks, beaten until thick
   and creamy

1 tablespoon orange blossom
   water

1 cup light rum

■ Mexican-style Eggnog, or *Rompope,* is originally from Spain. It is very popular in Puebla, where it is a common aperitif or after-dinner drink. In addition, it is used as a sauce and ingredient in desserts. ■

In a large saucepan over medium heat, mix the milk and sugar and bring to a simmer. Add the cinnamon, cloves, nutmeg, and baking soda, and simmer the mixture for 7 minutes, then remove from the heat. Add the almonds, return to the heat, and simmer 3 more minutes. Allow the mixture to cool to 160 degrees. Whisk ½ cup of the milk mixture into the egg yolks, then another ½ cup, then stir the resulting mixture into the saucepan. Stirring constantly, bring the temperature up to 175 degrees, or until the mixture begins to thicken. Then immediately remove it from the heat. Quickly strain the mixture, add the orange blossom water and rum, allow it to cool, and then place it in the refrigerator. Makes 8 to 10 drinks.

✴ PIRATE'S COCKTAIL

■ According to legend, in the old days bartenders in waterfront *cantinas* of the walled port city of Campeche stirred their drinks with a branch from a plant called *cola de gallo*, or cock's tail, and English sailors translated this into a generic name for mixed drinks, or "cocktails." ■

Fill a cocktail shaker with ice, add the remaining ingredients, shake, and serve. To obtain the coconut water, strike a skinned coconut with the blunt side of a cleaver about a third of the way down from the "eyes" until it cracks. Pry off the top and pour the water into a container. If this fails, drill the eyes with a large-diameter drill bit and drain off the water. Makes 1 drink.

Ice
5 mint leaves
2 teaspoons sugar
1½ shots gin
½ cup coconut water

GLOSSARY

Abulón: Abalone.

Acelgas: Swiss chard.

Achiote: A paste used in the Yucatán made by grinding the seeds of the annato tree with spices and lime juice or vinegar.

Acocil: Small, freshwater crustacean.

Adobo: A chile-based marinade or sauce. Similar to the Yucatán *recado*.

Aguamiel: The sweet juice of the maguey plant, which when fermented produces *pulque*.

Aguardiente: Brandy.

Aguas frescas: A genre of soft drinks made by infusing water with various flavorings.

Aguja: A cut of chuck steak that is one of the favorite *al carbón* specialties of northern Mexico.

Ahumar: To smoke foods.

Ajo: Garlic.

Ajonjoli: Sesame.

Alas: Wings.

Albahaca: Basil.

Albaricoque: Apricot.

Albóndiga: Meatball.

Al carbón: Cooked over charcoal or wood coals.

Al pastor: Middle Eastern style of spit cooking.

Alegría: A traditional Mexican sweet dating from pre-Hispanic times.

Almeja: Clam.

Almendra: Almond.

Almíbar: Syrup.

Almuerzo: Traditionally a midmorning meal.

Al vapor: To steam.

Anaheim chile: Long thin chiles used to make dried New Mexican chiles.

Ancho chile: Dried *poblano* chile.

Añejo: Aged, as in aged liquor or cheese.

Anís: Aniseed.

Antojito: Appetizer or snack. The term comes from the Spanish word *antojo* which means whim. (See burrito, *cazuelita*, *chalupa*, *chilaquile*, chimichanga, *empanada*, enchilada, *enfrijola da*, *entomatada*, *envuelto*, *flauta*, *garnacha*, *gordita*, *molote*, *pambazo*, *panucho*, *papadzules*, *pellizcada*, *peneque*, *picada*, *quesadilla*, *sopa*, taco, *taquito*, tamale, *tlacoyo*, *torta compuesta*.)

Apio: Celery.

Arrachera: Skirt steak.

Arriera: Mule driver. Several dishes were named after these colorful characters.

Arroz: Rice.

Asada: Broiled.

Asadero: A barbecue or grill. Also a type of cheese.

Asar: To broil.

Ate de membrillo: A thick paste of quince with the texture of a thick purée.

Atole: A thick Mexican drink or porridge, dating from pre-Hispanic times, made with ground corn.

Ayocote: A large type of bean.

Azafrán: Saffron.

Azúcar: Sugar.

Bacalao: Dried cod fish, a traditional Spanish Christmas dish.

Balché: A Mayan alcoholic beverage made from the bark of the balché tree and honey.

Barbacoa: Meat cooked in an underground pit, usually wrapped in maguey or sometimes banana leaves.

Betabel: Beet.

Birria: A *barbacoa* specialty of Jalisco made with lamb or goat.

Bistec: Beefsteak.

Bizcocho: A cookie, often flavored with aniseed.

Biznaga: A type of cactus, resembling a barrel cactus.

Blanco de Pátzcuaro: A mild-flavored fish from Lake Pátzcuaro in Michoacán.

Blanquear: To blanch.

Blanquillo: A Mexican euphemism for egg. Used to avoid double entendre.

Bocadillo: Snack or finger food.

Bolillo: A French-style crusty roll made in the shape of a bobbin, served with entrées.

Borracho: Refers, in the culinary sense, to sauces and foods made with alcohol.

Borrego: Sheep.

Botana: A snack or appetizer.

Brasear: To braise.

Brocheta: Shish kebab or skewer.

Budín: Pudding.

Buñuelo: A fritter made of wheat flour.

Burrito: A filling wrapped in a large flour tortilla.

Cabrito: Kid.

Cacahuate: Peanut.

Cacerola: Casserole dish.

Café de olla: Mexican-style coffee made in a clay pot.

Cajeta: A confection made by simmering goat's milk and sugar to a thick paste. A specialty of Guanajuato.

Calabacita: Squash.

Calabaza: Pumpkin or very large squash.

Calamar: Squid.

Caldo: Soup or broth.

Camarón: Shrimp.

Camote: Sweet potato. Also refers to the sweets of Puebla made with sweet potatoes.

Canela: Cinnamon.

Capeado: A method of frying small morsels of food covered in batter.

Capirotada: A pudding of bread, fruit, and syrup.

Capulín: A type of fruit resembling a wild cherry.

Caramelo: Caramel.

Carne: Meat.

Carne asada: Broiled meat.

Carne de puerco: Pork.

Carne de res: Beef.

Carne molida: Ground meat.

Carnitas: Pork simmered in fruit juice and used as a filling for tacos. A specialty of Michoacán.

Carnero: Mutton.

Cascabel chile: A dark red small chile of medium heat used in salsas for meats.

Cazuela: A large, clay cooking vessel that is much wider at the top than at the bottom.

Cebiche/cheviche: Raw fish marinated in lime juice.

Cebolla: Onion.

Cebollitas de cambray: Green onions or scallions.

Cecina: Razor-thin piece of dried beef or pork.

Cedazo: Strainer or sieve.

Cena: Supper.

Cerdo: Pig.

Cerveza: Beer.

Chalupa: Fried stuffed corn tortilla.

Chambarete: Shank of beef.

Chamberete de carnero: Lamb or mutton shank.

Champurrado: An atole flavored with chocolate.

Charral: Minnow-sized dried fish.

Chaya: Large-leafed vegetable used in salads.

Chayote: A vine-grown type of squash.

Chía: A plant whose seeds have been used in Mexico since pre-Hispanic times. The oil is used in cooking.

Chícharo: Pea.

Chicharrones: Pork rinds that are deep-fried.

Chicozapote: Small brown-skinned fruit with a flavor somewhat like a pear.

Chilaquile: Crisp, fried tortilla quarters served as an appetizer or with breakfast.

Chilatole: An *atole* flavored with tomatoes and chiles.

Chilhuacle chile: A medium-sized brown and red chile from Oaxaca.

Chilmole: A flavoring paste from the Yucatán made with dried roasted chiles.

Chilocuil: Red maguey worms.

Chilorio: A northern meat filling usually made with pork that is boiled, shredded, then fried with ground chiles and other spices.

Chilpachol: A soup made with crabmeat and tomato.

Chimichanga: Deep-fried burrito, usually filled with shredded or dried meat.

Chipotle: A dried smoked jalapeño chile.

Chirimoya: A fruit also called custard apple.

Chirmol: A *mole* from the state of Tabasco made with beef, pumpkin seeds, and roasted tortillas.

Chirmole: Yucatán black *mole*.

Chivo: Goat.

Chorizo: Highly seasoned Mexican- or

Spanish-style sausage. The Spanish version is usually dried and flavored with paprika. The Mexican-style is sold fresh and is flavored with hot chiles.

Chorote: An *atole* served in the state of Tabasco.

Chuleta: Chop, as in *chuleta de puerco* or pork chop.

Cilantro: Coriander.

Ciruela: Plum; prune.

Clavetear: To decorate.

Clavo de olor: Clove.

Cocada: A sticky sweet made with coconut.

Cocido: A Mexican boiled dinner.

Cochinita pibil: Steamed barbeque of pork.

Codorniz: Quail.

Col: Cabbage.

Colonche: An alcoholic beverage of northern Mexico made from fermented cactus tuna.

Colorín: Edible red flower from the tree of the same name.

Comal: A griddle made originally from clay but now more usually from iron, steel, or aluminum.

Comida: A meal, usually the principal one eaten in the mid- or late afternoon.

Comino: Cumin.

Conejo: Rabbit.

Conserva: Preserved food.

Cordero: Lamb.

Corunda: A type of tamale that is a specialty of Michoacán.

Costillas: Ribs.

Cotija: An aged cheese often called *queso añejo*.

Crema: Cream.

Crepa: Crepe.

Damiana: A plant found in Baja California that is said to have aphrodisiacal qualities. It is used as an ingredient in a sweet liquor of the same name.

Dátil: Date.

De árbol: A very hot chile shaped like a small cayenne pepper.

Diezmillo: Chuck steak.

Dorado: Dolphin.

Dulce: Sweet or candy.

Dulcería: Candy shop.

Durazno: Peach.

Dzotobilchay: A tamale from the Yucatán wrapped with *chaya* leaves.

Ejote: Green bean.

Elote: Fresh corn, as opposed to maíz or dried corn.

Embutido: Cold meat; sausage and the making of sausage.

Empanada: Pastry turnover filled with either meat or fruit and other sweets.

Empanizar: To fry items such as meat that have been coated with breadcrumbs.

Enchilada: Corn tortilla dipped in a sauce and wrapped around cheese or shredded meat.

Enchilado: Meat, cheese, or other foods coated with chile paste or powder.

Enfrijolada: Appetizer similar to an enchilada except covered with thinned, refried beans and often folded into a triangle shape.

Ensalada: Salad.

En su jugo: Meat or poultry cooked in its own juice.

Entomatada: An enchilada served with a tomato sauce.

Entrada: Entrée.

Envuelto: Another name for a taco that is filled and fried.

Epazote: An herb found wild throughout North America used extensively to flavor soups, stews, and quesadillas.

Escabeche: A mixture of vinegar, oil, herbs, and seasonings used to preserve or "pickle" meats and vegetables or other foods.

Escamoles: Ant eggs; a pre-Hispanic delicacy.

Espagetti: Spaghetti.

Espelón: A small black bean from the Yucatán.

Espinazo: Spine.

Estofado: A stew; stewed or braised.

Estragón: Tarragon.

Falda: Literally "skirt"; refers to the cut of beef of the same name (also called *arrechera*).

Fécula: Starch.

Fiambre: A mixture of various foods such as fruits, vegetables, meats, and cheeses marinated in a dressing.

Fideo: Noodles or pasta; usually refers to a coil of dried pasta.

Filete: Filet.

Flan: Custard or dessert made with milk or cream and eggs.

Flauta: A long corn tortilla rolled around a filling and deep-fried.

Flor: Flour.

Flor de calabaza: Squash blossom.

Fogón: Hearth.

Fondo: Broth or consommé made from bones. Reduced stock.

Fresas: Strawberries.

Frijoles: Beans.

Frijoles borrachos: Beans cooked with beer or *pulque*.

Frijoles colados: Beans cooked then strained before frying.

Frijoles maneados: Beans fried with cheese from Sonora.

Frijoles refritos: Refried beans.

Fritada: Northern Mexican dish made by cooking kid in blood.

Frito: Fried.

Fruta: Fruit.

Garnacha: An appetizer of the *gordita* family from the Yucatán.

Gelatina: Gelatin.

Golosina: Candy or sweet.

Gordita: Appetizer made with tortilla dough patted into circles then cooked on a *comal* and sometimes deep-fried as well.

Granada: Pomegranate.

Grasa: Grease or fat.

Guacamole: Avocado ground to a paste, sometimes mixed with onions, chiles, tomato, lime juice, and cilantro.

Guajillo: A dried chile of medium heat with a smooth skin.

Guajolote: Turkey.

Guanábana: Soursop. A medium-large fruit with custard-like flesh.

Guarnición: Accompaniment to the main entrée, such as vegetables.

Guayaba: Guava apple. A yellow fruit with a fresh, almost sour, taste. It is often used in preserves, candy, and fruit.

Guisado: Stewed.

Gusanos de Maguey: Agave worms considered a delicacy when fried. The worms are often found in bottles of mescal.

Haba: Fava bean.

Habanero chile: The hottest chile pepper known. Use sparingly.

Harina: Flour.

Harina de maíz: Flour made from nixtamalized corn for making *masa* for tortillas and tamales.

Harina de trigo: Wheat flour.

Helado: Ice cream.

Hierbabuena: Mint (also spelled *yerbabuena*).

Hierba: Herb.

Hígado: Liver.

Hojaldre: Puff pastry.

Hoja santa: A plant whose large, soft leaves have the flavor of aniseed and are used to flavor stews and tamales. Especially popular in Oaxaca.

Hongo: Mushroom. Also referred to as *champiñon*.

Horchata: Soft drink prepared by blending water or juice with melon seeds or rice.

Huachinango: Red snapper.

Huauhtli: Amaranth.

Huauzontle: Leaves of a plant resembling amaranth.

Hueso: Bone.

Huevo: Egg. See *blanquillo*.

Huitlacoche: The very black, mushroom-like corn smut used in Mexican cooking.

Jaiba: Crab.

Jalapeño: A medium hot chile.

Jalea: Jelly or marmalade.

Jamoncillo: Confection or candy made from sugar and milk or from fruits and pumpkin seeds.

Jarabe: Syrup.

Jarra: Pitcher.

Jengibre: Ginger.

Jícama: An edible root.

Jugo: Juice.

Jumil: An insect eaten both alive and dried. A specialty of Taxco.

Langosta: Lobster.

Laurel: Bay leaf.

Leche: Milk.

Leche quemada: Literally "burned milk"; another term for *cajeta*.

Lechuga: Lettuce.

Leguado: Flounder.

Legumbre: Vegetable.

Lenteja: Lentil.

Licor: Liquor.

Lima agria: The sour lime found in Yucatán and used in the region's cuisine.

Limón: Lime.

Limonada: Limeade.

Lomo: Pork loin.

Longaniza: A sausage flavored with chiles and other spices.

Machacar: To mash or shred.

Maguey: Agave.

Mango: Mango.

Mantequilla: Butter.

Maíz: Dried corn.

Mamey: A tree that bears edible fruit. It is a favorite ingredient in ice cream.

Manchego cheese: Spanish cheese made with sheep's milk—also made in Mexico in a softer version with cow's milk.

Manitas: Often refers to *manitas decende* or pig's feet.

Manjar: A delicacy.

Manteca: Lard.

Manzana: Apple.

Mariscos: Seafood.

Marquesote: A sweet bread or tort.

Masa: Dough of ground nixtamal from which tortillas are made.

Mejorana: Marjoram.

Melaza: Molasses.

Melón: Melon.

Memela: Oval-shaped thick corn tortilla.

Membrillo: Quince.

Menudencias: Giblets.

Menudo: Soup or stew made with tripe and flavored with chiles.

Meocuil: The white maguey worm.

Merienda: A light meal or snack eaten either between the *almuerzo* and *comida* or between the *comida* and the *cena*. Similar to an English high tea.

Mermelada: Marmalade.

Mero: Grouper.

Metate: The three-legged stone implement used for grinding.

Mezcal/Mescal: Distilled liquor made from the juice of various agaves.

Mezclar: To mix.

Miel: Honey.

Milanesa: A cutlet of meat that has been breaded or floured and fried.

Milpa: Cornfield. Often beans, squash, *tomatillos*, tomatoes, and chiles are grown amidst the corn.

Miltomate or tomate de milpa: *Tomatillo.*

Mixiote: Thin, parchment-like membrane of the maguey; used to wrap meats and vegetables cooked in a barbecue pit or steamed.

Mojo de ajo: Garlic sauce.

Molcajete: Stone mortar used principally to prepare sauces.

Mole: From the Nahuatl word *molli*, or sauce. Now refers to a traditional stew.

Molido: Ground.

Molinillo: Wooden chocolate beater.

Mollete: A dish of buttered and toasted rolls with refried beans and cheese.

Molote: Corn *masa* for tortillas, sometimes with some wheat flour added.

Molusca bivalvo: Scallop.

Morcilla: Meat, often entrails, cooked in blood or stuffed into intestines and grilled or broiled.

Mostaza: Mustard.

Mulato: A dark version of the chile ancho.

Muslo: Thigh.

Naranja: Orange.

Nata: Skin or cream. The top skimmed off milk or cream.

Natillas: Custard.

Nixtamal: Corn boiled in lime water from which a paste (masa) is made for tamales or tortillas.

Nogada: A sauce made from peeled, ground walnuts.

Nopal: The cactus, either the whole plant or the leaf.

Nopalitos: Nopal leaves chopped into pieces. Thought to lower cholesterol.

Nuez: Literally nut. In the north it usually refers to pecans.

Nuez moscada: Nutmeg.

Olla: Pot.

Olla podrida: A stew of boiled meats and vegetables.

Ostión: Oyster.

Ostionería: Small café specializing in seafood.

Palomita: Popcorn.

Pambazo: Cheap bread made with inferior wheat, but for our purposes refers to a type of sandwich made from a medium to small French type roll.

Pámpano: Pompano.

Pan: Bread.

Panela: Diamond-shaped sponge cake.

Panela cheese: A dry, medium-flavored cheese like feta in texture but more mild.

Panucho: A specialty from the Yucatán made by filling puffs from tortilla dough as it cooks, then frying it to a golden brown.

Papa: Potato.

Papadzules: A Yucatán dish of rolled soft corn tortillas filled with various ingredients and topped with pumpkin seed and tomato sauces.

Papa frita: French fry.

Parilla: A grill that is placed over hot coals.

Pasilla: A long, thin dried chile that is nearly black in color.

Pastel: Cake.

Pato: Duck.

Pavo: Turkey.

Pechuga: Breast, as in chicken breast or *pechuga de pollo*.

Pejelagarto: A type of alligator gar eaten in Tabasco.

Pellizcada: A type of *gordita* with the dough pinched-up around the edges to contain the filling.

Peneque: An antojito similar to a *gordita* that is both fried and simmered in tomato sauce.

Pepino: Cucumber.

Pepita: Squash seed.

Perejil: Parsley.

Pequín chile: A tiny, football-shaped very hot pepper.

Pescado: Fish.

Pibil: Barbeque pit used in the Yucatán.

Picadillo: Filling made of ground meat.

Picante: Hot as in chile.

Pierna: Leg as in leg of lamb.

Piloncillo: Unrefined cane sugar.

Pimienta dulce: Allspice.

Pimienta negra: Black pepper.

Pimientón dulce: Paprika.

Piña: Pineapple.

Pinole: Flour made from roasted, dried corn. Used to make a drink flavored with sugar, cinnamon, and aniseed.

Piñones: Pine nuts.

Pipián: A fricassee or stew, similar to a *mole*, usually containing ground squash seeds and nuts.

Pitaya: Fruit from a type of prickly pear cactus.

Pizca: Pinch of an herb or seasoning.

Plátano: Plantain or banana.

Poblano: One of the oldest chiles indigenous to Mexico. It is used to make stuffed chiles.

Pollo: Chicken.

Ponche: Punch, usually with liquor such as brandy or rum and fruit, and usually served hot.

Porro: Leek.

Pozole: Soup made with meat, usually pork,

and unground nixtamalized corn kernels.

Postre: Dessert.

Puchero: A large dish or stew.

Puerro: Green onion.

Pulpo: Octopus.

Pulque: A mildly alcoholic drink made by fermenting aguamiel, the juice of the maguey plant.

Pulquería: A bar where pulque is sold.

Quelite: Generic name for edible wild plants; used much the way we use the term "greens."

Quesadilla: A corn or flour tortilla grilled with cheese.

Queso: Cheese.

Queso fresco: A semi-soft white cheese.

Rábano: Radish.

Rajas: Sautéed slices of skinned, fried *poblano* chiles.

Raspada: Shaved ice flavored with syrup.

Recado: Yucatán-style seasoning paste usually smeared on meats prior to cooking.

Refresco: Soft drink.

Refrigerador: Refrigerator.

Relleno: Filling, stuffing.

Repostería: Confectionary. The art of making desserts and pastries.

Res: Beef, as in *carne de res*.

Riñon: Kidney.

Robalo: Snook.

Romerito: A wild herb that looks much like rosemary.

Romero: Rosemary.

Rompope: Mexican-style eggnog.

Ropa Vieja: Literally old clothes; refers to a stew made with shredded meat.

Sábana: Literally sheet. Tenderloin steak pounded paper thin and briefly seared.

Salbute: A *chalupa*-like *antojito* filled with shredded beef and vegetables. It is a specialty of the Yucatán.

Salchicha: Sausage.

Salmón: Salmon.

Salpicón: Mixture of finely chopped or shredded ingredients.

Salpimentar/Salpimienta: To salt and pepper an item.

Salsa: Sauce.

Salsa mexicana: Uncooked relish made with diced tomato, onion, and fresh chiles.

Sandía: Watermelon.

Sangría: Drink of Spanish origin made with fruit juice, fruit, and rum, brandy, or wine.

Sangrita: A combination of orange juice, grenadine, chile powder, and sometimes tomato juice that is the favorite accompaniment to tequila in Mexico.

Seco: Dry.

Serrano chile: A favorite chile of northern Mexico and one of the hottest.

Sesos: Brains.

Sopa: Soup. The word *caldo,* or broth, is often used.

Sopa seca: Literally "dry soup"; includes rice and pasta dishes.

Sopera: Soup bowl.

Sope: Another name for *gordita.*

Taco: Corn or flour tortilla wrapped around a filling.

Tacos a la plancha: Tacos made with meats cooked on a griddle.

Tacos al carbón: Tacos filled with char-broiled meats; a specialty of northern Mexico.

Tacos al pastor: Tacos filled with thin slices of marinated pork cooked *al pastor* style.

Tacos de barbacoa: Tacos filled with pit-cooked meat.

Tacos de carnitas: Tacos made with *carnitas.*

Tacos de cazuela: Tacos filled with ingredients, usually a stew of some sort.

Tacos de harina: Tacos made with flour tortillas.

Tacos de maíz: Tacos made with corn tortillas.

Tacos dorados: Tacos named after the golden crisp-fried corn tortilla that encloses them.

Tamale: Appetizer made by placing some tortilla dough on a fresh corn husk, adding a filling of meat, vegetable, or fruit, wrapping the husk, and steaming it.

Tamarindo: Tamarind.

Taquería: A taco stand.

Taquito: "Little taco" made by deep frying a corn tortilla that has been wrapped around a filling. A small version of the *flauta.*

Tasajo: Thinly sliced, dried or partially dried beef or pork often flavored with chile.

Té or thé: Tea.

Tejocote: A tree which produces edible fruit.

Tejolote: The pestle used with a *molcajete*.

Telera: A type of roll usually used to make *tortas*.

Tepache: An alcoholic beverage made from pineapple and sugar.

Tequesquite: Rock salt.

Tequila: Liquor distilled from the juice of the blue "tequila" agave.

Tesgüino: Beer made from corn, principally by the Tarahumara Indians, who live in the mountains of Chihuahua.

Tiburón: Shark.

Tlacoyo: One of the oldest appetizers made by rolling tortilla dough around a filling of squash blossoms, *huitlacoche*, or mushrooms, then cooking the mixture on a *comal*.

Tocino: Bacon.

Tomatillo: Relative of the gooseberry family. Resembles a small green tomato.

Tomillo: Thyme.

Toronja: Grapefruit.

Torta: Literally a pie or tort; also refers to a Mexican-style sandwich.

Torta compuesta: Mexican version of the sandwich.

Tortilla: Flat, thin bread made from nixtamalized corn. The most important ingredient of Mexican cooking.

Tortillería: An establishment where tortillas are made and sold.

Tortuga: Turtle.

Tostada: Fried corn tortilla chips; fried corn tortilla with toppings.

Totoaba: A fish with delicately flavored flesh found in the Sea of Cortés.

Trigo: Wheat.

Tripas: Tripe.

Trucha: Trout.

Tuba: Alcoholic beverage made from fermented palm juice.

Tuna: The fruit of the nopal cactus.

Uchepo: Michoacán-style tamale made from fresh rather than dried corn.

Uva: Grape.

Uva pasa: Raisin.

Vainilla: Vanilla.

Vasija: Vessel or container.

Venado: Deer.

Verdolaga: Purslane.

Verdura: Vegetable.

Vinagre: Vinegar.

Vinatería: A wine shop.

Vino: Wine.

Xnipec: A relish common in the Yucatán.

Xoconostle: A type of cactus tuna.

Zacahuil: A gigantic tamale often filled with a suckling pig or whole turkey and cooked in a pit.

Zanahoria: Carrot.

Zapote: Trees which produce fruits, both yellow and black.

BIBLIOGRAPHY

Andrews, Jean. *Peppers.* Austin: University of Texas Press, 1984.

Beltrán, Lourdes. *La cocina jarocha.* Veracruz: Editorial Pax México, 1991.

Campos, Laura B. de Caraza. *La cocina de Laura.* Mexico City: Editorial Patria, 1997.

Coe, Sophie D. and Michael D. *The True History of Chocolate.* London: Thames and Hudson, 1996.

Coe, Sophie D. *America's First Cuisines.* Austin: University of Texas Press, 1994.

Coté, Ray, and Melva Sannebeck. *Villa Montaña Cuisine.* Morelia, Mexico: Raymond J. Coté, 1962.

De'Angeli, Alicia and Jorge. *Epazote y molcajete, productos y técnicas de la cocina mexicana.* Mexico City: Ediciones Larousse, 1993.

De'Angeli, Alicia and Jorge. *El gran libro de la cocina mexicana.* Mexico City: Ediciones Larousse, 1988.

DeWitt, Dave, and Nancy Gerlach. *The Whole Chile Pepper Book.* Boston: Little, Brown, 1990.

Díaz del Castillo, Captain Bernal. *The True History of the Conquest of Mexico, Written in 1568.* Translated by Maurice Keating. New York: Robert M. McBride, 1927.

Farga, Amando. *Historia de la comida en México.* Mexico City: José Inés Loredo y José Luis Loredo, 1980.

Fehrenbach, T. R. *Fire and Blood: A History of Mexico.* New York: Bonanza Books, 1985.

Fernández, Miguel Angel, and Víctor Ruiz Naufal. *Mesa mexicana.* Mexico City: Grupo Financiero Bancomer and Grupo Azabache, 1993.

Flores y Escalante, Jesús. *Brevísima historia de la comida mexicana.* Mexico City: Asociación Mexicana de Estudios Fonográficos, 1994.

Foster, Nelson, and Linda S. Cordell, eds. *Chiles to Chocolate: Food the Americas Gave the World.* Tucson: University of Arizona Press, 1992.

Grupo Voluntariado Bancomer. *La cocina regional de México.* Mexico City: Grupo Voluntariado Bancomer, 1993.

Heiser, Charles B., Jr. *Seed to Civilization: The Story of Food.* Cambridge, Mass.: Reprinted by permission of Harvard University Press, 1975, 1981, 1990.

Hernández Díaz, Gilberto, and Roberto Acevedo Escamilla. *Los primeros panaderos de Oaxaca, origen y características.* Oaxaca, Mexico: Gilberto Hernández Díaz and Roberto Acevedo Escamilla, 1992.

Katz, S. H., M. L. Hediger, L. A. Valleroy. "Traditional Maize Processing Techniques in the New World." *Science* (May 1974).

Kennedy, Diana. *The Cuisines of Mexico.* New York: Harper & Row, 1972.

Knab, Dr. T. J., ed., and Thelma D. Sullivan, trans. *A Scattering of Jades: Stories, Poems, and Prayers of the Aztecs.* New York: Simon & Schuster, 1994.

Lagasse, Emeril, and Jessie Tirsch. *Emeril's New New Orleans Cooking.* New York: William Morrow, 1993.

Landa, Friar Diego de, William Gates, trans. *Yucatan Before and After the Conquest.* New York: Dover Publications, 1978.

León-Portilla, Miguel. *The Broken Spears: The Aztec Account of the Conquest of Mexico.* Boston: Beacon Press, 1990.

Leonard, Irving A. *Baroque Times in Old Mexico.* Ann Arbor: University of Michigan Press, 1959.

Long, Janet, Coordinación. *Conquista y comida.* Mexico City: Universidad Nacional Autónoma de México, 1996.

Long Solís, Janet. *El placer del chile.* Mexico: Editorial Clío, 1998.

Malmström, Vincent H. *Cycles of the Sun, Mysteries of the Moon.* Austin: University of Texas Press, 1997.

Martínez Llopis, Manuel. *Historia de la gastronomía española.* Madrid: Ministerio de Agricultura, Pesca y Alimentación y Ediciones La Val de Onsera, 1995.

Molinar, Rita. *Dulces mexicanos.* Mexico City: Editorial Pax-México, 1991.

Molinar, Rita. *Antojitos y cocina mexicana.* Mexico City: Editorial Pax Mexico, 1975, 1990.

Palazuelos, Susanna. *Lo mejor de la cocina internacional: México*. San Francisco: Weldon Owen, 1994.

Palazuelos, Susanna. *Mexico: The Beautiful Cookbook*. San Francisco: Collins Publishers, 1991.

Paz, Octavio. *Mexico: Splendors of Thirty Centuries*. New York: The Metropolitan Museum of Art, 1990.

Revel, Jean-François. *Culture and Cuisine*. Garden City, N.Y.: Doubleday and Company, 1982.

Sahagún, Bernardino de, Arthur J.O. Anderson, and Charles E. Dibble, trans. *The Florentine Codex: General History of Things in Spain*. Santa Fe, N. M. and Salt Lake City, Utah: School of American Research and the University of Utah, 1970.

Sahagún, Bernardino de, Arthur J.O. Anderson, and Charles E. Dibble, trans. *The Florentine Codex: General History of Things in Spain, Book 1–The Gods*. Santa Fe, N. M. and Salt Lake City, Utah: School of American Research and the University of Utah, 1970. Reprinted by permission from the School of American Research.

Sahagún, Bernardino de, Arthur J.O. Anderson, and Charles E. Dibble, trans. *The Florentine Codex: General History of Things in Spain, Book 2–The Ceremonies*. Santa Fe, N. M. and Salt Lake City, Utah: School of American Research and the University of Utah, 1981. Reprinted by permission from the School of American Research.

Sahagún, Bernardino de, Arthur J.O. Anderson, and Charles E. Dibble, trans. *The Florentine Codex: General History of Things in Spain, Book 8–Kings and Lords*. Santa Fe, N. M. and Salt Lake City, Utah: School of American Research and the University of Utah, 1954. Reprinted by permission from the School of American Research.

Scott, Natalie V. *Your Mexican Kitchen*. New York: G. P. Putnam & Sons, 1935.

Soustelle, Jacques. *Daily Life of the Aztecs*. Stanford, Calif.: Stanford University Press, 1993.

Stoopen, María. *El universo de la cocina mexicana*. Mexico City: Fomento Cultural Banamex, 1988.

Taibo I, Pablo Ignacio. *Encuentro de dos fogones*. Mexico City: Promoción e Imagen, 1992.

Tedlock, Dennis, trans. *Popol Vuh: The Mayan Book of the Dawn of Life*. New York: Simon and Schuster, 1996.

Van Rhijn Armida, Patricia. *La cocina del maíz*. Mexico City: Ma. Angeles González, 1993.

Verti, Sebastián. *Esplendor y grandeza de la cocina mexicana.* Mexico City: Editorial Diana, 1994.

Villaseñor V., Ignacio. *Gastrosofía de la comida mexicana.* Guadalajara, Mexico: Editorial Conexión Gráfica, 1992.

Viola, Herman J., and Carolyn Margolis. *Seeds of Change.* Washington, D.C.: Smithsonian Institution Press, 1991.

Whitlock, Ralph. *Everyday Life of the Maya.* New York: Dorset Press, 1987.

The following list is from a series of monographs on the history of Mexican cooking. The series title and title on each edition is *La cocina mexicana a través de los siglos.* The subtitles, authors, and publication dates are given below. The series was published by Editorial Clío in cooperation with Fundación Herdez, A.C.

Brokmann Haro, Carlos. *Mestizaje culinario,* 1996.

Carreño King, Tania. *El pan de cada día,* 1997.

González, de la Vara, Fernán. *Epoca prehispánica,* 1996.

González, de la Vara, Martin. *Tiempos de guerra,* 1997.

Long, Janet. *La nueva españa,* 1997.

Rabell Jara, René. *La bella época,* 1996.

Sugiura, Yoko, and Fernán González de la Vara. *México antiguo,* 1996.

The following list is from a series of monographs *Guía Gastronomía* on the cooking of various Mexican states published by Mexico Desconocido. The various authors, titles, and publication dates are given below.

Luna Parra, Georgina, and Laura B. de Caraza Campos. *Comida campechana,* 1995.

Luna Parra, Georgina, and Laura B. de Caraza Campos. *Comida chihuahuense,* 1994.

Luna Parra, Georgina, and Laura B. de Caraza Campos. *Comida guanajuatense,* 1995.

Luna Parra, Georgina, and Laura B. de Caraza Campos. *Comida michoacana,* 1994.

Luna Parra, Georgina, and Laura B. de Caraza Campos. *Comida yucateca,* 1994.

OTHER COOKBOOKS FROM RED CRANE BOOKS
TO ORDER CALL 1-800-922-3392

LA COCINA DE LA FRONTERA
Mexican-American Cooking from the Southwest

by James Peyton
photography by Michael O'Shaughnessy

*"Likely to be the definitive book in the field, here's the most
scholarly, thoughtful, and authentic treatment
of Mexican-American cooking yet printed, and
one of the finest cookbooks of the year."*
—Travel Books Worldwide

Winner of the Border Regional Library Association
Southwest Book Award, 1995

8x9, 352 pages
12 color photos, drawings
$22.50 paper
1-878610-34-1

EL NORTE
The Cuisine of Northern Mexico

by James Peyton

"If you want one beautiful book about Mexican food and how to prepare it authentically, get EL NORTE."
—Texas Books in Review

"Detailed cooking instructions and a fascinating personal narrative set this collection apart. The 'Mexican food' lover will discover nuances in ingredient selection and preparation that will transform ordinary southwestern cooking."
—The Bloomsbury Review

8x9, 256 pages
12 color photos, 9 b/w
$22.50 paper
1-878610-58-9

FILIPINO CUISINE
Recipes from the Islands

by Gerry G. Gelle
photography by Michael O'Shaughnessy

*"Beautifully produced and
highly recommended."*
—Library Journal

*"...This is one of the most interesting
of all books on this cuisine."*
—A World of Cookbooks

*"An interesting and informative book for cooks
who want to expand their horizons and
familiarize themselves with another aspect
of Asian cooking."*
—Country Living

8x9, 304 pages
24 color photos
$29.95 cloth
1-878610-63-5

A PAINTER'S KITCHEN
Recipes from the Kitchen of Georgia O'Keeffe

by Margaret Wood
food photography by Michael O'Shaughnessy

*"Lavishly sprinkled with black-and-white photographs
of the artist as well as full-color food photos,*
A Painter's Kitchen *is a feast for the eyes
as well as the mind and the stomach."*
—Mail Order Gourmet

"Step into A Painter's Kitchen *and accept an invitation
to meet Georgia O'Keeffe, an intriguing,
striking individual who had definite ideas about
food and life. Try a recipe or two and add
simple elegance to your next dinner.*
—Southwest International Food & Wine Review

REVISED EDITION
8x9, 128 pages
8 color and 8 b/w photos
$14.95 paper
1-878610-61-9

YUCATÁN COOKBOOK
Recipes and Tales

by Lyman Morton
photography by Michael O'Shaughnessy

"This is not a cookbook for the person in a hurry. It is for the culinary artist, the closet anthropologist."
—Albuquerque Monthly

"...following the author's instructions, the truly adventuresome can cook up rare treats."
—Booklist

8x9, 256 pages
12 color photographs, map
$24.50 paper
1-878610-51-1